Digital Leisure Cultures

The digital turn in leisure has opened up a vast array of new opportunities to play, learn, participate and be entertained – opportunities that have transformed what we recognise as leisure. This edited collection provides a significant contribution to our changing understanding of digital leisure cultures, reflecting on the socio-historical context within which the digital age emerged, while engaging with new debates about the evolving and controversial role of digital platforms in contemporary leisure cultures.

This book also demonstrates the interdisciplinary nature of studying digital leisure cultures. To make sense of how individuals and institutions use digital spaces it is necessary to draw on history, science and technology, philosophy, cultural studies, sociology and geography, as well as sport and leisure studies. This important and timely study discusses both the promise of the digital sphere as a realm of liberation, and the darker side of the internet associated with control, surveillance, exclusion and dehumanisation.

Digital Leisure Cultures: Critical perspectives is fascinating reading for any student or scholar of sociology, sport and leisure studies, geography or media studies.

Sandro Carnicelli is the Programme Leader for Events Management and Tourism Management at the University of the West of Scotland, UK. Sandro has published articles in international journals, including *Annals of Tourism Research*, *Tourism Management*, *Annals of Leisure Research*, *Journal of Teaching in Travel & Tourism*, and *World Leisure*. He is also a member of the ABRATUR (International Academy for the Development of Tourism Research in Brazil), and he is on the Executive Board (Treasurer) of the Leisure Studies Association and on the Advisory Board of the *Annals of Leisure Research*.

David McGillivray holds a Chair in Event and Digital Cultures in the School of Media, Culture and Society at University of the West of Scotland, UK. His research focuses on two main areas of activity. The first area of interest is the contemporary significance of events and festivals (sporting and cultural) as markers of identity and mechanisms for the achievements of wider economic, social and cultural externalities. The second area relates to the affordances of digital culture, especially related to understandings of digital citizenship, participation and the role of everyday digital media platforms and practices in enabling (or restricting) voices within an increasingly saturated media landscape. He has published extensively on these themes and been involved in research and knowledge exchange activities that take as their focus the *affordances of digital culture*, including sub-themes of digital citizenship (see digital commonwealth.co.uk), digital participation, digital storytelling and alternative/community media and digital sport media. He is currently Deputy Editor of the *Annals of Leisure Research*.

Gayle McPherson holds a Chair in Events and Cultural Policy within the School of Media, Culture and Society at the University of the West of Scotland, UK. Her research interests revolve around the interventions of the local and national state in events and festivity of all types and the social and cultural impacts of events on communities. She is involved on the international collaborative research project Leveraging Parasport Events: for sustainable community participation. She has recently completed a digital literacy practice research project around the Commonwealth Games 2014. She is a member of the European Cultural Parliament and teaches at the Institute of Cultural Diplomacy in Berlin. She has published widely in the events, culture and festivals area, including recently as a co-author (2015) *Young People, Media Making and Critical Digital Citizenship*, and regularly publishes in journals such as *Cultural Trends*, *Managing Leisure*, *Journal of Policy Research in Tourism, Leisure and Events* and *Leisure Studies*.

Digital Leisure Cultures
Critical perspectives

**Edited by
Sandro Carnicelli,
David McGillivray
and Gayle McPherson**

LONDON AND NEW YORK

First published 2017
by Routledge
2 Park Square, Milton Park, Abingdon, Oxon OX14 4RN

and by Routledge
711 Third Avenue, New York, NY 10017

Routledge is an imprint of the Taylor & Francis Group, an informa business

© 2017 Sandro Carnicelli, David McGillivray and Gayle McPherson

The right of the editors to be identified as the authors of the editorial matter, and of the authors for their individual chapters, has been asserted in accordance with sections 77 and 78 of the Copyright, Designs and Patents Act 1988.

All rights reserved. No part of this book may be reprinted or reproduced or utilised in any form or by any electronic, mechanical, or other means, now known or hereafter invented, including photocopying and recording, or in any information storage or retrieval system, without permission in writing from the publishers.

Trademark notice: Product or corporate names may be trademarks or registered trademarks, and are used only for identification and explanation without intent to infringe.

British Library Cataloguing-in-Publication Data
A catalogue record for this book is available from the British Library

Library of Congress Cataloging in Publication Data
Names: Carnicelli, Sandro, editor. | McGillivray, David, editor. | McPherson, Gayle, 1968– editor.
Title: Digital leisure cultures : critical perspectives / edited by Sandro Carnicelli, David McGillivray and Gayle McPherson.
Description: Abingdon, Oxon ; New York, NY : Routledge, 2016. | Includes bibliographical references and index.
Identifiers: LCCN 2016009874| ISBN 9781138955073 (hardback) | ISBN 9781315666600 (ebook)
Subjects: LCSH: Internet–Social aspects. | Digital media–Social aspects. | Leisure. | Internet entertainment. | Information society.
Classification: LCC HM851 .D539 2016 | DDC 302.23/1–dc23
LC record available at https://lccn.loc.gov/2016009874

ISBN: 978-1-138-95507-3 (hbk)
ISBN: 978-1-315-66660-0 (ebk)

Typeset in Times New Roman
by Wearset Ltd, Boldon, Tyne and Wear

Contents

List of figures	vii
List of tables	viii
Notes on contributors	ix
Foreword	xii
KARL SPRACKLEN	

1 Introduction   1
SANDRO CARNICELLI, DAVID MCGILLIVRAY AND GAYLE MCPHERSON

2 Gigs will tear you apart: accelerated culture and digital leisure studies   13
STEVE REDHEAD

3 3D printed self-replicas: personal digital data made solid   26
DEBORAH LUPTON

4 'I'm selling the dream really aren't I?' Sharing fit male bodies on social networking sites   39
ALISON WINCH AND JAMIE HAKIM

5 Experiencing outdoor recreation in the digital technology age: a case study from the Port Hills of Christchurch, New Zealand   53
CAROLINE DÉPATIE, ROSLYN KERR, STEPHEN ESPINER AND EMMA J. STEWART

6 GoPro panopticon: performing in the surveyed leisure experience   66
ANJA DINHOPL AND ULRIKE GRETZEL

vi Contents

7 **Serious leisure, prosumption and the digital sport media economy: a case study of ice hockey blogging** 80
   MARK NORMAN

8 **The (in)visibility of older adults in digital leisure cultures** 94
   SHANNON HEBBLETHWAITE

9 **Demystifying digital divide and digital leisure** 107
   MASSIMO RAGNEDDA AND BRUCE MUTSVAIRO

10 **Understanding cyber-enabled abuse in sport** 120
   EMMA KAVANAGH AND IAN JONES

11 **Consuming authentic leisure in the virtual world of gaming: young gamers' experience of imaginary play in second modernity** 135
   MICHAEL WEARING

12 ***E'gao* as a networked digital leisure practice in China** 152
   HAIQING YU AND JIAN XU

13 **Teju Cole's *small fates*: producing leisure space and leisure time on Twitter** 166
   STUART J. PURCELL

14 **Street hauntings: digital storytelling in twenty-first-century leisure cultures** 179
   SPENCER JORDAN

15 **Literary work as a leisure activity: amateur literary forums on the Czech internet** 193
   KAREL PIORECKÝ

16 **Sexual desire in the digital leisure sphere: women's consumption of sexually explicit material** 207
   DIANA C. PARRY AND TRACY PENNY LIGHT

17 **Concluding remarks** 222
   SANDRO CARNICELLI, DAVID MCGILLIVRAY AND GAYLE MCPHERSON

   Index 225

Figures

3.1	A 3D self-replica sitting on the 3D printer that fabricated it	31
3.2	3D self-replicas in various forms	33
10.1	A typology of virtual maltreatment in sport	124
12.1	Transplantation of head images of Chen Luyu and Guo Degang into the anchors of CCTV's *Network News*	157
12.2	*Dormitory Network News*	158
12.3	Design of the 'never colliding high-speed train'	161
12.4	Movie poster of *Fatal Bullet Train*	162
14.1	Paddle post in the subway under the A470	185
14.2	Extant crane post in Canal Park	186
14.3	The start of the journey, the Grangetown War Memorial	188

Tables

5.1 Activity types of research sample 57
5.2 Digital devices carried by recreationists 58

Contributors

Caroline Dépatie is a PhD Candidate at Lincoln University, Christchurch, New Zealand, researching the significance of digital technology in users' experience of outdoor recreation in peri-urban settings. She is a Faculty member at Capilano University, British Columbia, Canada where she teaches in the Department of Outdoor Recreation.

Anja Dinhopl is a PhD Candidate in Tourism at the University of Queensland, Australia. She studies consumer culture in the context of tourism and technology, and focuses on understanding consumers' use of new technologies for taking pictures and recording videos.

Stephen Espiner is a Senior Lecturer in Parks, Recreation and Tourism at Lincoln University, New Zealand. His current research interests focus on the human dimensions of protected natural area management, with particular reference to nature-based recreation and tourism, and associated conservation, community and visitor management issues.

Ulrike Gretzel is a Professor of Tourism at the University of Queensland, Australia and a member of the Smart Tourism Research Centre at Kyung Hee University, South Korea. Her research focuses on technology use in tourism, with an emphasis on social media, both from organizational as well as consumer perspectives.

Jamie Hakim is a Lecturer in Media Studies at the University of East Anglia and a Teaching Fellow in Culture, Media and Creative Industries at King's College, London. He is currently working with Dr Alison Winch on a project entitled 'Digital Masculinities in the Age of Austerity'.

Shannon Hebblethwaite completed her BA and MA in Recreation and Leisure Studies at the University of Waterloo and her PhD in Family Relations at the University of Guelph. Her research focuses on social inclusion and the impact of leisure on well-being in a variety of contexts, including older adults, grandparents, first-time mothers and individuals with disabilities.

Ian Jones is an Associate Professor within the Department of Sport and Physical Activity at Bournemouth University. His teaching and research interests are

x   *Contributors*

largely focused on sport fan behaviour. He is author of *Research Methods for Sport Studies* and co-author of *Qualitative Research in Sport and Physical Activity*.

Spencer Jordan is Deputy Director for Drama and Creative Writing in the School of English, University of Nottingham. His expertise includes fiction (the novel and the short story); historical and experimental writing; digital/hypertext fiction; and literary geography, particularly as it relates to the digitally enhanced context of the smart city.

Emma Kavanagh is a lecturer in Sports Psychology at Bournemouth University. Her current research interests are focused on the maltreatment of athletes, human rights in sport and athlete well-being. She is part of a number of international research networks, which have a clear vision to enhance the climate and environment for athletes across the world of sport.

Roslyn Kerr is a lecturer in Sport and Recreation at Lincoln University, New Zealand. She holds a PhD in Sociology of Sport from the University of Canterbury. Her research interests include sport and technology, the use of actor-network theory within sports sociology, and the history and workings of the sport of gymnastics.

Tracy Penny Light is Executive Director of the Centre for Student Engagement and Learning Innovation and Associate Professor of History at Thompson Rivers University, Kamloops British Columbia, Canada. She has published widely on the ways in which gender and sexuality are represented in various discourses, including medicine and the media.

Deborah Lupton is Centenary Research Professor in the Faculty of Arts and Design, University of Canberra, Australia. Her current research interests focus on critical data studies and personal data practices. Her latest books are *Digital Sociology* (2015) and *The Quantified Self: A Sociology of Self-tracking Cultures* (2016).

Bruce Mutsvairo (PhD, Leiden University, The Netherlands) is a former journalist with the Amsterdam Bureau of the Associated Press (AP). He is currently a Senior Lecturer in Journalism at Northumbria University, UK, where he conducts research on social media activism.

Mark Norman completed his PhD in Sociology of Sport in 2015. Among his research interests is the impact of new media on sport culture and fandom. He is currently a sessional instructor at Ryerson University and a research assistant at the Centre for Sport Policy Studies at University of Toronto.

Diana C. Parry is an Associate Professor in the Department of Recreation and Leisure Studies and Special Adviser to the President on Women's and Gender Issues at the University of Waterloo, Waterloo, Ontario, Canada. She has published widely on women's leisure experiences and feminism.

Karel Piorecký is a literary historian and theorist, and a researcher in the Institute of Czech Literature of the CAS. His main area of research is the poetry of the twentieth and twenty-first centuries, and the relationship of literature and new media. He is author of the monograph *Czech poetry in the Postmodern Situation* (2011).

Stuart J. Purcell holds degrees in Business Law and Marketing, and English Literature from the University of Strathclyde, and a MLitt in Modernities from the University of Glasgow. He is currently undertaking an AHRC-funded interdisciplinary PhD in English Literature and Media Theory at the University of Glasgow, focusing on the intersection of print and digital media through the lens of contemporary literary practice.

Massimo Ragnedda (PhD) is a Senior Lecturer in Mass Communication at Northumbria University, Newcastle. He has authored six books with some of his publications appearing in numerous peer-reviewed journals and book chapters in English, Spanish and Italian.

Steve Redhead is currently Adjunct Professor in the Graduate Studies Programme in Humanities in the Faculty of Graduate Studies, York University, Ontario, Canada. He has published 16 books, including *Football and Accelerated Culture: This Modern Sporting Life* (Routledge, Research in Sport, Culture and Society Series, 2015). His personal website is www.steveredhead.zone.

Emma J. Stewart is a Senior Lecturer in Parks, Recreation and Tourism at Lincoln University, New Zealand, as well as a Research Associate with the Arctic Institute of North America. Her research interests include polar tourism, cruise tourism, human dimensions of climate change, outdoor recreation and participatory research methodologies.

Michael Wearing is a Senior Lecturer in Arts and Social Sciences, University of New South Wales, Sydney. He is the author of several books and over 70 publications in the areas of youth justice, youth leisure and tourism, and socio-legal policy. His research interests include youth leisure and crime.

Alison Winch is a Lecturer in Media Studies at the University of East Anglia. She has published journal articles on female sociality and branding in film, television and online, as well as a monograph *Girlfriends and Postfeminist Sisterhood* (Palgrave, 2013).

Jian Xu is a joint Visiting Fellow in the Centre for Global Communication Studies and the Centre for the Study of Contemporary China at the University of Pennsylvania. He was a 2015 Endeavour Postdoctoral Research Fellow at the University of Technology Sydney. He is the author of *Media Events in Web 2.0 China: Interventions of Online Activism* (Sussex Academic Press, 2016).

Haiqing Yu is Senior Lecturer of Contemporary Chinese Media and Culture in the School of Humanities and Languages, University of New South Wales, Australia. She is the author of *Media and Cultural Transformation in China* (Routledge, 2009) and co-author of *Sex in China* (with Elaine Jeffreys, Polity Press, 2015).

Foreword
Karl Spracklen

Leisure studies has often been seen outside of its own subject field as being focused too narrowly on sports, active recreation and individual experiences of leisure. But the internet and other digital spaces and activities are forms of leisure, and as such they should be if interest to leisure scholars. My own work on digital leisure (Spracklen, 2015) has started to map out the implications of the technological and cultural shifts that have surrounded us, while fixing the theory of digital leisure in the realm of leisure more broadly. Digital leisure has the appearance of novelty, and online spaces seem to be public spheres through which we can build a common culture and destiny. But the internet and digital cultures more generally are commercialised and controlled; that is, digital leisure is just another form of leisure, albeit one that has significant opportunities for communicative action and counter-hegemonic resistance. Digital cultures have been explored within wider social sciences and humanities research, especially in media studies and communication studies, but also cultural studies – but here the idea that these spaces and activities are forms of leisure has been accepted with a superficial theorisation of leisure. This edited collection is a significant contribution to understanding digital leisure cultures and may be seen as evidence of the growing interest in digital leisure. It presents the best of the wider 'digital studies' tradition, while rooting that tradition in debates about leisure and culture. It is important because it shows the depth and vitality of the research, and the complexity of the theoretical tools applied to understanding digital leisure cultures. This book's contributors show the complex struggles for power over digital leisure cultures, the struggles for and against commercialisation and state control. They show also a strong awareness of the interdisciplinary nature of studying digital leisure cultures. To make sense of how people and institutions use the internet it is necessary to draw upon history, science and technology studies, philosophy, cultural studies, sociology, political studies and geography, as well as leisure studies. Hopefully this book will be the first of many such projects as the study of digital leisure cultures becomes as established as any other study of leisure or culture.

Reference

Spracklen, K. (2015) *Digital Leisure, the Internet and Popular Culture.* Basingstoke: Palgrave.

1 Introduction

Sandro Carnicelli, David McGillivray and Gayle McPherson

The rise in the use of the term 'digital leisure cultures' has gained prominence in academic circles over the past few years (Spracklen, 2015). The idea for this book arose out of a specially convened digital cultures stream and subsequent discussions that took place at the Leisure Studies Conference at the University of the West of Scotland in 2014. Since then a number of articles, events and scholarly debates have focused on the digital turn in the study of leisure (here we include sport, events, festivity, tourism and recreation). We want to contribute to the emergent critical research agenda on digital leisure cultures, drawing upon theoretically informed analyses that consider social forces, power relations, socio-spatial inequalities, marginalisations, exclusions, contradictions, crisis tendencies and lines of potential or actual conflict. In this introductory chapter, we reduce these complexities to a focus on the transformations and tribulations associated with the digital turn upon the leisure sphere before illustrating how the selection of chapters contributes to these important debates.

Why digital leisure cultures?

This book focuses on the changing nature of leisure cultures brought about, intensified or accelerated in a digital world. The digital turn in leisure has opened up a vast array of new opportunities to play, learn, participate and be entertained – opportunities that have transformed what we recognise as leisure pastimes and activities, no longer bound by geography, but increasingly framed by the technological tools and practices that mediate our experience of social life. People are communicating with each other in different ways, more intensively and at greater speed. Technological advances enable people to create and distribute music, videos, images and ideas on a handheld device at the touch of a button or swipe of a touchscreen (Solis, 2012). Within the rhetoric of consumer as king we have endless choice, are able to make our own decisions about when and where we listen to our favourite artists, the number of episodes of our favourite TV series we can binge on and on what device. But, while endless possibilities are evident, there are also marginalisations and exclusions that make it necessary to give critical consideration to the 'costs' associated with digital leisure cultures on individuals, organisations and societies – those related to narratives of control, surveillance, alienation, atomisation or dehumanisation. Within pervasive digital cultures, institutional and corporate regulation of individual and social life is increasingly continuous and unbounded, characterised by the disappearance of gaps, open spaces and times. Thus, on the one hand, the promise of the digital sphere is of liberation, of a universal sharing of knowledge and creativity and of greater spreadability, which is both empowering and exciting. At the same time it is also clear that the digital sphere may be read as a space of intensified regulation and governance where every engagement is tracked, captured, used and, increasingly, sold to those with an interest in extracting commercial value from our communications.

Digital transformations: (re)conceptualising leisure in the digital age

As academics interested in the digital sphere and its affordances (boyd, 2014), the focus of this text has strong parallels with our recent experiences of the digital academy. Academic practice, for some, has been altered significantly by the availability of digital platforms and its impact on the production, circulation and consumption of knowledge. It is now possible to craft a curated online academic profile with the tools and technologies available. Lecture and conference presentation slides may be shared on multiple platforms such as Slideshare. Scholars now regularly blog about their research on their personal academic blogs, tweet links to their imagined audience, upload papers to Research Gate or Academia.edu – all with the intention of extending the reach and impact of their work. These cultural practices mirror the experiences that many now take for granted as they participate in digital leisure cultures. Like the digital academic, this participation requires continual cultivation and labour. As academics, we need to expend academic labour into maintaining our online profiles, to participate actively in scholarly conversations, and to manage the relationship between our public (professional) and private lives. We are also creating a digital footprint which will have a persistent presence extending well into the future, allowing others to survey our performance at the click of a button. Persistence, curation, surveillance, connectedness – these are just some of the terms we feel are relevant to discussions of leisure cultures in the digital sphere and that provide the focus of the contributions to this book.

We came to this book as a group of scholars interested in what the digital age means for what we understand as leisure culture in the early part of the twenty-first century. Historically, leisure has been viewed in opposition to work or having a relationship to work that included clear demarcations, whether by space or time. In the early 1990s we became interested in the way in which everyday domestic and consumer technologies were impacting upon the relationship between previously 'differentiated spheres' of work/leisure and public/private. Ken Roberts (1999) considered the increasing prevalence of *destandardised lives* and the loss of *sacrosanct time* and *spaces* where people had previously spent time with their families and enjoyed collective leisure experiences. In the early

2000s, Foley and McGillivray (2000) suggested, tentatively, that the mass availability of consumer technologies (laptops and mobile telephones at that time) meant that people would (and were) increasingly finding *surrogate workplaces* within which to carry out their work – the train, the coffee shop, the kitchen. At the same time, they were also using workspaces (and time) to participate in what could be described as leisure pastimes – gaming, surfing the net, researching and booking holidays. Over the past 20 years, in affluent economies in particular, we no longer question whether or not work can be performed flexibly in a mobile fashion or whether the train, the meeting room or the airport lounge represents a place for leisure and consumption to take place. For those with the right devices and connectivity (not available for all, as we will see later) it is possible to watch the football World Cup live on a smartphone, place a bet on who will score the next goal, hook up with colleagues for a Google Hangout, share a filtered image with 'friends' across the world via Instagram, and even create and edit a short film for circulation to a potential audience of millions via YouTube – all as they travel to and from work.

Fixed understandings of time, space and geography are challenged in a digitally mediated world. As (apparently) free, empowered and liberated (consumer) citizens we are encouraged to interact with whom we choose, pursue the leisure interests that suit us, and visit places, physically or virtually, when we so desire. There is certainly no need to be in the same place, or timezone, as others to share experiences, and that will only become more likely with the renewed thrust for immersive virtual reality and related technological developments. Through the development of mobile technology in our pockets, fans and consumers are now able to engage in, and to some extent determine, leisure trends. Artists, for example, in the music industries have embraced the idea of Direct to Fan (D2F), reducing the time and space from production to consumption (Tessler and Flynn, 2015).

Keeping to the theme of transformation (liberatory) social media as a form of leisure culture has seen an exponential increase over the past decade. Collectively, social media are 'the sites and services that emerged during the early 2000s, including social network sites, video sharing sites, blogging and microblogging platforms that allow participants to create and share their own content' (boyd, 2014: 6). boyd has argued that the emergence and establishment of social media was also accompanied by a cultural mindset that shifted the emphasis from those early adopters of the internet who avoided local communities by hanging out in chat rooms and bulletin boards, to younger people going online to connect to the people in their community. In her analysis of this influential leisure practice, boyd argues that the main change is that young people's online participation is 'not eccentric; it is entirely normal, even expected' (boyd, 2014: 6). The cultural mindset or set of social behaviours we refer to are not reliant on the use of a specific technology but rather represent 'spaces' where people congregate, complementing or supplementing face-to-face encounters. For what has recently been called 'Generation Moth' that congregate around screens, a digitally mediated presence already feels completely natural. The spaces of social media are interesting because they have distinctive features which mean that behaviours and practices have a persistent quality. As boyd (2014) again suggests, mediated environments created by social media are defined by *persistence* (the durability of online expressions and content), *visibility* (the potential audience who can bear witness), *spreadability* (the ease with which content may be shared) and *searchability* (the ability to find content easily). These four 'affordances' as boyd calls them impact upon the way in which we access, participate, record and think about our online leisure lives. But they also draw our attention to the fact that our everyday leisure practices are not without implications. We leave a residue when we share, collaborate, like and retweet that is worthy of further scrutiny here.

Digital tribulations: the dark(er) side of digital leisure

Forty years ago those offering a leisure society thesis promised us more time to be at leisure, to recuperate from the grind of work and to have psychological space to be free of a productive logic. Those optimistic forecasts were left unfulfilled and the problem of time in the contemporary period is exacerbated by endless choice, pressures for constant connectivity and normalisation of multi-device usage. The title of Judy Wajcman's (2014) recent book *Pressed for Time: The Acceleration of Life in Digital Capitalism* illustrates the concern among scholars about the inherent tensions between time-saving technological advances and their everyday use which can lead to extension of work and production logics.

Whereas in previous decades there were more clearly demarcated places and periods when one was at rest – before work, after work, at the weekend, on holiday – in recent years there has been a shift to a state of play whereby 'nothing is ever fundamentally "off" and there is never an actual state of rest' (Crary, 2013). There is now a pressure to be connected continuously, to take advantage of the plethora of ways to 'participate' digitally and not miss out on the myriad experiences available to us. There is a permeability, even indistinction, between the hours of work and leisure, especially as being connected is esteemed in our current period. The protected, or sacrosanct, spheres and periods of life that marked previous historical epochs have been dissolved, or at least weakened, in the digital age where so many of us own a device capable of securing access to a network, enabling us to connect wherever we are and at whatever time we wish. We expect responses to emails immediately, to be able to download and upload a file within seconds, to watch a film online or to catch up on the latest TV blockbuster on our tablets. Speed and instantaneity are emblems of our time (Virilio, 2000).

But, of course, there are many who decry the cult of connectivity, arguing that it leads to the atrophy of shared physical experiences and a continual dissatisfaction that brings about disjunctions, fractures and continual disequilibrium. Turkle (2011), for example, has expressed concern at this cult of connectivity, where we create, analyse and perform our emotional lives through the medium of technology. She is sceptical of the implications of 'continuous connection:

always on and always on them' (Turkle, 2011: 17). While we are cautious here not to contribute to moral panics over the alienating nature of digital platforms, we do recognise that the mass availability of domestic and consumer technologies, social media platforms and their ownership in the hands of a relatively few global conglomerates provides the conditions for what we refer to as the darker side of digital. The example of social media provides an illustration of the double-edged sword of the digital (leisure) world. The sheer pervasiveness of some social media platforms, especially Facebook, and their call to 'engage' leads to accusations of the constant socialisation of users and their life activity (Halpin, 2013). This desire to socialise its users is common to most corporate social media platforms, motivated by the need to extract (ultimately) commercial value from its users through advertising and other techniques of monetisation (Andrejevic, 2009; Fuchs, 2014).

In order to extract this commercial value, there is a need for the constant shepherding of our activities as proprietary platforms (e.g. Facebook, Google or Twitter) participate in the 'ownership of memories, in the form of documents, photos and videos' (Halpin, 2013: 18). To secure access to our collective memories these platforms need to intrude into the apparent banalities of everyday life. Any sense that the everyday (and informal leisure) was *outside* what was organised and institutionalised around work and consumerism is rendered unsustainable. We now know that corporate social media harvest information about the people sending the message out, who receives it and what they do or do not do with it. Yet, as invaluable participants in the creation of these big data about our leisure practices, we are often left unsure about who *owns* our data and what they can and cannot do with it. We remain uncertain about what a cookie is, what it does and whether we should accept its presence as we surf online. As new platforms emerge, we are uncertain of who owns them, how to judge their intentions, and why they are changing their terms and conditions and privacy settings 'for our benefit' or 'to improve the service they can offer'. As a result of this confusion created by owners of the proprietary platforms as users, we 'passively and often voluntarily ... collaborate in one's own surveillance and datamining' (Crary, 2013: 46). We frequently present and curate our life stories and personal biographies online. The personal is increasingly publicly mediated, as we grant others access to information about our leisure lives, habits and behaviours. This information is used to predict and, some would argue, modify our behaviours. We have all received the advertisements that best reflect our apparent wants and desires, the songs we must hear or the books we really ought to have read. With digital traces assembled by personalisation engines our most intimate behaviours are uncovered and reflected back at us. But, of course, this is a filtered lens on reality and one that, in effect, leaves an algorithm to decide what stories from our news feeds our social media guardian angel thinks we ought to see.

When thinking about digital tribulations, we also need to reflect on the fact that an economic, social and cultural gap still exists between those that are able to reap the benefits of participation in the digital leisure sphere and those that are not. While on one level choices appear endless, in reality not being digitally active (even if by choice) makes participating in economic, social and cultural life more difficult than ever before. The evidence suggests that those people least likely to be online are those facing other, often multiple, forms of social isolation and in possession of different forms of capital (Willig *et al.*, 2015). As Willig *et al.* stress,

> Internet access may not, in and of itself, level the playing field when it comes to the potential payoffs of being online. Instead, those from more privileged backgrounds may reap more of its benefits if they are more likely to use it in potential beneficial ways.
>
> (Willig *et al.*, 2015: 5)

In a similarly Bourdieusian-informed analysis, Danielsson (2011) highlights the continuation of class-distinctive habituses that impact upon what he calls 'privileged' and 'disprivileged' males' approach to leisure (and education). He suggests that the privileged (digitally literate) view spare-time activities as 'a scarce resource to be strategically invested in (digital) goods and practices with the capacity to generate profit in the field of education and the general social field' (p. 68). Strategic practices include learning, and producing digital content. In contrast, the disprivileged disregard the moral order of digital goods and practices, participating in digital activities that appear to oppose an educational outcome – those that have as their core function entertainment (he uses the example of video games). What is important here is that the affordances and possibilities of digital leisure practices are unequally experienced and interpreted, and therefore it cannot be taken for granted that they are empowering, liberatory or can address existing systemic societal inequalities.

Digital leisure cultures and creative resistance

Although it is sometimes tempting to take the critical perspectives put forward by some scholars of the digital as evidence of a *fait accompli* whereby we are all enmeshed in a web of surveillance, handing over our data voluntarily to corporations who use it to generate significant profit, it is also important to recognise that digital spaces are sites of negotiation, where struggles over ideology, representation and power take place. These spaces are defined by complexity, diversity and contradiction, and they contain cultural practices that can both repress and empower. Thus, rather than merely viewing those participating in, for example, regular Facebook activity as passive consumers, we may instead ask: To what extent do individuals and collectivities have the power to hold these corporations to account? Like in all forms of leisure behaviour, attempts to regulate and control behaviour also produce its 'other'. Informed by critical theory and cultural studies, this approach to analysing digital leisure is consistent with the history of the study of leisure where there has long been a concern to investigate the subcultural or counter-cultural forces that co-exist with dominant or parent culture and through which individuals and others negotiate their identities (see Clarke and Critcher, 1985). The digital sphere is no different, with the affordances of digital cultures such as self-production and self-publishing enabling people to engage creatively and critically with media production outside of the commercial domain. With relatively inexpensive equipment and software, it is now possible to create, distribute and sell music without engagement with global music labels. Or one can use photo- or video-sharing capacities and the power of social media to 'hack' or hijack the agendas of others, whether that be global conglomerates or media events like the Olympic Games (Price, 2008).

These struggles over control, rights and freedoms in the leisure sphere are not new. In the 1990s, leisure businesses in the creative sphere (music, film, video, gaming) lost out commercially when a culture of peer-to-peer free sharing first took hold. This loss was related to the inability to maintain control of content in the digital sphere. As Rojek (2005) noted, P2P file sharing was considered a novel leisure form that raised significant issues about the ownership and control of intellectual and artistic property, access and the regulation of leisure choices. Of course the creative industries developed new business models to negate some of this 'everything-for-free' culture that was taking hold at that time, but there remain constant tensions between a culture of openness, sharing and hacking the system and the ability of others to protect, commercialise and monetise the digital sphere.

One leisure sphere where the digital realm contributes to creative resistance is the landscape of major sporting and cultural events. Event owners seek to control how their events are defined, and sanctioning bodies use their powers to secure and protect these media assets from being ambushed or hijacked by others. However, the now ubiquitous digital and online platforms already enable vast networks to be activated in a manner unheard of before and with great immediacy. That, in itself, holds the authorities to account, as they find it more difficult to control the media message with such a diversity of platforms available and distributed so widely. In a number of recent practice research projects (see McGillivray and Jones, 2013; McGillivray and Frew, 2013; McGillivray, 2014; McGillivray et al., 2015) we have explored how everyday digital technologies (e.g. smartphones and tablets) may be used to enhance digital media literacy, lowering the threshold for involvement in creative media production using the focus of a major event. We have sought to create and support media collectives to demonstrate the power of citizen-oriented storytelling, emphasising the power people have in their pocket, promoting digital cultures as enabling, fostering decentralised and distributed structures, where individuals and groups can interact with a network public to amplify their messages through a shared, and free, communication platform. The accessibility of social media increasingly blurs the boundaries between the producers and consumers of content (Ritzer and Jurgenson, 2010), drawing attention to competing claims and affirmations, and acting to at least unsettle the unchallenged deployment of power which has previously existed. Established media institutions struggle to cope with an amorphous and deterritorialising medium. Institutional strategic narratives and control attempts collide with that of digitally empowered citizens, producing counter-movements that organise, mobilise and amplify locally derived content. If well organised and with a collective interest at their heart, digital infrastructures can offer citizens new channels for speaking and acting together, *lowering the threshold for involvement* (Bakardjieva *et al.*, 2012).

We are not forwarding this example from one leisure sphere to suggest that citizen/community-focused initiatives of this sort alter mega-event narratives or automatically lead to people using the power in their pocket to produce some sort of digital disruption that is sustainable and meaningful in political terms. There are plenty of powerful critiques of the liberatory political potential of new media platforms whereby the internet contributes to a consumerist protest mentality, devoid of risk and commitment on behalf of participants (Hands, 2011; Morozov, 2011). What we are suggesting is that the digital sphere offers new possibilities of co-creation, co-production and co-authoring (Solis, 2012), themes that will be addressed in this collection.

Book structure

It is our contention that by looking at the leisure aspects of digital cultures (as opposed to their expression in labour or production) we can generate useful insights that have not always been the focus of other disciplines and fields. Those in the 'new' fields of digital humanities or digital sociology (Lupton, 2014) certainly consider what we view as digital leisure practices in their work, but they are rarely pulled together into one volume. Moreover, in this text we also wanted to enable our contributors to highlight the range of experiences that producers, consumers and regulators can encounter within one apparently liberating leisure practice. For example, digital games, from one theoretical perspective, are creative, sociable and educational, while from another they reflect an alienated and atomised fantasy world with negative social implications. The leisure practices our contributors consider in this text can be empowering or destructive, depending on the preferred theoretical interpretation. In this book three main themes emerged from the contributions: *reconceptualising digital leisure, digital tribulations and creative resistance*. Each chapter advances both a theoretical and empirical contribution and the topics covered include sport blogging, outdoor recreation, online gaming, body modification, 3D self-replicas, literary practice and social media as a leisure practice.

Reconceptualising Digital Leisure is the theme that emerged from *Steve Redhead's* contribution as he focuses on the theoretical gaps in what he terms 'digital leisure studies' and makes a strong argument that we look for theories from outside the field in order to move this emergent field forward. Drawing upon an eclectic range of social theorists, including Baudrillard, Badiou, Virilio and Žižek, Redhead explores the concepts of 'accelerated culture' and 'claustropolitanism', and proposes a theoretical framework that can provide the foundation for the further development of digital leisure studies. In his chapter Redhead points out many contradictions that can be linked to the digital divide which we will see emerge in other chapters in the book.

Body and body image in a technological world provides the theme of *Deborah Lupton's* chapter. Looking at advancements in 3D printing of body parts and self-replicas, Lupton reflects upon the physical materialisation of digital data that is gathered in all the devices around human beings. These 3D printing self-replicas as well as other digital objects and data can become invested with selfhood based in the personal information gathered and stored, this may include personal and professional information, images of the self and of others as well as memories of leisure experiences and life histories. Lupton points out that 3D printing technologies are still relatively new and there are still a lot to be developed and researched and with still broader questions remaining to be answered.

The body and digital leisure culture is also the focus of *Jamie Hakim* and *Alison Winch's* chapter. The focus of this chapter is on the emergence of self-branding techniques and the sharing of body image on social networks, particularly Instagram. The authors look into the practices of going to the gym and posting photos of one's body as neoliberal labour based on an entrepreneurial project of the self. To Winch and Hakim, this neoliberal labour and self-promotion of body images is penetrating social life and leisure time. The chapter also assesses the importance of men feeling impelled to perform traditionally feminine body work, illustrating how successfully the logistics of neoliberal labour are penetrating the leisure time, intimate worlds and everyday lives of a social group historically immune to them.

Building on Lupton's and Hakim and Winch's chapters, *Caroline Dépatie, Roslyn Kerr, Stephen Espiner and Emma Stewart* focus on the use of digital devices during outdoor recreation in New Zealand and draw upon actor-network theory (ANT) to explore how non-humans act as intermediaries or mediators through facilitating or disrupting experiences. They argue that technological devices are not only manufactured or 'non-natural' instruments but non-human agents acting as social forces that have the power to reveal different realities. They found that in peri-urban settings the behaviour of participants in outdoor activities emulated that of urban settings, having multiple reasons for having the technology with them at all times, including safety, entertainment (music) and as a memory keeper (for time and to take photos).

Anja Dinhopl and Ulrike Gretzel take as their theoretical focus ideas around performativity, surveillance and, in particular, the concept of performing authenticity to consider the behaviour of snowboarders as their practices become inseparable from their engagement with emerging technologies. They suggest that the panopticon gaze of GoPro wearable video cameras does not always allow participants to know when they are being filmed. Focusing on the unannounced recording of images, the authors draw attention to the complexity of performing authenticity and the ethical dilemmas that are brought to the surface in the process.

Mark Norman uses the concepts of serious leisure and prosumption to explain the growing phenomenon of sports blogging – focusing specifically on ice hockey. Norman uses the idea of prosumption to explore the duality between production and consumption in online environments and also looks to the six characteristics of serious leisure that help explain the activities of bloggers (the development of careers in leisure pursuit; perseverance through difficult circumstances; large amounts of effort and the development of specialised skills or knowledge; variety of individual benefits; emergence of a unique ethos around the practice; strong identification with the activity).

A second theme that emerged from the contributions regards *digital tribulations*. *Shannon Hebblethwaite* focuses on digital exclusion and, in particular, on digital ageism. She argues that older adults have been rendered invisible in dominant discourses about technology and the digital world and, in particular, on the role of technology in the context of leisure for older adults. Drawing upon critical theory, she interrogates ageist assumptions in relation to leisure and digital media use (or non-use) and proposes that older adults are agentic in their choices around media use.

Following Hebblethewaite, *Massimo Ragnedda* and *Bruce Mutsvairo*'s chapter also focuses attention on social inequalities and the nature of access and participation in digital leisure. They explore how inequitable access to and use of digital technologies influences the consumption of leisure, arguing that social and digital inequalities are inseparable. They conclude by arguing that being excluded from leisure cultures, both in socio-economic and educational terms, will have consequences in terms of full participation in virtual communities.

Focusing on an increasingly prevalent tribulation intensified by the affordances of digital leisure cultures, *Emma Kavanagh* and *Ian Jones* consider the ethical and legal dimensions of online abuse of elite sport athletes carried out on the social network, Twitter. They suggest that online environments create an optimal climate for abuse and, as a result, social media sites are increasingly providing an outlet for a variety of types of hate to occur, and it is evident that such environments 'enable' abuse rather than act to prevent or control it.

Michael Wearing's chapter focuses on another form of online leisure practice that has flourished in recent years: virtual gaming. He contextualises the growth of this phenomenon and highlights how conventional parental and governmental wisdom, tainted by the knowledge of more violent games, is that role-play and multiple video gaming itself creates social and personal risks as well as significant financial outlays for young people in this global digital leisure activity. He then presents an analysis framed by ideas around risk, authenticity and second modernity to demonstrate the complexities of young people's use and identity formation through virtual gaming culture internationally.

A final theme emerging from the chapters regards creative resistance and digital leisure cultures. *Haiqing Yu and Jian Xu's* chapter exploring E'gao practices in China. Focusing on E'gao as a spoofing practice, the authors present a digital leisure practice that uses humour and satire to challenge power discourses and play with the establishment of culture and structure in a country where the online world is constantly under surveillance.

Whereas in *Kavanagh and Jones* Twitter was considered as an online environment optimised for abuse, *Stuart Purcell's* chapter provides a more creative and agential counterpoint. Purcell posits that Twitter can, in fact, be used as a creative literary tool to produce new leisure practices and to develop the liberal arts. raws on Teju Cole and the small fates project to argue for the dynamic and recursive nature of digital tools' development, highlighting how these developments are not purely deterministic but instead may be restructured through forms of engaged practice that expose and challenge the spatial and temporal biases of digital tools. If the temporal and spatial dimensions of digital tools can be restructured, then a place for leisure can be carved out within their environs.

The literary practice present in Purcell's chapter is only one example of possible links between digital practices and literary work. *Spencer Jordan*'s chapter draws upon digital storytelling practices from two case studies in Wales, to demonstrate how the use of digital technology can support the creation of bottom-up community-based 'landscapes of memory'. Using audio, video and social media platforms, he argues that digital storytelling can reconnect what is left of the physical space with human memory.

Continuing with the literary leisure theme, *Karel Piorecký* explores the role of online forums as a space to develop literary work and participate in serious leisure practices based on amateur activities and community sharing. He argues that these literary forums are democratic spaces where people can share their writings but also facilitate editing and review.

The final contributors, *Diana Parry* and *Tracy Penny Light*, return to the theme of the body in their chapter on women's sexually explicit material (SEM). They use a cyberfeminist approach to examine and discuss the use of digital technology by women consuming SEM and the changing nature of the leisure culture related to women's sexuality. Digitally mediated, they argue that online sites and services represent a place of resistance for women where they can challenge patriarchal ideologies related to their sexual behaviour and their bodies.

References

Andrejevic, M. (2009) Exploiting YouTube: Contradictions of User Generated Labor. In P. Snickars and P. Vonderau (eds) *The YouTube Reader* (406–423). Stockholm: National Library of Sweden.

Bakardjieva, M., Svensson, J. and Skoric, M. (2012) Digital Citizenship and Activism: Questions of Power and Participation Online. *JeDEM*, 4(1): i–v.

boyd, d. (2014) *It's Complicated: The Social Lives of Networked Teens*. London: Yale University Press.

Clarke, J., and Critcher, J. (1985) *The Devil Makes Work: Leisure in Capitalist Britain*. Basingstoke: Macmillan.

Crary, J. (2013) *24/7 Late Capitalism and the Ends of Sleep*. London: Verso.

Danielsson, M. (2011) Digital Media as Classified and Classifying: The Case of Young Men in Sweden. *PLATFORM: Journal of Media and Communication* ECREA Special Issue (November): 57–71.

Foley, M. and McGillivray, D. (2000) Absence *from* or Absence *of* Work in the 'Leisure Industries': Free Time or Displacement? *Managing Leisure*, 5(4):163–180.

Fuchs, C. (2014) *Social Media: A Critical Introduction*. London: Sage.

Halpin, H. (2013) Immaterial Civil War: The World Wide War on the Web. *Culture Machine*, 14(1–26). Available at: http://culturemachine.net/index.php/cm/article/view/509/524.

Hands, J. (2011) *@ is for Activism*. London: Pluto Press.
Lupton, D. (2014) *Digital Sociology*. London and New York: Routledge.
McGillivray, D. (2013) Digital Cultures, Acceleration and Mega Sporting Event Narratives. *Leisure Studies*, 33(1): 96–109. DOI: 10.1080/02614367.2013.841747.
McGillivray, D. and Frew, M. (2013) The Olympic Torch Relay: Activating Citizen–Consumer Discourses. *Lusophone Journal of Cultural Studies*, 1(2): 232–251.
McGillivray, D. and Jones, J. (2013) Events and Resistance. In R. Finkel, D. McGillivray, G. McPherson and P. Robinson (eds) *Research Themes for Events* (129–141). Oxford: CABI Publishing.
McGillivray, D., McPherson, G., Jones., J. and McCandlish, A. (2015) Young People, Digital Media Making and Critical Digital Citizenship. *Leisure Studies*. Available at: www.tandfonline.com/doi/full/10.1080/02614367.2015.1062041.
Morozov, E. (2011) *The Net Delusion*. London: Penguin Books.
Price, M. (2008) On Seizing the Olympic Platform. In M.E. Price and D. Dayan (eds) *Owning the Olympics: Narratives of the New China* (86–114). Michigan, OH: Digitalculturebooks.
Ritzer, G. and Jurgenson, N. (2010) Production, Consumption, Prosumption: The Nature of Capitalism in the Age of the Digital 'Prosumer'. *Journal of Consumer Culture*, 10(1): 13–35.
Rojek, C. (2005) P2P Leisure Exchange: Net Banditry and the Policing of Intellectual Property. *Leisure Studies*, 24(4): 357–369.
Roberts, K. (1999) *Leisure in Contemporary Society*. Oxford: CABI Publishing.
Solis, B. (2012) Meet Generation C: The Connected Customer. Available at: http://pandodaily.com/2012/03/06/meet-generation-c-the-connected-customer/ (accessed 16 February 2016).
Spracklen, K. (2015) *Digital Leisure, the Internet and Popular Culture*. Basingstoke: Palgrave.
Tessler, H. and Flynn, M. (2015) From DIY to D2F: Contextualizing Entrepreneurship for the Artist/Musician. In A. Dumbreck and G. McPherson (eds) *Music Entrepreneurship* (47–74). London: Bloomsbury.
Turkle, S. (2011) *Alone Together: Why We Expect More from Technology and Less from Each Other*. New York: Basic Books.
Virilio, P. (2000) *A Landscape of Events*. London: MIT Press.
Wajcman, J. (2014) *Pressed for Time: The Acceleration of Life in Digital Capitalism*. Chicago, IL: University of Chicago Press.
Willig, I., Waltorp, K. and Hartley, J.M. (2015) Field Theory Approaches to New Media Practices: An Introduction and Some Theoretical Considerations. *MedieKultur*, 58: 1–12.

2 Gigs will tear you apart

Accelerated culture and digital leisure studies

Steve Redhead

Introduction

This chapter looks at perceived gaps in the recent theoretical development of work on digital leisure cultures and how to address them. Drawing upon empirical examples of digital leisure cultures, my aim is to produce a more robust theoretical approach to the so-called 'digital turn' in various disciplines. After pioneering work on the nature and contours of 'digital sociology' by academics such as Deborah Lupton (Lupton, 2014) it is possible to envisage an emerging digital leisure studies to which this chapter, and this book, contributes and defines (Spracklen, 2015). In this chapter I want to consider new directions in critical perspectives in digital leisure cultures because the present routes forward are often confused, stymied and unsatisfactory, reflecting a more general concern in the population as a whole about our digitised world and how to come to terms with this condition. Urgent questions on digitisation remain unanswered, as they do on globalisation. Specifically, as far as digital leisure cultures are concerned, the crucial question for this chapter is: What are gigabytes doing to us and how can we explain this process? Echoing Manchester United soccer fans' chant about former player and assistant coach Ryan Giggs, 'Giggs Will Tear You Apart' (aimed at opposing fans and based on Joy Division's classic 'Love Will Tear Us Apart'), I am asking: Will these 'gigs' tear us apart? We have certainly become so addicted to the hyperspeed of electronic digital connection that we all feel that familiar sickening stomach churning while we wait for our screens (on whatever platform) as almost a global cultural condition, yet we greedily binge-watch whole series of our favourite television shows in one day once the connection is eventually made a few seconds later. We are back in the realms of asking whether we are now at long last living today in the 'leisure society' predicted for us in the 1980s, enabled by globalisation, 'free markets' and digitisation.

On the bright side of the road in the new dark ages

Digital leisure cultures as a term is fraught with difficulty. But I would argue that it covers some of the following technologies and practices which have built cultures around them: namely apps (applications), smartphones, online games, interaction on some form of social media, and the downloading of films, live televised sports events and music. Traditional notions of legal intellectual property have been thrown into disarray by these developments in digital leisure cultures. Entertainment and Sports Law has become an important part of the legal curriculum worldwide. Digital fan cultures in sport and music have subsequently developed and been an object of study – witness academic work on fan forums and fan identities (Redhead, 2014). Sports personalities have also featured strongly in the new celebrity culture promoted by social media. However, in cyberculture there are video gamers *and* cyber football hooligans, and there are campaigners for social justice *and* hate crime promoted by trolls and cyber bullies. Although we may not have labelled them in this way, 'digital leisure cultures' have been around for at least some of the past 15 years since the millennium but the years between the global financial crisis of 2007/2008 and today have been fundamental in the digital turn, especially in their inexorable speeding up. I call this widening process 'accelerated culture' and have developed a theoretical framework for explaining its development more generally in our contemporary society, drawing upon theorists such as Paul Virilio and Jean Baudrillard (Redhead, 2004a, 2004b, 2008) and Alain Badiou and Slavoj Žižek (Redhead, 2011, 2015). Certainly, there is a global recognition that we are living through significant changes, but there is uneven social and technological development and a questioning of 'globalisation' as a consequence. Academics and commentators write as if *everyone* in the world is digitally connected. Journalist and broadcaster Paul Mason has argued that 'the simultaneous arrival of tablets, streaming video and music and the takeoff of social media between 2009 and 2014 will be seen as the key moment of synergy' (Mason, 2015: 125) when we come to look back on the contemporary capitalist present which he sees as moving in the near future into a 'PostCapitalist' nirvana full of an 'Internet of Things' (Mason, 2015: 125). This imagined reality of coming decades, combined with the astonishing acceleration of high-end computing, is a modern technological revolution in anyone's language, and one occurring within a very short space of time, but there is little study of what it actually means for us as leisured citizens. Are the internet and the web part of a sinister movement from the dark side designed to enslave us in what the 'Slovenian Lacan' Slavoj Žižek has called a 'new dark ages' (Žižek, 2014b), or are they instead somehow hiding in the light on the bright side of the road, as Van Morrison once put it? The study of leisure, and 'digital leisure cultures', has in some ways come late to this debate about the good and evil sides of digitisation, but widespread, furious engagement continues elsewhere and we need to take account of it in general as far as we can. To this end I want to single out several important theorists who are not often used regularly within the study of leisure to move the debate further on up the digital road. In the case of my own theoretical perspective which I draw upon here, I want to identify Paul Virilio, Jean Baudrillard, Alain Badiou and Slavoj Žižek as theorists who may illuminate the path ahead (though they are not without their own flaws). They are a necessary, if insufficient, resource for the millions of followers who gather on the rather precarious vantage point of the narrow ledge of social media and other virtual communities following the uneven global shocks of the recent past. Theories, and theorists, are no longer optional or marginal, if they ever were: they are central to reconstruction, political, economic, cultural, social, in what Slavoj Žižek has called 'postmodern capitalism' (Žižek, 2013, 2014b).

How can we theorise digital leisure cultures?

The idea of digital leisure studies requires critical theory, and critical theorists, to sustain it. Fortunately we live in what are, in my view, 'theoretical times'.[1] Study has attached itself to what I call 'post-theory' (Redhead, 2011) and to contemporary critical theorists on a completely new scale. Theorists mentioned in this chapter are in many ways on opposite sides of the debate about the good and evil narrative in digitisation. Slavoj Žižek (2014b), for example, has occasionally lauded the internet – and its supposed associated postmodern freedoms where 'everyone gets a chance' (Žižek, 2013: 34; Hamza, 2015) – as part of a neo-communist future which he has promoted with fellow 'new left' theorists like Alain Badiou (Ruda, 2015; Badiou, 2010a; Bartlett and Clemens, 2010). Furthermore, Žižek has reflected, in answering chapter-length questions from Yong-june Park (Žižek, 2013), on the rapidly changing internet and its promotion of postmodern leisure pursuits. Žižek muses on the acceleration of digital leisure cultures, and the attendant homogenisation, miniaturisation and digitisation:

> Let's see what is now happening on the internet. We get, more and more, to serialise our lives: we go to see the same movies and we watch the same news. People describe it as a movement towards the clouds: cloud computing. We no longer need a big computer to play video games, like the one I have in my room to have fun with my son.
> (Žižek, 2013: 6)

In Žižek's view:

> A decade ago, a computer was a big box on one's table, and downloading was done with floppy disks and USB sticks; today, we no longer need strong individual computers since cloud computing is internet based – ie. software and information are provided to computers or smartphones on demand, in the guise of web-based tools or applications that users can access and use through a browser as if were a programme installed on their own computer. In this way, we can access information from wherever we are in the world, on any computer, with smartphones putting this access literally into our pocket.
> (Žižek, 2013: 6)

For Žižek, though he is a fan of the digital world, there is a perceived danger in the virtual – homogenisation, monopoly and standardisation in the internet and the web. He worries that:

Everything happens out there. Are people aware how this will standardise everything? We will only be connected to one single provider, like Google or iTunes, but we are limited to their choices. Our struggle should thus focus on those aspects that pose a threat to the transnational public sphere. Part of this general push toward the privatisation of the 'general intellect' is the recent trend in the organisation of cyberspace towards 'cloud computing'.

(Žižek, 2013: 6–7)

In general, despite his misgivings, Žižek is in favour of the accelerated culture that is being generated by these technological changes. On the other hand, self-styled 'left wing militant Christian' Paul Virilio (Virilio, 2011) is more pessimistic and sceptical, envisaging the high-speed accidents of technology as 'events' (Žižek, 2014a), as part of the dangers of the 'futurism of the moment' (Virilio, 2011, 2012) where wars (real on battlefields and virtual on gamers' screens) are fought at the 'speed of light' (Redhead, 2004a, 2004b, 2011). Virilio in particular has seen events in our digitised world as partially the result of 'automatic speculation in the futurism of the instant' (Virilio, 2012: 34). For Virilio, the aim of shrinking time and space has 'arrived' in the modern world, but his own avowed political economy of speed is often flawed, with surprisingly little empirical evidence brought forward to support his aphoristic commentary. The accelerated culture of the past four decades (Redhead, 2004a, 2004b) which Virilio sometimes obliquely captures in his uniquely singular way is, however, absolutely at the heart of the crisis of our condition. Virilio has, for instance, pointedly claimed that:

The economic crash that we experienced in 2007–2008 was a systemic crash with a history, a history going back to the early 1980s when a global stock exchange was first connected in real time. This connection called 'Program Trading', also had another, highly suggestive name: the Big Bang of the markets. A first crash in 1987 confirmed and concretised the impossibility of managing this speed. The crash in 2008, which was partially caused by 'flash trading', or very fast computerised listings done on the same computers as those used in national defence.... Our reality has become uninhabitable in milliseconds, picoseconds, femtoseconds, billionths of seconds.

(Virilio, 2012: 34–35)

Virilio is on the more cynical side of the argument about the merits of digitisation, despite celebrating the 'city of the instant' which the online world has supposedly brought us – 'live' broadcasting, with everyone watching at the same time, of, for instance, a soccer World Cup replacing the real community of the past with a virtual community of today. For the anarchistic Christian Paul Virilio, there is a 'communism of affect' in the 'city of the instant', so there is also a hopeful, optimistic side to his thoughts. Although politically on different parts of the left, and on different sides of the good-and-evil-of-digitisation debate, both Žižek and Virilio suffer at times from a pervasive libertarianism which is part of the contemporary politics of digital leisure cultures (Spracklen, 2015), and the questions of identity and community which accompany this politics. It certainly mirrors the free-market dominance of neoliberalism in the wider world and it is this aspect of political economy rather than a spuriously attributed 'postmodernism' that matters for our discussion here.

Paul Virilio's friend and colleague the late Jean Baudrillard, as critical commentators have noted, casts a more complicated shadow over the good-and-evil narrative conflict around digitisation, and over the ideas of postmodernity and postmodernism. Baudrillard often endured a reading of his work which highlighted 'postmodernism' (and also ideas like 'simulation' and 'hyperreality'), whereas 'impossible exchange', 'dystopia' and 'apocalyptism', conditions more attuned to the 2008 global financial crisis, were actually much more commonly applied in Baudrillard's work. Such concepts were used explicitly and implicitly by Baudrillard in the few years before his death much more than the more commonly attributed ideas of postmodernism, simulation and hyperreality. As reinterpreters of Baudrillard and his global significance have rightly pointed out, the term 'postmodernism' is not an accurate portrayal of Baudrillard's work or of Jean Baudrillard himself. Baudrillard utterly rejected it in many interviews during his lifetime (Smith and Clarke, 2015). I have myself referred to Baudrillard as 'non-postmodernist' and, further, a theorist of 'non-postmodernity' (Redhead, 2008) to further clarify his position on this. Regarding digitisation, Jean Baudrillard has distinguished himself from Paul Virilio on the specificity of 'digital' virtualisation. Baudrillard, who died from cancer in 2007 but left several important works to be published posthumously (Redhead, 2012), argued that his friend Paul Virilio was correct in seeing great risks in developing the internet but that there was a more complex series of questions at play in what Baudrillard saw as the 'radical uncertainty' of the contemporary world. In an interview warning against simple pessimism in response to the rapid changes the world is undergoing, a position associated with Virilio, Baudrillard points out:

> Monsieur Virilio is right that there is a risk of the subject being taken hostage, in a way, by his own tool. However, I do not see a doom-laden phenomenon there. I would side more with Leo Scheer, when he says that virtuality, being itself virtual, does not really happen. To make the network operate for the network, by a machine whose end is to operate at all costs, is not to give it a will.
>
> (Smith and Clarke, 2015: 110)

Baudrillard argues for seeing a radical uncertainty in the world which is not just about good or evil, dark side or bright side:

> I don't think it is possible to find a politics of virtuality, a code of ethics of virtuality, because virtuality virtualises politics as well; there will be no politics of virtuality because politics has become virtual; there will be no code of ethics of virtuality, because the code of ethics has become virtual, that is,

there are no more references to a value system. I am not making a nostalgic note there: virtuality retranscribes everything in its space; in a way, human ends vanish into thin air in virtuality. It is not a doom-laden danger in the sense of an explosion, but rather a passage through an indefinable space, a kind of radical uncertainty.

(Smith and Clarke, 2015: 110)

The fourth theorist I want to cite in this debate is Alain Badiou. For Badiou, who was a student of Louis Althusser's in the 1960s and for a time a committed Maoist, the debate about the global 'virtual' society is a matter of seeing the potential in global and local organisation for a neo-communism of the future which the internet provides, and indeed he envisages nothing less than a global 'resurrection of communism' with an organised global politics to sustain it. For Badiou, interviewed by Peter Engelmann, a former prisoner of the Stasi, the 'Idea of Communism' (Badiou, 2010b):

can be discussed at a global level with anyone. By contrast, in terms of concrete political experiments, I think we have to give local experiments the time to develop, and we should try to learn what they're about. What I kind of had in mind was to try to create a global space that would simply be a place for exchanging experiences, where everyone would describe their own way of activating the idea of emancipation, what specific activities they've carried out and how they've managed to keep violence in check. It would be a place to report on experiences that have been very interesting in this regard.

(Badiou and Engelmann, 2015: 92)

For Badiou, who is interested in universalism rather than the failed experiment of 'globalisation':

There's a lot to report on and talk about if we're to enter a new era of politics that isn't a politics of representation.... Where what people describe has a universal value, where you can ask them questions.

(Badiou and Engelmann, 2015: 92)

Whether or not he is fully aware of it, Alain Badiou is actually describing, quite powerfully, some political and social aspects of the contemporary internet and social media – universal and full of potential for radical change, in among the ubiquitous trolling, bullying and outright discrimination. Badiou has gone further and envisaged the 'resurrection of communism' in these conditions:

This is what I call reactivation or resurrection. Incidentally, when I suggest returning to the word 'communism', it's an attempt at resurrection. I'm well aware that Stalin killed off communism, but I think it can come back to life.

(Badiou and Engelmann, 2015: 101)

Let us see what these various theorists have to offer us and in particular how we might generate concepts out of aspects of their work which will better reframe theories of digital leisure cultures. Indeed, contemporary digital leisure studies needs theory and theorists from outside of itself to move forward in this rapidly accelerating culture.

Critical study of digital leisure cultures

Empirically, in this realm of emerging digital leisure studies, there are also plenty of contemporary examples of digital leisure cultures to get our theoretical teeth into. In digital soccer cultures, for instance, an event I have called the 'First Twitter World Cup' in the football tournament in Brazil in 2014 (Redhead, 2015), what has also been referred to as 'The Last World Cup' in some quarters because of the social, economic and political costs of hosting such a mega-event, marks a watershed for social media and sport. Live tweeting of each match at a World Cup has not been witnessed before and sports journalism itself has been transformed by the notion of a 'city of the instant'. The tweets from the journalists at the games watching the matches are now more important than the match reports they eventually file. Social media (especially platforms like Twitter, Facebook, Snapchat and Instagram) and their regulation (social and legal) are a crucial part of the new media technologies which have transformed global soccer culture (or what we might refer to as 'digital soccer cultures'). Twitter has frequently become intertwined with civil law as well as criminal law. A prime example involved Ryan Giggs, then in the latter days of his career as a Manchester United player. Giggs, a married man, had an affair with a Big Brother TV contestant Imogen Thomas. His lawyers obtained a superinjunction from the high court, which banned the media from reporting anything to do with the alleged affair (and even that an injunction had been obtained) which was widely speculated upon (though without mentioning the names of the participants). When Twitter was eventually used to broadcast the name of Ryan Giggs as the footballer involved, almost instantly millions of people around the globe were informed without the need to have recourse to conventional media like television or newspapers. Giggs' lawyers' subsequent action was to launch a civil action against Twitter as a company, a classic case of trying to close the stable door when the horse had bolted. Battles over soccer clubs banning i-Pads from stadiums, or introducing Wi-Fi, or spectators attending matches virtually through Google+, may be set in a new context with these new theorists and new theories. New media technologies have remade our idea of what spectating at sporting events 'live' means. As well as Badiou and Žižek, Paul Virilio's ideas of the city of the instant and futurism of the moment and Jean Baudrillard's notion of impossible exchange are pregnant with possibility for analysing the relentless 24/7 accelerated culture which is global sport today. Sport and social media culture today are an integral part of what Virilio, dromological theorist of speed, power and technology (Redhead, 2004a, 2004b; Armitage, 2013), terms the 'city of the instant'. In this 'dromoscopy', amidst what he sees as the contemporary collapse of time and distance,

Virilio positions the city of the instant in a rapidly shrinking world of what I have called 'mobile city cultures' and 'accelerated culture' (Redhead, 2004a, 2004b, 2011). For Virilio, this prescient concept of the city of the instant connotes a 'live' audience of millions or, possibly, billions, watching events like sporting World Cups or the Olympics anywhere around the world, on various devices, all at the same time (with a smidgeon of digital delay). But it can equally register all the social networking sites of new media, globally connecting users all over the world, often in real time. In Virilio's writing ever since the 1950s it is frequently television which has been the main platform for such a broadcasting community or 'city of the instant'. In recent analyses, however, sports media analysts are increasingly writing about global sport after television. Digitisation and globalisation have changed the scene of digital leisure cultures as to make it almost unrecognisable. Utilising the theorists mentioned in this chapter anew when looking at, for example, sports consumption, sporting hooliganism, media simulation and mega-sporting events, or else the militarisation or technologisation of sport and leisure, is already being tried, with reasonable levels of success.

The main focus of this exploratory chapter is sport and sport media cultures which have a particular presence in new media technologies and social media platforms, but the theoretical argument I am making applies more widely to digital leisure cultures as a whole. It offers an outline of possibilities for a new direction in the *critical* study of digital leisure cultures. More specifically, the question is: Will the 'agony of power' and 'impossible exchange' (Baudrillard, 2010) of information overload in what I call 'non-postmodernity' (Redhead, 2008) tear us apart or bring us together as a collectivised community in the era of digital leisure? I have already suggested some critical theoretical perspectives we can bring to the field – in the study of sports, tourism, mega-events and so on. Now, we are 'after the goldrush'; as singer Neil Young once put it succinctly in the early 1970s when yet another 'capitalist crisis' was manifesting itself, there is radical rethinking across the board going on. We are also now, weirdly, 'post-catastrophe', as if we are aware we are living 'after postmodernity' as well as 'after the crash' (Redhead, 2011). What is more, a frantic search for *theory* is beginning again in an increasingly empiricist and business-oriented neoliberal global academy, tearing apart what we had settled on as satisfactory explanations for all sorts of phenomena. A veritable explosion of broadly critical work has been produced, veering off in various directions. In some ways, the new watershed for theory is the global financial crisis of 2008, beginning in 2007, which was followed by a brief 'global Keynesianism' before a return to the brutal neoliberalism now destroying the fabric of societies across the globe. Many of these works on new directions in critical thought have been published since the watershed, though much of the now published work was bubbling in the early years of the new century from the time of 9/11 onward. More generally in academic life globally, discipline after discipline has agonised over whether the tenets of yesteryear still hold good, and whether or not we need to return to the beginning or origin (Douzinas and Žižek, 2010: 209–226) of disciplines. For example, after Cultural Studies has, in the view of some participants, lost its way as we have known it, founding fathers have asked anxiously, 'what is the future of

Accelerated culture and leisure studies 21

Cultural Studies?' Economists have asked what is there left of economics after the (economic) crisis? Legal Studies has renewed its call for new critical legal theory and for 'law and critique' as never before. Philosophy has mused about whether it still has the power to explain events like the riots in the UK in 2011 and the ongoing Arab Spring in the way that, say, Karl Marx analysed the revolutions in Europe in 1848 and provided ethical and political intervention (Žižek, 2014b), reviving, for a new century, the question of the 'idea of communism' (Badiou, 2010a; Žižek, 2013) and the 'communist hypothesis' (Badiou, 2010a).

It is, in this context, worth taking stock of the relationship between the 'post-crash' global society and contemporary theory, and new disciplinary and interdisciplinary movements. What I label here 'digital leisure studies' is one such putative emerging subject within the more general field. It references global celebrity intellectual culture which has mushroomed partly as a result of burgeoning digital profiles, a consequence of our common tendency to live life online in a seemingly permanent state of 'play' and leisure, even if we are at 'work' and selling our 'labour power' in the same old way, as Karl Marx recognised 150 years ago. The celebrity intellectual culture, which has developed very quickly over the past few years since the millennium, has produced myriad YouTube appearances by myriad 'theorists as rock stars' as well as open access online journals devoted to these theorists and the minutiae of their theories. For instance, theorists mentioned in this chapter such as Jean Baudrillard, Alain Badiou and Slavoj Žižek have their own dedicated online open-access journals. The *International Journal of Baudrillard Studies* began in 2004, the *International Journal of Žižek Studies* began in 2007 and *Badiou Studies* began in 2012. A similar venture for the work of Paul Virilio seems to be only a matter of time. Dictionaries devoted to Žižek (Butler, 2014), Baudrillard (Smith, 2010), Badiou (Corcoran, 2015) and Virilio (Armitage, 2013) alongside other theorists have also started to be written, published and consumed to considerable international acclaim. The ideas of the theorists themselves have then been applied to what were once 'disciplines' – for instance, Virilio for architects (Armitage, 2015), Žižek for lawyers (De Sutter, 2015) and so on. In some senses, in the interstices of what I call 'accelerated culture', disciplines have been superseded. We have become post-disciplinary in our interdisciplinarity without even realising it. The study of leisure practices is no exception to these upheavals, and the 'digital turn' has simply emphasised the need for a new and more critical perspective and substantial innovative thinking. For theorists like Slavoj Žižek and Alain Badiou, a return to universalism, and universal concepts, following the relativist concepts of the so-called postmodern era, is absolutely crucial. For them globalisation is always something as part of the neoliberal era to be avoided; universalism is a part of the neo-communist fight-back. This issue of universalism and universality raises important issues on how, for instance, Baudrillard, Žižek or Badiou's work encompasses feminist or queer studies concerns. It also forces us to think how previously 'postmodernised' fields such as the study of leisure and subject areas such as digital leisure cultures can be transformed by the renewed use of universal concepts – such as, for instance, in the case of the four theorists I have selected, communism, justice, love and harm. Although pursuing different furrows ever since they first began to write, speak or photograph, Virilio and Baudrillard were friends and colleagues for many years until Baudrillard died from cancer in March 2007. Virilio is very much alive and still writing his provocative, pithy, short books as if they were positively envisaged to be written in consecutive 140-character tweets – almost the first Twitter philosophy books! Baudrillard, or 'post-Baudrillard' as we might describe recent posthumous ventures, lives on in some very significant short books which were written in the last two years of his life. Together, over a long period since the 1950s, Baudrillard and Virilio have a huge back catalogue which is only now being properly reassessed, and radically reinterpreted, by scholars in various disciplines. The same applies to the still-living Slavoj Žižek and Alain Badiou who have worked together (Badiou and Žižek, 2009) in the neo-communist cause for many years.

Towards a structure of feeling for digital leisure studies

In the concluding part of this chapter, I want to indicate how we might use these theorists and theories in pursuit of a new direction – namely a digital leisure studies. I did not choose the four theorists I selected for this chapter at random. The choice did not occur in a vacuum. I have for some time worked on these theorists and generated concepts out of a reading of their large body of work (Redhead, 2011, 2015, 2017). One of those concepts, 'accelerated culture', underpins the suggested new direction in critical perspectives on digital leisure cultures that we have investigated so far in this chapter. I want also to refer to another concept generated out of these readings: my concept of 'claustropolitanism'. This idea reimagines the post-crash cultural condition of our world in the context of the effects of digitisation – the narrative of good and evil, dark side and bright side – which has permeated this chapter. My notion of 'claustropolitanism' is intended to illuminate the global condition in these 'theoretical times' (Redhead, 2017), particularly in terms of the effects of rapid globalisation and digitisation in the whole of this century to date. It is veritably what Raymond Williams called a 'structure of feeling' (Williams, 2015) – a structure of feeling for the old, grey, capitalist world we inhabit, a structure of feeling at the end of the old world as a new one comes up. It emerges initially from Paul Virilio's slant on the term 'claustropolis'. Virilio's aphorism proclaims that we are moving, in our twenty-first-century world, from 'cosmopolis to claustropolis' (Virilio and Lotringer, 2008: 211), Virilio expanded on this pithy statement by relating it to 'new bunkers' and 'gated communities'. He has claimed:

> What I called claustropolis has replaced cosmopolis, where I'm from, since I'm the son of an illegal Italian immigrant *in France*. On the other hand, in Shanghai, in China, they're the avant-garde of modernity, in terms of claustropolis: *towerism*. They've got 4,000 towers overe there. Towers aren't just a matter of prestige. They're super-gated; except for Spiderman, no one is climbing up their facades.
>
> (Virilio and Lotringer, 2008: 211)

Accelerated culture and leisure studies 23

What Paul Virilio means by claustropolis is the gated community and the way in which the 'good life' is being colonised (literally, spatially) by the rich and powerful; for decades his own political work has involved 'housing for the poor' and started off with the Catholic worker-priests' movement in France. Although the Virilian notion is suggestive, my own recent work (Redhead, 2011, 2015, 2017) is about developing the idea of claustropolitanism as an element of a 'coming' claustropolitan society in the new dark ages envisaged so evocatively by Slavoj Žižek (2014b). I am arguing here for elements of a claustropolitan sociology to be outlined. More prosaically, 'claustropolitanism' embodies my idea of world society closing in (being foreclosed, in all sorts of senses), and builds on a global sense of 'claustrophobia' (Virilio himself is claustrophobic) which, as accelerated culture becomes more invasive and pervasive, we come to recognise more and more in our digital leisure practices. Claustropolitanism involves the idea that we want to leave the planet (which is shrinking technologically and materially as we write). Claustropolitanism as a concept for the contemporary post-crash condition has been given focus within socio-legal studies and criminology, especially ultra-realist criminology. For example, ultra-realist criminologists Steve Hall and Simon Winlow have argued that:

> Redhead's notion of *claustropolitanism* – based on Virilio's claim that humanity increasingly wishes to get off the planet and leave behind the depleting, overcrowded, gridlocked and corrupt world of neo-liberal megacities, resource wars, clamorous markets and petty consumerised struggles for social status – contextualises Atkinson's notion of the 'metropolitan cloud' as the first actual step, both metaphorically, and in some ways literally, in this process. In the vortices, the retreat of younger generations into subjectivity and fantasy is the pallid substitute for what the rich are beginning to do in reality ... Alain Badiou said something similar – at the moment judging by the way we think and what we desire, as disembodied subjects running away from reality we all, as Redhead implies, want to be 'out of this world'.
>
> (Hall and Winlow, 2015: 128–129)

Claustropolitanism, as a structure of feeling, can be usefully extended to other disciplines and subdisciplines, not least the study of leisure and digital leisure cultures.

This chapter has developed my concepts of 'accelerated culture' and 'claustropolitanism' in order to further illuminate the battle over how digital leisure cultures are viewed and what we may expect in an embryonic digital leisure studies from the coming struggles over various leisure concerns, areas and issues. Essentially, then, following the explorations in this chapter, I want to assert that we can indeed more satisfactorily reframe the study of digital leisure cultures for these accelerated cultural times.

Note

1 'Theoretical Times' is the title of one of my forthcoming books upon which I have drawn in this chapter for some of its new theoretical ideas. The process of writing *Theoretical Times* has been thoroughly 'digital'. It has, for example, been embedded in social media. There are 12 freely downloadable podcasts about its subject matter, recorded with Professor Tara Brabazon. These are focused on the theorists and theories I have discussed in *Theoretical Times*. These podcasts have been promoted on Twitter, Academia.edu and Facebook, and downloaded from various platforms many tens of thousands of times from all all around the world. I have taken into account diverse feedback (on social media or email) from those downloading the podcasts in the construction of *Theoretical Times*. For the podcasts, see my personal website (www.steveredhead.zone) and for the text see my forthcoming book *Theoretical Times* (Redhead, 2017).

References

Armitage, J. (ed.) (2013) *The Virilio Dictionary*. Edinburgh: Edinburgh University Press.
Armitage, J. (2015) *Virilio For Architects*. London and New York: Routledge.
Badiou, A. (2010a) *The Communist Hypothesis*. London and New York: Verso.
Badiou, A. (2010b) The Idea of Communism. In C. Douzinas and S. Žižek (eds) *The Idea of Communism*. London: Verso, pp. 1–14.
Badiou, A. and Engelmann, P. (2015) *Philosophy and the Idea of Communism*. Cambridge: Polity Press.
Badiou, A. and Žižek, S. (2009) *Philosophy in the Present*. Cambridge: Polity Press.
Bartlett, A.J. and Clemens, J. (eds) (2010) *Alain Badiou: Key Concepts*. Durham, NC: Acumen.
Baudrillard, J. (2010) *The Agony of Power*. Los Angeles: Semiotext(e).
Butler, R. (ed.) (2014) *The Žižek Dictionary*. Durham, NC: Acumen.
Corcoran, S. (ed.) (2015) *The Badiou Dictionary*. Edinburgh: Edinburgh University Press.
De Sutter, L. (2015) *Žižek and Law*. London and New York: Routledge.
Douzinas, C. and Žižek, S. (eds) *The Idea of Communism*. London: Verso.
Hall, S. and Winlow, S. (2015) *Revitalising Criminological Theory: Towards a New Ultra-realism*. London and New York: Routledge.
Hamza, A. (ed.) (2015) *Repeating Žižek*. Durham, NC, and London: Duke University Press.
Lupton, D. (2014) *Digital Sociology*. London and New York: Routledge.
Mason, P. (2015) *PostCapitalism: A Guide to Our Future*. London: Allen Lane.
Redhead, S. (2004a) *Paul Virilio: Theorist for an Accelerated Culture*. Edinburgh: Edinburgh University Press/Toronto: University of Toronto Press.
Redhead, S. (ed.) (2004b) *The Paul Virilio Reader*. Edinburgh: Edinburgh University Press/New York: Columbia University Press.
Redhead, S. (ed.) (2008) *The Jean Baudrillard Reader*. Edinburgh: Edinburgh University Press/New York: Columbia University Press.
Redhead, S. (2011) *We Have Never Been Postmodern: Theory at the Speed of Light*. Edinburgh: Edinburgh University Press.
Redhead, S. (2012) The Agony of Power/The Power of Agony: Post-Baudrillard Theory and Post-Political Politics. *International Journal of Baudrillard Studies*, Special Issue on Baudrillard and Politics, 9(3). Available at: www.ubishops.ca/baudrillardstudies/vol-9_3/v9-3-redhead.html.

Redhead, S. (2014) 'We're Not Racist, We Only Hate Mancs': Post-subculture and Football Fandom. In L. Duits, K. Zwaan and S. Rejinders (eds) *Ashgate Research Companion to Fan Cultures*. Aldershot: Ashgate, pp. 289–301.
Redhead, S. (2015) *Football and Accelerated Culture: This Modern Sporting Life*. London and New York: Routledge.
Redhead, S. (2017) *Theoretical Times*, London and New York: Routledge, forthcoming.
Ruda, F. (2015) *For Badiou: Idealism without Idealism*. Evanston: Northwestern University Press.
Smith, R. (ed.) (2010) *The Baudrillard Dictionary*. Edinburgh: Edinburgh University Press.
Smith, R. and Clarke, D. (eds) (2015) *Jean Baudrillard – From Hyperreality to Disappearance: Uncollected Interviews*. Edinburgh: Edinburgh University Press.
Spracklen, K. (2015) *Digital Leisure, the Internet and Popular Culture: Communities and Identities in a Digital Age*. Basingstoke: Palgrave Macmillan.
Virilio, P. (2010) *The Futurism of the Instant*. Cambridge: Polity Press.
Virilio, P. (2011) *A Winter's Journey: Four Conversations with Marianne Brausch*. Calcutta: Seagull Books.
Virilio, P. (2012) *The Administration of Fear*. Los Angeles: Semiotext(e).
Virilio, P. and Lotringer, S. (2008) *Pure War*, 3rd edn. Los Angeles: Semiotext(e).
Williams, R. (2015) *Politics and Letters: Interviews with New Left Review*. London and New York: Verso.
Žižek, S. (2013) *Demanding the Impossible*. Cambridge: Polity Press.
Žižek, S. (2014a) *Event: Philosophy in Transit*. London: Penguin.
Žižek, S. (2014b) *Trouble in Paradise: From the End of History to the End of Capitalism*. London: Allen Lane.

3 3D printed self-replicas
Personal digital data made solid

Deborah Lupton

Introduction

3D printing (also known as additive fabrication or additive manufacturing) is a method for generating three-dimensional objects that involves the use of computer-assisted design (CAD) software working with hardware to direct the sequential laying down of layers of materials to form the objects (Berman, 2012). The materials used, dispensed via nozzles, include plaster, resins, metals, ceramics, glass, plaster and even organic material such as living cells or edible substances (so-called 'bio-inks'). It has been claimed that the ability to generate rapid prototypes from 3D printing can facilitate novel approaches to making in both the workplace and the leisure sphere. 3D printing has been heralded as a 'disruptive' technology in various forms of industries and activities and even as generating a new industrial revolution (Lipson and Kurman, 2013; Petrick and Simpson, 2013).

A new way of representing selfhood and embodiment has emerged in the wake of the development of 3D printing technologies. This is the 3D printed self-replica, a fabrication using digital 3D body scans of people that produces a material artefact of a person's entire body or parts thereof. Full figurines of people made in this way are usually miniature in size, while separate body parts replicas, such as a head-and-shoulders 'bust', may be life sized. Such replicas, particularly of body parts, are now used in medical contexts for surgical, diagnostic and patient education purposes. The technologies to generate these artefacts are now also rapidly moving into a range of leisure domains, including sporting clubs and events, shopping centres, airports, concerts and amusement parks as well as fan cultures and marketing programmes. These artefacts are advertised as promoting opportunities for personal memorabilia and record-keeping about people's life events, interests and families. 3D printed self-replicas may be ordered from 3D printing companies and can even be made at home using a software package developed for the Xbox Kinect game box or a home 3D scanner in conjunction with a home 3D printer. Some commentators have begun to refer to the 3D printed self-replica as a new form of 'selfie' (the term now often used for a self-taken photographic portrait using a mobile device) – the '3D selfie'.

In this chapter, following an overview of the ways in which 3D printing technologies have become incorporated into leisure activities, I will focus on the 3D printed self-replica. As I will argue, there are deeper implications of these artefacts for the ways in which we understand not only the body, selfhood, personal memories, social relations and the engagement of people in leisure cultures but also people's entanglements with objects and personal digital data. I draw upon several theoretical perspectives to provide some insights.

The socio-material perspective, in its focus on humans' entanglements with nonhuman objects, is a good starting point. Socio-materialism incorporates the actor network approach from science and technology studies, Deleuzian theory, materialist feminist philosophy as well as various new materialist perspectives that have emerged from such areas as material cultures (principally developed in cultural anthropology), cultural geography and cultural studies (Latour, 2005; Coole and Frost, 2010). These perspectives move away from the focus on language and discourse that was a dominant feature of poststructuralist theorising to acknowledging the role played by nonhuman actors, including material objects, in human experience, embodiment and social relations. Related to socio-materialism is assemblage theory, which represents human bodies and other phenomena as hybrid, unstable and dynamic configurations of ideas, discourses, practices, biological matter and material objects (Marcus, 2006).

Several scholars have taken a socio-materialist perspective to contend that digital data are shared accomplishments between human and nonhuman actors (Ruppert, 2011; Rogers, 2013; Kitchin and Dodge, 2011). As human selves and bodies become increasingly digitised, they are rendered into digital data assemblages. The concept of code/space (Kitchin and Dodge, 2011) offers a way of articulating the manner in which human bodies intersect with and are produced by digital technologies. Code/space refers to the intertwinings of software code with spatial dimensions. It acknowledges that human bodies, and by extension selfhoods and identities, are increasingly configured through and with code and space. 3D self-replicas are specific examples of digital data assemblages: the enactment of code with space in ways that allow people to engage in self-expression and memorialisation. As a case study, they offer an opportunity to think through some of these intersections and entanglements of people with digital technologies and digital data.

3D printing in leisure domains

While 3D printing technologies were first developed in the context of industry, the manufacture and sale of 3D printers and software that people can use in their homes and the development of companies that offer to print objects for consumers have led to the proliferation of other sites and purposes for these technologies. As a result, the possibilities for 3D printing for contributing to and generating new leisure practices have expanded. There has been much speculation about the ways in which the technologies may be used by artists, designers and craft workers as well as by hobbyists (now often referred to as 'makers') to generate novel forms of art, craft and design. Other forms of leisure activities in which 3D printing technologies have been implicated include sports, food decoration and cooking activities, museum exhibitions and visitor engagement, children's craft and fan cultures.

3D printing technologies are used for leisure purposes across a range of domains. One of these is arts and crafts. The potential of 3D printing to contribute to the work of professionals in the creative industries has been discussed (Hoskins, 2013). With the use of these technologies, amateur makers can also begin to engage in the more sophisticated design and manufacture of objects. Some commentators have identified a 'maker movement' that has developed from the communal and participatory practices facilitated by digital technologies, the internet and the open source culture. This maker movement includes the exchange of information and experiences on social media as part of the sharing economy (John, 2013) in conjunction with novel digital devices such as 3D printing software and hardware (Tanenbaum et al., 2013; Shewbridge et al., 2014).

There are now dozens of books available directed at the lay user on how to use 3D printing technologies for DIY and crafting purposes, as well as several websites. Incorporating a social media element, companies such as Cubify not only offer the technologies for 3D printing (printing machines, cartridges, scanners and the relevant software) but also encourage the development of making communities. Cubify includes a section of its website and app, for example, where people can see what other people are making and download the CAD files to make the same objects themselves at home or to order products that are for sale. The MakerBot 3D printer company supports Thingiverse, another well-known website for 3D printing makers that promotes the objects made by community members and facilitates the sharing of designs. It is claimed on the website that over 130,000 members interact on the site and that over 100,000 designs are available there (Makerbot Thingiverse, 2015). People can join various specific interest groups to discuss issues and techniques. Thingiverse, therefore, combines social media community functioning and the sharing ethos with offering technical support (it also has Tumblr, Facebook and Instagram accounts for community members).

Digital fabrication has entered several areas of leisure. In the areas of sport and gaming, for instance, there are now many opportunities for entrepreneurs to market 3D fabricated objects to fans. The Shapeways and Cubify 3D printing company websites provide many such examples, offering the objects for sale and providing digital files of their prototypes for download by people who may want to fabricate them for themselves or learn from the design. These include files for 3D printed puzzles, game dice, poker chips, checkers and chess pieces, finger soccer pieces and tabletop ping-pong and bowling game pieces. Some companies have identified opportunities to use 3D printing to fabricate sporting equipment customised to the user, such as helmets, mouthguards, bicycle seats, goggles and protective masks and sports shoes.

3D fabrication entrepreneurs cater well for fans. On the Shapeways website alone there are specialised jewellery, model, dice and figurine ranges designed for fans of Harry Potter, League of Legends and Formula 1 motoring while the digital files for Box Trolls figurines may be downloaded free and fabricated at home. Fans can order classic model aeroplanes made on a 3D printer from one site. Makers are experimenting with fabricating custom Lego and sporting hero figurines. The most popular 3D printable model from one website offering over 200,000 of them in July 2015 included a Hillary Clinton action figure, a model of the New Horizons spacecraft and a Game of Thrones-themed iPhone case. The Pinshape website for 3D printing enthusiasts offers designs for many Dr Who artefacts (chess pieces, pen holders, logos, figurines, Tardises, jewellery and so on), as well as Pokemon, Star Wars and Minions objects.

Museums around the world are also beginning to incorporate 3D printing technologies not only as part of creating exhibits or demonstrating the capabilities of the technologies but also with the aim of enriching visitor experience or facilitating access to their collections. In 2012, the New York Metropolitan Museum of Art partnered with MakerBot to run a 3D scanning and printing hackathon. This event involved digital artists and designers scanning items in the collection and then fabricating them. The digital files are available on Thingiverse for others to use to print out their 3D copies of the artworks (Terrassa, 2012). The British Museum has released 3D printable scans of 14 objects from its holdings, available on the Sketchfab website (Cascone, 2014). Several other museums have featured exhibitions about 3D printing technologies and their applications.

The phenomenon of digital food printing has entered the domain of food and cuisine. 3D printers can use edible substances such as chocolate to produce novelty food items. The manufacturers of these technologies sometimes use the enticements of both creativity and gustatory pleasure in marketing them. Thus, for example, the Choc Edge company's website (Choc Edge, 2015) claims that its chocolate 3D printing machine allows users to engage in 'creating your chocolate in style' by engaging in 'choc art', thereby 'empower[ing] users to take chocolate creation to new levels'. Other companies offer 3D printing of objects using sugar or ice-cream, or manufacture machines that can generate biscuits, pasta or pancakes in customised shapes, or produce novelty shapes from food purees.

3D printing companies also cater for children's leisure activities. The Kids Creation Station website offers parents the opportunity to upload their children's drawings and turn them into 3D objects. It also provides 3D modelling software to download for free for children to experiment with, such as sketching, doodling, and modelling and design software to create and fabricate objects. The Shapeways website offers an online video tutorial to teach children how to use their 3D printing software. People may download the CAD files for various children's toys from Cubify.

Digital body objects in leisure domains

The human body has become increasingly rendered into digital form. People constantly emit digital data as they engage online, are tracked by the geolocation functions on their mobile devices, move around in sensor-embedded spaces, monitor themselves using self-tracking apps or wearable devices and generate images of themselves to share on social media sites (Lupton, in press). 3D fabrications of human bodies are becoming available in several contexts, including medicine (Lupton, 2015b). 3D scanning technologies for visualising human bodies, such as 3D sonography and computerised tomography, are now a feature of medical diagnostics. Medical professionals use the digitalised information from scans such as these to assist in decision-making, surgery and medical and patient education. Writers in the medical literature refer to 'patient-specific anatomical replicas' (Moody, 2014), or 3D printed objects fabricated from digital medical scans, including hearts, brains and other organs, as well as bones and joints. Doctors use these replicas, which are unique to each patient, to diagnose a medical condition, plan treatment, to refer to during surgery and as a means of informing the patient what the problem is and how it will be treated. They are now also used to demonstrate to patients what the effects of cosmetic surgery will be on their bodies. The replicas may be shown to patients so that they are able not only to see but also touch them, and their doctors can point to features on the replica to explain the problem and how they intend to treat it. Customised prosthetics of body parts are also manufactured using 3D printers.

Leisure activities have become another important domain for the creation of 3D fabricated digital body objects. The commercial production of self-replica figurines for novelty or marketing purposes has now been taken up by numerous companies. Some offer full body figurines while others generate busts or other parts of the body. Figure 3.1 shows an example of a self-replica figurine and the 3D printer that fabricated it. 3D full-body scanning booths are currently being rolled out in retail stores in the USA, with plans to expand to theme parks, airports and tourist destinations. A German 3D tech company, Doob Group AG, offers mobile 3D screening booths for clients to use at promotional events, concerts, sporting events and so on. Another company, Artec Group, as well as using 3D scanning booths, also sells a software package that allows users who own a Xbox Kinect game box to scan their bodies at home and print out a figurine using their own 3D printer or to send the digital files to the company for printing the figurine.

These initiatives are also beginning to emerge in marketing efforts as part of promotional campaigns. A recent example includes Coca-Cola's product launch of its new mini-size bottle of its product in Israel. The company invited people to visit its 3D printing lab to have 'mini-me' replica figurines made (Bilton, 2013). Japanese clothing company Uniqlo has offered customers the opportunity to be 3D scanned and rendered into figurines by providing scanning booths in selected stores (Thimmesch, 2014).

Medical imaging technologies are being used to create products for the commercial market as novelties. One company offers a service which turns MRI scans into full-scale replicas of an individual's brain, which can be mounted on a stand and displayed at home. The company also produces earrings, pendants and cufflinks for customers in the shape of their brains. As the company suggests, this process will allow customers to 'hold your brain in your hands!' and wearing the brain jewellery would be 'great for conferences and talks' (Brainform, 2015). Artist

3D: personal digital data made solid   31

Brendon McNaughton offers customers the opportunity to use their MRI heart scans to create a larger-than-life model of their hearts covered in shiny 22-carat gold leaf; enabling them to display their literal 'heart of gold'. 3D ultrasound imaging is now being used to produce life-sized figurines of human foetuses for their expectant parents to hold and display. A Californian company calling itself '3D Babies' offers this service, as well as fabricating newborn infant replicas using photographs supplied by the parents. These replicas are marketed on the company's site as offering an 'artistic sculpture for your display case', 'memorabilia for baby's room', centrepiece for baby shower', a way to 'share the news of your pregnancy' or to use at a 'gender reveal' party (3D Babies, 2014).

The family photograph has been reimagined in 3D, with services now offered for family members to have themselves scanned and then generated as figurines for display in the home in place of the traditional professional family portrait. It is easy to envisage people collecting figure replicas of themselves to mark important events, and to track children's physical growth and changes over their life course (from *in utero* onward, if services such as those offered by 3D Babies are used). Indeed, such uses have already been promoted by the companies who offer these services. The 3D Selfies website (3D Selfies, 2015), where the tagline is 'Revolutionizing the American Portrait', argues that replica figures of children can demonstrate their growth as well as memorialise children's favourite activities. The website displays examples of children dressed in sporting outfits with sports equipment, at birthday parties, recitals, confirmation ceremonies and bar or bat mitzvahs, in ballet garb or fancy dress. Customers are encouraged to partner with their children's sporting teams, dance schools, schools or scouting

Figure 3.1 A 3D self-replica sitting on the 3D printer that fabricated it. (Image credit: Goran Jonsson – 3-D printed by Daniel Noree on Replicator 2X. Available under a CC BY 2.0 licence. Image available at: https://plus.google.com/+DanielNoree/posts/C9Z7TwNzzrb).

organisations to sell the figurines, using a Kinect device or a scanner that works with an iPad to generate scans for printing. Other examples of self-replicas on this website include fabricating figures of pregnant women, people dressed in their military uniforms, people engaging in holiday events, for use as trophies and generating the replicas at corporate events as a keepsake for attendees.

Several of these companies provide self-replica figurines solely from digital photographs that customers send to them and, therefore, do not require 3D scanning technologies. Some companies allow customers to edit the figurines or busts that they generate. The FaceGen company's website offers services whereby customers can upload a digital image of their face and then manipulate it by changing the facial expression, skin colour, gender or age and adding facial hair or a different hairstyle. Customers of Cubify can scan in their face, choose a body prototype from the range offered by the company and then generate a figurine with their own facial features. The body prototypes include sports models such as beach volleyball player, surfer, swimmer and soccer player, costumes (rock guitarist, super-heroes, mythological figures, ninjas, pirates), jobs (doctor, police officer, firefighter, teacher), occasions (wearing formal wear, wedding dress, graduation robes) as well as a range of Halloween-style 'horror' outfits. Customers can then choose from a range of body sizes and height to make the model look more like themselves. The Choc Edge and 3D Selfies companies offer users the opportunity to generate edible self-portraits or figurines in chocolate. A variety of 3D printing companies offer services whereby people can have their faces superimposed onto Star Wars, GhostBusters and Star Trek figurines of their choice. Figure 3.2 shows some of these types of self-replica figurines on display.

Sexual activity, human genitalia and pornography have also been the targets of 3D printing initiatives. An enterprising Japanese artist, Megumi Igarashi, who specialises in artist portrayals of female genitalia, sought to raise money for her new art project by offering on a crowdfunding platform CAD files of her vulva for fabrication by customers. She was arrested by Japanese police and spent five days in jail on obscenity charges (Sevenson, 2014). Some people are dispensing entirely with the artistic impulse, scanning their genitals to give as gifts to their sexual partners. The sex toy industry is experimenting with 3D printing, promoting designs for sex toys that may be customised and made at home. The Makerlove website provides a range of free designs for download and encourages people to submit their designs to share. The Eroticart-shop company provides opportunities for customers to order customised body replicas of well-known female porn stars. These replicas may be fabricated as nudes or dressed in various provocative outfits.

Another form of 3D printed embodiment is that which uses digital data about the functions or activities of bodies rather than their appearance. Exploratory work on the part of some human–computer interaction research teams has begun to generate 3D objects created from digital biometric data. Researchers from The Exertion Games Lab at RMIT in Melbourne, for example, have experimented with using 3D printers in different ways to materialise personal body data. In one project, Edipulse, the team has fabricated chocolate using 3D printers and digital data of people's self-tracked heart rate following physical activity (Khot

3D: personal digital data made solid 33

Figure 3.2 3D self-replicas in various forms. (Image credit: 3D Printed Heroes – photograph by Maurizio Pesce. Available under a CC BY 2.0 licence. Image available at: www.flickr.com/photos/pestoverde/16863356645).

et al., 2015). Based on each individual's data, the 3D printer makes a customised chocolate in the shape of an emoticon or words providing encouraging messages (such as 'U Rock!'). The thickness of the sweet or the number of letters completed in each message varies according to the data (high levels of physical activity generate thicker chocolates, and a longer length of exercise produces a greater number of words fabricated). Different emoticons are printed out based on the intensity of exercise.

Another project by members of the Lab, SweatAtoms project, involved five different material manifestations of participants' physical activity fabricated on home 3D printers. These artefacts included a 3D graph of heart rate data, a flower shape where the length and width of the petals represent heart rate duration and intensity, a frog shape that changed in size according to the amount of physical activity carried out that day, a die representing the six zones of heart beat data and a ring displaying the number of hours the person was active (Khot *et al.*, 2013). The idea of such projects is to materialise personal bodily data in a way that people find more accessible than two-dimensional graphical representations or simple metrics. Some commentators have speculated that digital data could inform such practices as customised food fabrication, in which a person's physical activity or body weight data informs what type of food their personal kitchen-based 3D food printer makes for them (Lipson and Kurman, 2013).

Theorising the self-replica artefact

As sensor- and camera-embedded physical environments proliferate in both the domestic and public landscapes, the movements of human bodies in space and place are monitored, assessed and predicted by digital technologies. The mobile and wearable technologies that people carry around with them – their smartphones, smartwatches, tablet computers and digital self-tracking devices – constantly generate data about their movements and geolocation. People have become data-emitting nodes in the Internet of Things, exchanging data with other 'smart objects'. This vitality of digital data is a key element of contemporary digital data practices. The digital data economy involves the continual circulation of digital data across and between sites, platforms and devices (Beer, 2013; Lyon and Bauman, 2013; Andrejevic, 2013). Indeed, as I have previously argued, the personal data that are generated by digital technologies are 'lively' in several ways. These data are mobile as they circulate and are repurposed by different actors and agencies; they are about 'life itself' (people's activities, preferences, habits and bodies); they contribute to livelihoods (as the data-harvesting industry); and they are increasingly having effects on people's social interactions, relationships and life chances (Lupton, 2016).

Cultural analyses of material culture emphasise the importance of objects in constructing self-identity. Such objects may be directly representational of the self, such as photographic or video images featuring the self, or more symbolic of selfhood, such as favourite things (e.g. old toys, books, clothes, household objects, mementoes and sporting equipment) (Miller, 2010; Nippert-Eng, 1996; Keightley and Pickering, 2014; Turkle, 2007). Writers on material culture and affect have noted the entangling of bodies/selves with physical objects and how artefacts act as extensions or prostheses of the body/self, becoming markers of personhood. The objects that represent selfhood may be understood to extend the territory of the self beyond the fleshly body (Nippert-Eng, 1996).

In recent times, digital objects and digital data have become invested with selfhood. Smartphones, smartwatches or wearable self-tracking devices are carried on or close to people's bodies throughout the day, and have thus become part of their presentation of the self. The personal information stored in these devices is emblematic of the self (Lupton, 2015a, 2016; Hand, 2014). These include images of the self and of significant others, text messages and emails, calendar entries, geolocation information, details of physical activity and functions, and status updates on social media platforms. These digital data are a form of personal possession, unique to the individual, just as their photographs, home videos or diaries might be or commodities that they have customised as part of the appropriation of these objects into their everyday lives and life histories. As such, they are 'evocative objects' and 'things that we think with' (Turkle, 2007), repositories of emotion, memory and social relationships.

Visual representations of the body/self are an important element of the territories of the self. If the 3D printed self-replica is viewed as a type of selfie, it becomes not only a repository of emotion and intimate relations but also a prosthetic or technology of selfhood. Lury (1997) has written about the ways in which photographs act as a form of prostheses to the self, serving as a means of forming self-identity. She identifies the relationship between knowledge of the self and visual images that photography reinforces. Photographs of the self, she argues, are artefacts in which certain aspects of the self are fixed, framed or frozen. They contribute to the notion of the uniqueness of selfhood and embodiment. In the era of digital photography and the emergence of the selfie and other digitised personal photography practices, a far greater volume of photographic portrait images of the self and intimate others is now generated compared with previous generations and these images can more easily be shared with others. Using new digital media devices, self-portrait takers have more control over their images. They can employ devices such as cropping and filters and other photographic-editing technologies to manipulate easily the images and can decide with whom they want to share these images.

Some recent research has investigated the practices of using digital devices to take self-portraits and what people do with them. An academic literature on selfies and other forms of digital personal photography is beginning to emerge (Keightley and Pickering, 2014; Murray, 2008; Van House, 2011; Hess, 2015). It has been argued that through the practices of digital self-portrait taking and sharing, users engage in the performance of the body/self, configuring self-identity. While popular media coverage of the selfie phenomenon often focuses on the alleged narcissism and self-obsession that they promote, some scholars have theorised this practice as a Foucauldian technology of the self, involving self-reflection as well as self-expression and performativity. Personal photography, therefore, not only represents but enacts selfhood and self-identity (Tiidenberg, 2014; Tiidenberg and Cruz, 2015; Van House, 2011), including conveying information that represents the self in specific places and spaces (Hess, 2015).

The ease of the production and circulation of digital photographic portraits means that people now often have possession of many more images of themselves and intimate others. This volume, however, can be challenging for some people regarding developing strategies for managing the plethora of images. Digital images, if not printed out, may be considered to be more ephemeral, transitory, immediate and less proximate compared with analogue self and family photographs (Keightley and Pickering, 2014; Murray, 2008). It is here that 3D self-replicas offer a solution. One of the most intriguing aspects of 3D printing is the way in which it materialises digital data into solid objects, enacting them as less ephemeral than other digital self-portraits. These portraits are not constantly circulated through networked spaces like social networks in the same way as digital images are, but rather tend to remain *in situ*.

McCosker and Wilken (2014) refer to the tendency in data visualisation circles towards the fetishising and sublimity of 'beautiful data' as part of exerting mastery over the seemingly unlimited and thus overwhelming amounts of large digital datasets. Extending this logic, the physical materialising of digital data in the form of 3D printing may offer a solution to the anxieties of the volume, velocity and circulation of personal digital data. The Exertion Games researchers and others experimenting with these technologies (Stusak *et al.*, 2014) claim that the opportunity for people to handle – and even smell and taste materialisations of their personal bodily data – allows them to engage more readily and understand their data better. When it is one's personal data drawn from one's own flesh that is being manifested in a 3D digital data object, this may provoke a sense of mastery over what may be experienced as a continually data-emitting subjectivity.

Conclusion

The entry of 3D printing technologies into leisure cultures is still relatively new, and as yet there are few scholarly analyses of the ways in which these technologies have been dispersed and taken up in the kinds of domains that I have outlined in this chapter. How popular 3D printing or the other practices I have described may become is yet unknown, and remains the topic of no small degree of speculation. What I have attempted to do in this chapter, however, is to outline some of the leisure sites and cultures in which 3D printing is spreading, and, by using the 3D self-replica as a case study, begin to develop a critical sociocultural analysis of the phenomenon as a basis for further scholarly work.

Quite apart from the possible ways in which these artefacts may be taken up in leisure domains and how they may be used for marketing or promotional purposes in conjunction with leisure activities, broader questions remain concerning the ways in which people may enact themselves or intimate others via 3D self-replicas and the extent to which they are incorporated into practices of selfhood, embodiment, memory and social relations. As personal digital data 'made solid' or 'frozen', these artefacts offer new ways of thinking about the ways in which digital data may be employed to represent bodies/selves and become biographical objects, mementoes and signifiers of important or intimate events in people's lives. Their use is a form of data practice, a mode by which people interact with and make sense of personal digital data in an era in which such data are ceaselessly collected by and about them (Lupton, 2016). Not only can these artefacts serve to 'freeze' lively data, but they are also located in a physical space: on the mantelpiece at home, for example. The liquidity, flows and force of personal digital data become fixed in time and space in a material object.

The self-replica artefact is a tangible form of code/space that may be held, touched, displayed in various ways or placed next to other figurines of the self for comparison, just like analogue photographs that were printed on paper from negatives and enshrined in frames or photo albums. People may begin to use 3D self-replicas not only as a way of marking and measuring the growth and development of children, but also as material and tangible evidence of their own ageing processes, weight loss or physical fitness regimes, or even, in the case of 3D patient anatomical replicas, as memorabilia of how they or a loved one have overcome or succumbed to major surgery or disease (Lupton, 2015b). How evocative will these artefacts be for people and how will they interact with other objects in configuring personal memories? Will 3D self-replicas become incorporated into domestic spaces as mementoes of lives and bodies? In what ways will they represent the self and people's relationships with other people or with the objects or activities that are meaningful in their lives (including their leisure pastimes)? How will people learn about their bodies and their selves from the artefacts? Alternatively, will 3D self-replicas be short-lived as novelty items and fail to achieve persistent value? All of these questions remain to be explored.

References

3D Babies. (2014) *About Us*. Available at: www.3d-babies.com/about/.
3D Selfies. (2015) *3D Selfies*. Available at: www.3dselfies.com/index.html.
Andrejevic, M. (2013) *Infoglut: How Too Much Information is Changing the Way We Think and Know*. New York: Routledge.
Beer, D. (2013) *Popular Culture and New Media: the Politics of Circulation*. Basingstoke: Palgrave Macmillan.
Berman, B. (2012) 3-D printing: The new industrial revolution. *Business Horizons* 55: 155–162.
Bilton, R. (2013) Coca-Cola shows off the untapped potential for 3D printing in advertising. *Venturebeat*. Available at: http://venturebeat.com/2013/08/20/coca-cola-3d-printing/ (accessed 30 October 2014).
Brainform. (2015) *Brainform*. Available at: www.brainform.co.nz/.
Cascone, S. (2014) Recreate British Museum artifacts through 3-D printing. Available at: https://news.artnet.com/in-brief/recreate-british-museum-artifacts-through-3-d-printing-156270 (accessed 8 August 2015).
Choc Edge. (2015) *Choc Edge*. Available at: http://chocedge.com/.
Coole, D.H. and Frost, S. (2010) *New Materialisms: Ontology, Agency, and Politics*. Durham, NC: Duke University Press.
Hand, M. (2014) Persistent traces, potential memories: Smartphones and the negotiation of visual, locative, and textual data in personal life. *Convergence* online first.
Hess, A. (2015) The selfie assemblage. *International Journal of Communication* 9: 1629–1646.
Hoskins, S. (2013) *3D Printing for Artists, Designers and Makers*. London: Bloomsbury.
John, N. (2013) Sharing and Web 2.0: The emergence of a keyword. *New Media and Society* 15: 167–182.
Keightley, E. and Pickering, M. (2014) Technologies of memory: Practices of remembering in analogue and digital photography. *New Media and Society* 16: 576–593.
Khot, R., Mueller, F. and Hjorth, L. (2013) SweatAtoms: Materializing physical activity. In *Ninth Australasian Conference on Interactive Entertainment: Matters of Life and Death*. Melbourne: ACM Press, pp. 1–7.
Khot, R.A., Pennings, R. and Mueller, F.F. (2015) EdiPulse: Supporting physical activity with chocolate printed messages. *CHI'15*. Seoul: ACM Press, pp. 1391–1396.
Kitchin, R. and Dodge, M. (2011) *Code/Space: Software and Everyday Life*. Cambridge, MA: MIT Press.
Latour, B. (2005) *Reassembling the Social: An Introduction to Actor-Network-Theory*. Oxford: Clarendon Press.
Lipson, H and Kurman, M. (2013) *Fabricated: The New World of 3D Printing*. Indianapolis, IN: John Wiley & Sons.
Lupton, D. (2015a) *Digital Sociology*. London: Routledge.
Lupton, D. (2015b) Fabricated data bodies: Reflections on 3D printed digital body objects in medical and health domains. *Social Theory and Health* 13: 99–115.

Lupton, D. (2016) *The Quantified Self: A Sociology of Self-tracking.* Cambridge: Polity Press.
Lupton, D. (in press) Digital bodies. In D. Andrews, M. Silk and H. Thorpe (eds) *Routledge Handbook of Physical Cultural Studies.* London: Routledge.
Lury, C. (1997) *Prosthetic Culture: Photography, Memory and Identity.* London: Routledge.
Lyon, D. and Bauman, Z. (2013) *Liquid Surveillance: A Conversation.* Oxford: Wiley.
Makerbot Thingiverse. (2015) *Makerbot Thingiverse.* Available at: www.thingiverse.com/.
Marcus, G. (2006) Assemblage. *Theory, Culture and Society* 23: 101–106.
McCosker, A. and Wilken, R. (2014) Rethinking 'big data' as visual knowledge: The sublime and the diagrammatic in data visualisation. *Visual Studies* 29: 155–164.
Miller, D. (2010) *Stuff.* Cambridge: Polity Press.
Moody, M. (2014) How patient specific 3D printed organ replicas help patients reach informed decisions. *3D Print.com.* Available at: http://3dprint.com/9159/3d-printed-organ-replicas/ (accessed 24 October 2014).
Murray, S. (2008) Digital images, photo-sharing, and our shifting notions of everyday aesthetics. *Journal of Visual Culture* 7: 147–163.
Nippert-Eng, C. (1996) *Home and Work: Negotating Boundaries through Everyday Life.* Chicago, IL: University of Chicago Press.
Petrick, I.J. and Simpson, T.W. (2013) 3D printing disrupts manufacturing. *Research Technology Management* 56: 12.
Rogers, R. (2013) *Digital Methods.* Cambridge, MA: The MIT Press.
Ruppert, E. (2011) Population objects: Interpassive subjects. *Sociology* 45: 218–233.
Sevenson, B. (2014) '3D printed vagina' artist, Megumi Igarashi, speaks out after release from jail. *3D Print.com.* Available at: http://3dprint.com/9686/3d-print-vagina-igarashi/ (accessed 30 October 2014).
Shewbridge, R., Hurst, A. and Kane, S. (2014) Everyday making: Identifying future uses for 3D printing in the home. In *DIS 2014.* Vancouver: ACM Press, pp. 815–824.
Stusak, S., Tabard, A., Sauka, F., Khot, R.A. and Butz, A. (2014) Activity sculptures: Exploring the impact of physical visualizations on running activity. *IEEE Transactions on Visualization and Computer Graphics* 20: 2201–2210.
Tanenbaum, J.G., Williams, A.M., Desjardins, A. and Tanenbaum, K. (2013) Democratizing technology: Pleasure, utility and expressiveness in DIY and maker practice. In *CHI 2013.* Paris: ACM Press, pp. 2603–2612.
Terrassa, J. (2012) Met 3D: The Museum's first 3D scanning and printing hackathon. *The Metropolitan Museum of Arts.* Available at: www.metmuseum.org/about%20the%20museum/now%20at%20the%20met/features/2012/hackathon (accessed 8 August 2015).
Thimmesch, D. (2014) Trendy Japanese clothing retailer Uniqlo introduces the 'selfless selfie' via 3D printing. *3D Print.com.* Available at: http://3dprint.com/16667/uniqlo-3d-print-selfie/ (accessed 11 August 2015).
Tiidenberg, K. (2014) Bringing sexy back: Reclaiming the body aesthetic via self-shooting. *Cyberpsychology* 8: 3.
Tiidenberg, K. and Cruz, E.G. (2015) Selfies, image and the re-making of the body. *Body and Society* online first.
Turkle, S. (2007) Introduction: The things that matter. In S. Turkle (ed.) *Evocative Objects: Things We Think With.* Cambridge, MA: MIT Press, pp. 3–10.
Van House, N.A. (2011) Personal photography, digital technologies and the uses of the visual. *Visual Studies* 26: 125–134.

4 'I'm selling the dream really aren't I?'

Sharing fit male bodies on social networking sites

Alison Winch and Jamie Hakim

Introduction

This chapter explores the convergence between work and leisure time in neoliberal digital cultures by focusing on masculinity, gym culture and social networking sites, specifically Instagram and Facebook. We argue that the practices of men, both going to the gym and then posting images of worked-out bodies on social networking sites, are forms of neoliberal labour despite being conventionally understood as leisure practices. Therefore, we are interested in how labouring for an ideal fit body participates in the entrepreneurial project of the self. In the precarious climate of neoliberal austerity where we are encouraged to be creatives and artists, Instagram and Facebook are sites where new articulations of masculinity are displayed for the purposes of self-branding with the objective of being seen as a success in the everyday experience of promotional culture. This success is indexed through the lean, muscular body which denotes confidence, self-discipline, erotic appeal and different forms of value; the sharing of which has the potential to attract sexual partners, professional clients and strategic interpersonal relationships. This chapter looks at how young, white, middle-class men have begun to deploy neoliberal labour practices in what historically would have been understood as the recreational arena. More specifically, we examine the ways in which new forms of masculinity are produced within the world of fitness. In order to make an argument about the collapse of labour into leisure time through acts of digital self-branding (Hearn, 2008; Banet-Weiser, 2012), we draw on a wide range of theories: neo-Foucauldian theory (Rose, 1996, 1999), post-Fordism (Boltanski and Chiapello, 2007) and critiques of neoliberalism (Gilbert, 2013). We are also interested in both the gendered (Gill and Scharff, 2011) as well as the affective (Deleuze and Guattari, 1980) aspects of these processes. To do this we have conducted six semi-structured, in-depth interviews with young, white, middle-class men who are engaged with the 'fitness assemblage' in different capacities.

Labouring the neoliberal body

Jeremy Gilbert defines neoliberalism as distinct from other modes of capitalism. Whereas capitalism has historically denoted an economic system focused on the accumulation of capital, neoliberalism is a political philosophy and programme which extends capitalist conditions 'as far as possible into every domain of social life, by force if necessary' (Gilbert, 2013, 2015). In particular, markets dominated by large and unregulated corporations are favoured. Importantly for our purposes, the neoliberal programme penetrates not only the political and economic realms but also our intimate lives, including the relationship with one's self, one's body, the personal relationships we have with others and the leisure pursuits in which we engage. It attempts to create competitive individualistic social relations not just in economic markets but also in all areas of social life. What we are most interested in here is the extent to which labour is inscribed within and through these social relations. This manifests itself in a number of ways: the workplace as a holistic site that centres around and nurtures 'personal achievement' (Rose, 1999: 104); the subject as entrepreneurial project; and social networks as strategic sites of feedback and social capital which accrue value for self-brands.

Luc Boltanski and Eve Chiapello are two of the most significant critics to map the different ways in which labour and leisure have been conflated in post-1990s capitalism. In *The New Spirit of Capitalism* they explore how this happened by looking at managerial texts from the 1960s and 1990s. The discourses produced in the 1990s, with their claims to authenticity and freedom, aimed to blur the distinction between leisure and work (Boltanski and Chiapello, 2007). Prior to the period identified by Boltanski and Chiapello, Fordism had created leisure as a separate sphere to labour so that workers could be rejuvenated and more effectively contribute to the accumulation of capital. This separation of the two was criticised as 'dehumanising' by radicals in the 1960s. Boltanski and Chiappello point out how capitalist institutions incorporated this critique into their interests in a way that was more dehumanising than was imaginable under Fordism. The new professional mechanisms that came into place to do this 'penetrate more deeply into people's inner selves – people are expected to "give" themselves to their work' (Boltanski and Chiapello, 2007: 98). Under supposedly more free working conditions, professional life has become precariously organised as a portfolio of projects and thus '*[l]ife* is conceived as a *succession* of projects' (Boltanski and Chiapello, 2007: 110, emphasis added). Moreover, these projects depend on interpersonal networks that combine both friendships and professional or useful relations (Boltanski and Chiapello, 2007).

Anthony Giddens and Nikolas Rose have written about the rise of the entrepreneurial subject (Giddens, 1991; Rose, 1996, 1999) in which the self is constantly worked on and where both the image of the individual at work as well as outside work are aligned 'with the human technologies for the government of enterprise' (Rose, 1999: 104). Consequently, citizens are made accountable for their self-regulation, in the Foucauldian sense. In particular, subjects are expected to assume a reflexive selfhood through which they must constantly invent themselves in response to the labour market. As traditional institutions are erased, so the focus shifts to the self as an entrepreneurial subject. According to

Giddens, the self is 'made'; it is an undertaking that is continuously worked and reflected upon. The made self is produced through a reflexive understanding of one's biography that is created, monitored and revised through sets of narratives that explain one to oneself as well as to others. We take this understanding of the self, both in the workplace as well as outside it, as a project in perpetual process. Under such conditions, the protestant work ethic has penetrated into people's inner selves to the extent that recreational time is configured, experienced and marketed as labour.

Another significant way in which neoliberal labour practices have penetrated our intimate and personal lives is through practices of self-branding (Hearn, 2008; Banet-Weiser, 2012). Banet-Weiser maintains that 'areas of our lives that have historically been considered non-commercial and "authentic" – namely religion, creativity, politics, the self – have recently become branded spaces'. They are 'often created and sustained using the same kind of marketing strategies that branding managers used to sell products'. Moreover, they are 'increasingly only legible in culture through and within the logic and vocabulary of the market' (Banet-Weiser, 2012: 14). Self-branding strategies come into play across multiple but related platforms in contemporary media convergence culture. Online and offline spaces interconnect as 'resources for self-work' (Ouellette and Wilson, 2011: 559). Ouellette and Wilson look at the gendered dynamics of these practices and show how women's cultures no longer provide time out. Instead, traditional televisual cultures designed 'to be watched in a state of distraction' have recently transitioned to 'purposeful, multiplatform, "on demand" domestic media' (Ouellette and Wilson, 2011: 550): 'women's interactivity can be mobilized as a gendered requirement of neoliberal citizenship, an ongoing, mundane regimen of self-empowerment' (Ouellette and Wilson, 2011: 549).

Banet-Weiser extends this analysis of postfeminist digital culture where body image is maintained and controlled to argue for the harnessing of marketing strategies in order to create and sustain the self-brand. Significantly, she focuses on peer-to-peer networks which provide useful feedback and evaluation:

> Self-branding, much like the branding of other products, only works if you enable other people to rank your product, which in this case is yourself.... Self-branding does not merely involve self-presentation but is a layered process of judging, assessment, and valuation taking place in a media economy of visibility.
>
> (Banet-Weiser, 2012: 87)

Ouellette and Wilson (2011) and Banet-Weiser (2012) examine how femininities are constructed in neoliberal media convergence cultures. Gill and Scharff ask whether 'neoliberalism *is always already gendered*' and whether 'women are constructed as its ideal subjects?' (Gill and Scharff, 2011: 7). They argue that to a 'much greater extent than men, women are required to work on and transform the self, to regulate every aspect of their conduct, and to present all their actions as freely chosen' (Gill and Scharff, 2012: 7). We would not dispute this. However, we are fascinated by the ways in which certain demographics of men have also recently been captured by the health, beauty and well-being market. In a similar fashion to how neoliberal postfeminist culture addresses women as brand managers in their personal lives encouraging them to cultivate their bodies as brands (Winch, 2013), these men experience their bodies as sites of regulation, scrutiny, competition and value. As we will go on to argue, the men who we interviewed feel ambivalent about these techniques of self-promotion and self-work. In addition, they often describe their affective experience of labouring on and displaying their bodies with recourse to hyper-masculine discourses such as being machine-like or 'cavemen'.

The fitness assemblage

Following Deleuze and Guattari (1980), we use the term *assemblage* to describe the world of fitness and the relations within and around it. We identify the fitness assemblage as an element in the much wider beauty-health-lifestyle industry complex. It has its own heroes, celebrities, logics, internal rules, flows of communication, events, brands, products, modes of embodiment, structures of feeling, norms, ideals and hierarchies of power. Rather than being self-contained it links into other assemblages such as the wider promotional cultures. Our interview with our participant Davide may be used to illustrate how an individual might engage with the fitness assemblage. Davide is a fitness professional. He competes in events hosted by the corporation World Beauty Fitness and Fashion inc. Competing in these events helps him secure contracts such as becoming the face of performance-enhancement supplements and appearing as a model in the men's health and fitness press. He has modelled for titles such as *Men's Health*, which is the highest-selling magazine in the men's magazine market. Through the position he occupies within semio-capitalist promotional culture (Lazzarato, 2014), he possesses an idealised male body that non-professionals might aspire to emulate. Indeed, two of the other men who we interviewed (one other fitness professional, one non-professional) follow Davide on Instagram and Facebook where he shares images of his body. Davide does not receive direct payment for sharing these images in the same way as his contract work. Nevertheless, they are vital in building up his brand and maintaining his employability. In addition, he does not own these online images. Instead, this image production and distribution – or 'content' – is a form of free labour that feeds into the capital accumulation of social networking sites (Taylor, 2014). This in turn creates profit for the industries that buy advertising space on these social networking sites.

In recent years the fitness assemblage has expanded in size. There are a number of indicators to evidence this. For example, the UK government-commissioned Active People Survey (2014) found that between 2008 and 2014 there has been a 7 per cent increase in 16- to 25-year-old men going to the gym at least once a week. Since 2009, men's fitness magazine *Men's*

Health has been the bestselling publication in a rapidly declining men's magazine market – doubling its circulation and selling twice as many as its nearest competitor *GQ* (Brook, 2009). In 2014 the sorts of sports nutrition products that are designed to strip fat and build muscle increased their sales by 40 per cent in the ten top supermarkets. In the same year the term *healthie* was coined to signify a fitness-related selfie. At the time of writing, a substantial number of 'healthies' have aggregated around the following hashtags on popular social networking site Instagram: #fitness (91,612,347), #fitfam (26,221,853), #fitspo (21,488,398) and #muscle (12,628,642). During the same period of time, the fitness assemblage has also moved from the margins to the centre of contemporary visual culture. For example, in the past, muscle-building protein powders used to be advertised in specialist publications using images of the tub in which the powder was sold. More recently, the styles and tropes of glossy fashion photography have been used to sexualise images of the nude male body on billboards and viral marketing campaigns, becoming what Orbach (2009) has called 'the visual muzak' of public space. The #revealyourself advertising campaign by Bulk Powders is the most high profile of these campaigns at the time of writing.

Researching fit male bodies

The research process for this chapter commenced in 2014 when we began to notice more men posting images of their worked-out bodies in the newsfeeds of the social networking sites to which we subscribed. Around the same time, a media figure called the 'spornosexual' (Simpson, 2014) emerged in the media, initially in the *Daily Telegraph* (Stanley, 2014; Wotherspoon, 2014), and then in the *Guardian* (Moore, 2014), *Esquire* (Olesker, 2015) and Vice.com (Martin, 2014). The spornosexual is a term used to denote a man who exercises in order to look like a hybrid of a sportsman and a porn star, and who shares images of his body on social networking sites. Most of the coverage coded spornosexuals as working class, and as improperly embodied. In other words, the fact that they accrued cultural value through their bodies marked them as deviant. What we are interested in here is why men in different class positions have started to use their bodies to render themselves legible in contemporary British culture when historically this has been a strategy deployed by less privileged groups, primarily women. It is important to note that historically masculine discourses of the body have not been indexed through the same signifiers of shame, repulsion and monstrosity as the female body. In addition, men have not been marketed to by the beauty, fitness and health industries in the same ways – or for as long as – as women. For these reasons – and because maleness is associated with subjectivity and the mind – the body practices in which 'spornosexuals' engage incite anxiety in the mainstream press.

Starting from a broadly cultural studies perspective that understands analyses of cultural phenomena as being able to illuminate the much wider dynamics of social formations, we decided to use mixed methods: (1) semi-structured in-depth interviews with men who share images of their worked-out bodies on social networking sites, and (2) textual analysis of the content (images and text) they had shared. The process of data collection was guided by the question: What can the recent emergence of these practices reveal about living in the current neoliberal moment, and to what extent are they gendered? In terms of the interviews, we were interested in what these practices consisted of, what motivated the men who engaged in them, what discourses they used to make sense of them and how engaging in such practices made them feel. This was supplemented by textual analysis that looked for the recurring motifs within the images and text that our participants posted. The data was rich with a number of themes emerging that has meant utilising a variety of theoretical concepts to interpret them. Elsewhere we have used concepts of affect (Berlant, 2011) and value (Skeggs, 2014) to analyse the data (Hakim, 2015). For reasons explained above, here we have used perspectives taken from the debates relating to neoliberal labour and leisure.

Our sample of participants was constructed through snowballing from personal contacts. Although, on the one hand, this method of sample construction has potential limits, these were outweighed by the benefits of having built up the long-term trust required for discussing intimate matters, such as body image, relationships and the interviewees' affective lives. Two of the interviewees (Colin and Jonny) engaged in spornosexual practice as a leisure activity. Three of them work as fitness professionals (Matt, Davide, Oskar). Mark is a journalist who 'became spornosexual' for three months in order to write an experiential magazine feature. All the interviewees identify as white. All identify as middle class (although Colin says he is from a working-class background). All of them are aged between 20 and 35. Three of the interviewees identify as gay and three as heterosexual. This difference was introduced into the sample because the construction of 'spornosexual' as a discursive category relies on the softening of difference between homo- and heterosexuality which the popularisation of the metrosexual has naturalised in contemporary cultures of consumption (Mort, 1996; Nixon, 1996). Interestingly, the data revealed little difference between the heterosexual and gay participants. The biggest difference was between the fitness professionals and those who engaged in these practices for other reasons, hence the focus of the chapter. All the interviewees are employed in either the promotional/creative or fitness industries – either on a freelance basis or on permanent contracts. This is significant because we can see how marketing strategies employed in the workplace are redeployed in personal time. The introduction of practices of labour into areas historically understood as leisure time emerged most prominently in the interviews around the following themes. The first related to the strategic practices involved before and during our interviewees' holidays. The second related to work and the consumption of food, and the third related to the complex marketing strategies our interviewees used to brand themselves in their everyday lives.

'Selling the dream' and becoming 'beach body ready'

Jonny and Colin were the interviewees who talked most about the labour involved in getting 'beach body ready'.[1] Neither Jonny nor Frank are fitness professionals and as such their engagement with the fitness assemblage is through their 'leisure' time. Nevertheless – as PR professionals – this distinction between work and leisure is not tenable because they employ the promotional strategies learned at work in both their interpersonal lives and in relation to their bodies. For instance, Colin increases the frequency of his work-out regime prior to going on holiday. During the interview, he talked in detail about the labour involved in producing the digital imagery of his body on holiday that he felt was so crucial to the self-branding strategies he deployed on social media. He or a friend will use a smartphone – often with a filter – to take several shots of one pose that he feels most effectively displays his worked-out body. He then selects one photograph that he thinks he looks 'hottest' in; crops the image to increase the appearance of musculature; and posts it to Instagram. He claims to be aware of the best time to post images in order to maximise the amount of likes, re-grams and comments he will receive (during the morning and evening commutes and during lunch hour). When asked why he performed so much labour while on holiday, he answered:

> I mean I'm selling the dream really aren't I?
> **What do you mean?**
> [Laughs] That this is the great lifestyle that is possible if you are Colin…
> **[Interviewer laughs]**
> I mean, I didn't think that I looked awful there. You are only going to publish the pictures that you like.

In this quote we can see that Colin is deploying the skills of an art director he uses in his paid work to promote himself. He art directs a photo shoot and then chooses the image which he feels best 'sells the dream' of the project that is 'Colin'. The phrase 'selling the dream' concisely expresses the logics of marketability and the entrepreneurial self, as well as self-branding. Interestingly, by doing so, he participates in and is complicit with neoliberal aspirational discourse; the digital content of his life is evidence as to its apparent truths. Nevertheless, his laughter may be interpreted as revealing a discomfort or self-consciousness about his participation in the fitness assemblage, and we discuss this further below.

For Jonny, the labour involved in becoming 'beach body ready' also begins in the gym. Jonny attends the gym regularly anyway – going as frequently as five times a week. In the weeks prior to his holiday he will increase the frequency of his gym attendance to ten times a week:

> If I'm going abroad and there's somewhere that I want to take my top off I would do a cardio session in the evening and a weights session in the morning.

In the interview he goes so far as to claim that all his labour in the gym is directed towards displaying his fit body while on holiday:

> What's your goal?
> ... At this very moment in time I am going on a cruise for work and if I'm very honest my goal would be leaner in a course of a week and realistically that's not going to happen so my goal is to be as lean as possible in the time frame that I have.
> ...
> So there's no ultimate goal?
> No. For me the goal is driven by a beach or an opportunity.

By 'opportunity' (which could be as part of a professional assignment such as on a cruise or could be part of a beach holiday, though as a PR manager the assignment would not require him to have a fit body in the same way as it would for fitness professionals Davide or Oskar), Jonny refers to displaying his fit body and sharing this through social media. The logic underpinning Jonny's statement illustrates Boltanski and Chiapello's (2007) discussion of the project as part of contemporary labour practices. Jonny talks about preparing for this 'opportunity' as a short-term project that involves achieving a goal within a certain time frame. What is significant here is that the 'opportunity' to share his fit body – and therefore to work on his self-brand – is a form of labour that feeds from both his professional and recreational life. The blurring of these two spheres is further evidenced in his Facebook profile which has multiple images of him topless on the beach and which contains both personal and professional contacts.

'I ate some boring shit'

Food was a recurrent theme in the interviews and it appeared in two ways. The first was materially: the 'right' sort of nutrition was as necessary as the right sort of exercise regime in order to achieve the bodies the men were happy sharing as images on social networking sites. The other was discursively: images of the 'correct' kinds of meals were posted on Instagram as part of the self-branding strategies that both the professionals and non-professionals deployed within digital space. All of the interviewees who mentioned food in relation to their work-out regimes spoke of sacrificing the pleasure of eating for a rigorously disciplined work ethic, although each had a different affective response to this sacrifice.

Perhaps because Davide occupies such a prominent – if precarious – position within the power structures of the fitness assemblage, he applies neoliberal work ethics to his eating most rigorously as well as claiming to have the most positive affective experience of it. Aside from the modelling work Davide is paid for and the fitness competitions in which he competes, Davide was also studying for a nutrition degree at an elite university at the time of interview. The reason he gave for studying for this degree was that he wanted to train 'normal people who want to be better and more beautiful'. Subsequently he follows both a strict exercise and nutrition regime:

> I always see myself in the mirror and I'm always looking better and better and know this is all to do with my nutrition and my training and I keep doing it to get better and better. I know if I stop one of the factors in this process I'm not going to have the results that I'm having.

The labour involved in maintaining the eating regime is extensive and the language that Davide employs reflects the business framework through which he cultivates his body as self-brand. Food is a 'factor' and he scrutinises the 'process' through which he sculpts his body for 'results' in order to 'get better and better'. His body, which is his livelihood, is 'like a good machine: you have to give it good fuel'.

> It's like two years now that I'm waking up an hour before to cook all my meals for the day.... So that's pretty admirable from outside because it's so hard to do if you're not passionate about something ... diet is the basis of everything. You have to eat seven or eight meals a day so every two hours three hours I'm eating something.

Davide discusses the sacrifice involved in following this regime for two years – 'I sacrifice sometimes nice dinners' – but he claims it does not take an affective toll. In fact he asserts quite the opposite:

> because I'm understanding that I'm living a really healthy and good life as a result of this kind of body and this kind of mentality. I never feel bored or sad. I always feel grateful for the food I'm eating. Sometimes if I feel tired I know what type of food to put in, the kind of the work to put in. Even to change my mood. So it helps me. So the health makes me feel better.

Mark is a journalist who practised a similarly strict diet and exercise regime as Davide for three months for the purposes of writing an experiential magazine feature (another example of work saturating private life). Nevertheless, he has always regularly attended the gym, having trained as a wrestler at school and then working out as a young adult, 'a normal amount I guess. I would go to my local gym twice a week.' He describes the affect produced by this frequency of gym practice in the following way: 'I quite enjoyed the working out – clearing the mind and feeling slightly better about myself afterwards.' Motivated only by the purposes of writing a magazine feature, Mark's experience of the eating and exercising required to achieve a body like Davide's was considerably less joyful than the fitness professional who enjoys such a prominent position within fitness assemblage:

> I despised everything about the food regime. It's so deadening and wretched to eat things you have been prescribed. Even if you are not a great *gourmand*

or *bon vivant*, if you think about it everything you eat you make that choice. Three times a day you make a choice to eat a thing that pleases you. You make a qualitative decision: 'I shall have that.' And having that totally removed from you I found harrowing. I ate some boring shit.... I spent hours ... I tried to cook as correct a thing I could within as little time as possible. But every night I had to measure and weigh and the whole thing was just boring and awful and the food was unsatisfying and that just really took its toll psychologically.

Here Mark is describing the same practice of eating as labour in which Davide participates: the punishing schedule, the precise quantification of foodstuffs and the eating of foods that enable the production of a body that is deemed successful in accordance with the ideals of the fitness assemblage. He uses the French terms *gourmand* and *bon vivant* to describe the pleasures of eating as a leisure pursuit, as well as eating as one of simple pleasure or choice. During his three-month exercise regime, eating as labour is clearly a negative affective experience for Mark, revealing one of the problems of leisure becoming work under neoliberalism. It is also worthwhile reflecting here how a work project so deeply penetrated Mark's personal time and intimate life.

The networked self-brand

The ultimate goal for all the interviewees when they post images of their worked-out bodies on social networking sites is to receive as many likes, comments, tags and/or shares as possible. In order to do this they utilise various strategies on social media. For instance, Colin spends considerable time following different profiles on Instagram and liking as many pictures as possible so that the people who posted them will follow him and like the images he shares in return. Colin follows 'hot' guys to whom he is attracted (and sometimes chats to or flirts with) but who also inspire him to go to the gym and get fitter, and whose imagery on Instagram he emulates. He will consequently post these images of his fit body in order to cultivate 'likes' as indexes of value: 'If I Instagrammed a picture of something and there was tumbleweed it would make you feel *shit*. You'd think Instagram was broken.' This echoes techniques of digital self-branding identified by Banet-Weiser. For example, she discusses how 'prosumers' use the internet to 'rank their product'; that is, themselves.

Davide tags more successful bodybuilders in his Instagram posts in order to make his images visible to as wide an audience as possible, and he also helps other participants in the fitness assemblage by 'giving' them followers. As part of his self-branding strategy, Davide posts images of 'my life' – such as the books he is reading, the food he eats – as well as his professional life, which is his body: 'I wake up – body shot – and other stuff.' As stated above, both Matt and Colin are aware of the best times to post in order to maximise the amount of likes their pictures receive: during the morning and evening commutes and during the lunch hour. Matt has a complex social media strategy in order to give the impression that he is not trying too hard:

> My approach in life is that if you're trying too hard people are going to see and it's going to look obvious. I try and do things naturally. I know the best time to post something is 9 or 10 because people are at work and they've checked their emails and just go on Facebook quickly. And because I work with two different timezones South Africa and here.... And because I know that if I start getting likes it goes higher up on people's newsfeeds and stuff. I know if I release something on South Africa time and it gets likes it means it goes higher up on people's newsfeeds in the UK. I know that. And if, I wouldn't say ... I suppose there is a slight influence. The majority of the time I go out, I take a picture and I put it up straight away. I do post bad pictures of myself as well. I don't do a photo shoot. Every now and then I think 'that's a good picture I'll put that one up' but I do put bad pictures up as well.

This strategic creation and manipulation of networks echoes Boltanski and Chiapello's identification of the importance of creating interpersonal networks as part of the 'life as project' in neoliberal labour practices. The difference between Boltanksi and Chiappelo's 'projective' subject and our interviewees is that the former strategically cultivate networks in order to advance their careers and sustain their livelihoods, whereas the latter are also doing it to market themselves as successful projects and, as Matt succinctly articulates, 'to get laid'. More specifically, they illustrate what Banet-Weiser identifies as strategies of self-branding.

Significantly, the interviewees have complex attitudes about their participation in the fitness assemblage. Matt and Davide, for example, explain their processes of self-branding through recourse to hyper-masculine tropes. Davide talks about his body as a machine that gets 'better and better', while Matt associates his paleo diet and his desire to self-promote and be attractive to being a caveman':

> My philosophy is that whatever a guy does, it's to get laid. And you can take that back to work so that he can ... It's our primal basic instinct. We want to procreate and it's through all the animal kingdom and we are animals.

These ways of describing their digital embodiment distinguishes their behaviours from the criticisms directed at women; that is, that they are vain, narcissistic, objectified. Indeed, the associations with feminine behaviours mean that Colin and Mark express an ambivalence over their participation in the fitness assemblage and often disassociate from – or 'other' – those men who appear to be more invested. Colin begins the following quote talking about someone who engages in the same leisure-as-labour practices as him, and finishes reflecting on his own:

> But what annoys me about that is that he's pulling a funny face but *actually* just trying to show off his body. He's just trying to sell this weird dream. It's just very constructed. Which maybe mine looks but....

Colin's refrain 'selling the dream' which says so much about the neoliberal labour practices in which he engages reappears in this quote but with its inauthenticity explicitly drawn out; an inauthenticity that recognizes as 'maybe' being present in his use of social networking sites.

What Colin identifies as 'weird' is felt much more strongly by Mark who is very articulate about the affective spaces he entered near the end of his three-month stint working out in the ways that our other participants do in their everyday lives:

> It forced me into the genuine mindsets of people who have become obsessed by their bodies because I knew that any time I wanted to jack it in that regardless I would have to take these [topless] photos [for the magazine feature] and suddenly I was looking at [my personal trainer's] website and looking at all his other body transformations and trying to work out whether my fat loss had been as good as that guy's fat loss or had my biceps ... I got into *mental* stuff. Who cares? But for a while I was 'oh he's get two inches on his trapezius muscles' you know you go down this rabbit hole of obsessive stuff [emphasis in original].

Mark describes the digital media practices he engaged in at this point in his programme more forcefully than Colin as '*mental*', 'obsessed' and like going down 'this rabbit hole of obsessive stuff'. Despite participating so actively in these digital-leisure-as-labour practices, he displays a self-consciousness of both the peculiar affectivity they generate, as well as recognizing how little they matter – 'who cares?' What has been most revealing about the interviews is this degree of self-consciousness that many of the participants exhibited about their engagement in these practices. This brings us back to the discomfort in Colin's laughter that we highlighted earlier when he expresses an ironic reflection about 'selling the dream':

> I mean I'm selling the dream really aren't I?
> **What do you mean?**
> [Laughs] That this is the great lifestyle that is possible if you are Colin.

His laughter suggests that although he engages in these practices he does not buy into the logics that underpin them wholesale; that there is something comic – or unsettling – about the labour regimes to which he subjects himself in pursuing the entrepreneurial project of the self.

Conclusion

In this chapter we have used the recent rise in men working out and posting images of their bodies on social networking sites as evidence of the way in which neoliberal labour practices have penetrated areas of social life historically understood as leisure time. We have done this using three different examples of practices historically understood as leisure time: holiday, the consumption of food and networked interpersonal relationships. What we have been particularly concerned with is how these neoliberal leisure-as-labour practices have been gendered. In an attempt to engage with Gill and Scharff's question whether 'neoliberalism *is always already gendered*' and whether 'women are constructed as its ideal subjects' (Gill and Scharff, 2012: 7), we have chosen men as the subject of our investigation and found that like the women to whom Gill and Scharff refer, the men who we interviewed feel 'required to work on and transform the self, to regulate every aspect of their conduct, and to present all their actions as freely chosen' (Gill and Scharff, 2012: 7). Nevertheless, we do not want to argue that men are experiencing this regulation in the same ways as women. The negative portrayals of 'spornosexuals' in the mainstream media, as well as the ambivalence expressed by our interviewees, reveal that these behaviours are not easily considered to be normative. That is, masculinity does not easily or neatly denote extensive body monitoring and display in the same way that femininity does. However, the fact that some men are beginning to feel impelled to perform traditionally feminine body work at all is culturally significant, as it attests to how successfully the logics of neoliberal labour are penetrating the leisure time, intimate worlds and everyday lives of a social group historically immune to them. Moreover, it is the digital that is becoming an important medium through which this is happening. It seems that the marketisation of intimate lives, including our relationships to our bodies and to others, is reconfiguring gender.

Note

1 This phrase refers to having a body which sufficiently conforms to hegemonic beauty norms that it is ready to be revealed in swimwear on a beach. Use of this term is widespread in popular culture – reaching its peak in April 2015 when gym supplement company Protein World ran a controversial, high-profile marketing campaign using the phrase as its slogan.

References

Active People Survey. (2014) Available at: www.sportengland.org/research/who-plays-sport/ (accessed 9 August 2014).

Banet-Weiser, S. (2012) *Authentic: The Politics of Ambivalence in a Brand Culture*. New York: New York University Press.

Berlant, L. (2011) *Cruel Optimism*. Durham, NC: Duke University Press.

Boltanski, L. and Chiapello, E. (2007) *The New Spirit of Capitalism*. London: Verso.

Brook, S. (2009) Men's magazines and women's glossies share the pain of recession. *Guardian*. Available at: www.theguardian.com/media/2009/aug/13/magazine-abcs-mens-womens (accessed 30 June 2015).

Deleuze, G. and Guattari, F. (1980) *A Thousand Plateaus: Capitalism and Schizophrenia*, translated by Brian Massumi. Reprinted New York: Continuum, 2004 [1987].

Giddens, A. (1991) *Modernity and Self-identity: Self and Society in the Late Modern Age*. Palo Alto, CA, and London: Stamford University Press.

Gilbert, J. (2013) *Common Ground: Democracy and Collectivity in an Age of Individualism*. London: Pluto Press.

Gilbert, J. (2015) 'Neoliberalism' and 'capitalism' – What's the difference? Available at: https://jeremygilbertwriting.wordpress.com/2015/07/14/neoliberalism-and-capitalism-whats-the-difference/ (accessed 21 August 2015).

Gill, R. and Scharff, C. (2011) *New Femininities: Postfeminism, Neoliberalism and Subjectivity*. Basingstoke: Palgrave.

Hakim, J. (2015) 'Fit is the new rich': Male embodiment in the age of austerity. *Soundings* 61: 84–94.

Hearn, A. (2008) Variations on the branded 'self': Theme, invention, improvisation and inventory. In D. Hesmondhalgh and J. Toynbee (eds) *The Media and Social Theory* (pp. 194–210). London: Routledge.

Lazzarato, M. (2014) *Signs and Machines: Capitalism and the Production of Subjectivity*. Los Angeles: Semiotexte(e).

Martin, C. (2014) How sad young douche bags took over modern Britain. Vice.com, 13 March. Available at: www.vice.com/en_uk/read/anatomy-of-a-new-modern-douchebag (accessed 16 May 2016).

Moore, S. (2014) The decay of women is obsessively charted. Now men are finding out how it feels. Available at: www.theguardian.com/commentisfree/2014/jul/30/decay-women-men-finding-out (accessed 4 August 2014).

Mort, F. (1996) *Cultures of Consumption: Masculinities and Social Space in Late Twentieth-century Britain*. London: Routledge.

Nixon, S. (1996) *Hard Looks: Masculinities, Spectatorship and Contemporary Consumption*. London: UCL Press.

Olesker, M. (2015) The rise and rise of the spornosexual. Available at: www.esquire.co.uk/culture/features/7588/the-rise-and-rise-of-the-spornosexual/ (accessed 31 January 2015).

Orbach, S. (2009) *Bodies*. London: Profile.

Ouellette, L. and Wilson, J. (2011) Women's work: Affective labour and convergence culture. *Cultural Studies* 25(4–5): 548–565.

Rose, N. (1996) *Inventing Our Selves: Psychology, Power, and Personhood*. Cambridge: Cambridge University Press.

Rose, N. (1999) *Powers of Freedom: Reframing Political Thought*. Cambridge: Cambridge University Press.

Simpson, M. (2014) The metrosexual is dead. Long live the 'spornosexual'. Available at: www.telegraph.co.uk/men/fashion-and-style/10881682/The-metrosexual-is-dead.-Long-live-the-spornosexual.html (accessed 17 July 2014).

Skeggs, B. (2014) Values beyond value? Is anything beyond the logic of capital? *The British Journal of Sociology* 65(1): 1–22.

Stanley, T. (2014) 'Spornosexuality': An evolutionary step backwards for men. Available at: www.telegraph.co.uk/men/fashion-and-style/10881682/The-metrosexual-is-dead.-Long-live-the-spornosexual.html (accessed 17 July 2014).

Taylor, A. (2014) *The People's Platform: Taking Back Power and Culture in the Digital Age*. New York: Fourth Estate.

Winch, A. (2013) *Girlfriends and Postfeminist Sisterhood*. Basingstoke: Palgrave Macmillan.

Wotherspoon, J. (2014) Meet the new breed of chest-waxing, hair-straightening, weight-lifting spornosexuals. Available at: www.telegraph.co.uk/men/thinking-man/10954865/Meet-the-new-breed-of-chest-waxing-hair-straightening-weight-lifting-spornosexuals.html (accessed 17 July 2014).

5 Experiencing outdoor recreation in the digital technology age

A case study from the Port Hills of Christchurch, New Zealand

Caroline Dépatie, Roslyn Kerr, Stephen Espiner and Emma J. Stewart

Introduction

The outdoor recreation literature provides a wealth of evidence for the health benefits of spending leisure time in natural resource settings (Driver, 1998). Among the positive outcomes are documented improvements in physical, social, mental and spiritual well-being which have been linked to the opportunity for individuals to disconnect from their day-to-day lives and to experience valued interactions with each other and with the physical environment (Devlin *et al.*, 1995; Louv, 2009; Manning, 2011; Pigram and Jenkins, 2006; Plummer, 2009).

Today, over half of the world's population live in urban areas, making access to rural or otherwise unmodified areas such as national parks challenging for some (Louv, 2011b; Miller and Spoolman, 2009). In New Zealand alone, more than 80 per cent of people reside in urban areas (Field *et al.*, 2013). For those seeking outdoor recreation experiences, the extent of urbanisation has increased the recreational value of open spaces located on the urban fringe. These highly accessible spaces, referred to here as 'peri-urban' locations, are the interaction zones where urban and rural activities are juxtaposed (Douglas, 2006), and form an increasingly important component of urban recreational systems (Liu *et al.*, 2010). Alongside urbanisation, a digital technology revolution may be reshaping recreation participation and experience, with some commentators observing the potential for such developments to undermine the principal values of nature-based interactions (Louv, 2005, 2011a) or to prevent people from using natural areas altogether (Pergams and Zaradic, 2006).

This chapter reports on the case of the Port Hills in Christchurch, New Zealand, and considers how the outdoor recreation experience is transformed by technology use and how recreationists, including hikers, runners, mountain bikers and rock climbers, negotiate the dichotomy between experiencing the natural environment while using technology. A main premise of the research was to examine the possibility that the overall experience of outdoor recreation in peri-urban settings was changing as a result of developments in technology and, more specifically, because of the use of digital portable devices such as smartphones, music players, cameras and self-tracking devices (e.g. GPS, cycle computers, heart rate monitors). In this setting, reliable access to wireless networks allowed recreationists to use many functions on their digital devices.

Digital cuture and the outdoor recreation experience

With the evolution of digital technology, portable digital devices now accompany individuals everywhere they go. Gere (2008) writes that 'we live in a society supersaturated with digital technology' (p. 201) and, with technology present in every aspect of our life, it is becoming a world of digital nature. Indeed, in digital culture research, digital technology has been described as a form of human extension offering the potential to be connected at all times and the ability to experience a sense of individualised control over social space, ultimately changing the way we interact with each other and with our environments (Bull, 2005; Campbell and Park, 2008; Creeber and Martin, 2009; Gere, 2008; Young, 2012). Campbell and Park (2008) discuss a shift from mass to individualised consumption that is well illustrated through communication technology, where home phones, PCs and CD players have been replaced by mobile phones, laptops and iPods. The authors argue that we are experiencing a movement towards a personal communication society and highlight how the mobile phone allows for individualised control through choosing how it looks, sounds and operates. Furthermore, the phone is integrated with the senses as it moves with the body, allowing for emotional attachment and a perpetual sense of connection (Campbell and Park, 2008; Young, 2012). Similarly, Bull (2005) in his study on the iPod and the culture of mobile listening in an urban environment, argued that technology gives users control over their experience of space and time, as well as blurring the lines between what is considered private and public.

Along with digital devices providing users with individualised control, they can also 'act' to impact upon experiences. This view reflects the concept of 'agency' found in Latour's work on actor-network theory (ANT), where it is argued that non-humans act as intermediaries or mediators through facilitating or disrupting experiences (Latour, 2005). Technological devices are not only manufactured or 'non-natural' instruments but non-human agents acting as social forces that have the power to reveal different realities (Matthewman, 2011; VanLoon, 2002). Mobile phones, for instance, have been identified as acting as safety devices, in allowing young people, particularly girls, to access a wider variety of locations (Foley *et al.*, 2007; Pain *et al.*, 2005). At the same time, studies acknowledge that the phone provides a false sense of security, as its ability to act is limited to the user's opportunity to use it (Pain *et al.*, 2005). Thus, rather than directly altering user experience, the phone is acknowledged as presenting users with new challenges and forms of negotiation.

Within the outdoor recreation literature, some authors have long argued that the use of technology has changed the experience of and the relationship to the natural environment (Devlin, 1993; Ewert and Shultis, 1999). This is emphasised by Ewert and Shultis (1999) who demonstrated that the wilderness experience has been fundamentally altered by technological changes in transportation, safety, comfort, communication and information sectors. The relevance of digital technologies within this framework is easy to see, for example, in the development of communication devices such as enhanced two-way radios, personal locator beacons and cellular telephones which have significant implications for personal safety and for how (and when) information is transmitted. For Ewert and Shultis (1999), changes in technology may have facilitated the ability of the public to engage in backcountry recreation, but the use of these technological agents has raised concerns among some recreationists about threats to the wilderness experience (Wray *et al.*, 2010) and changed the way in which users view and appreciate natural environments and protected areas. Building on his earlier research, Shultis (2001) questioned the growing relationship with our technological devices in wilderness settings and commented that 'recreationists and recreation managers will both be attracted and repelled by the recreation technology that affects the outdoor recreation experience and recreation management in both a positive and negative manner' (p. 56).

In writing about the virtual self and the digital ability to self-track or self-quantify, Young (2012) argued that the connection to our digital devices extends the self out into the world. Self-tracking is a way of 'keeping a record of information about yourself, in a format that can be expressed in statistical ways and that can be shared with others via online services' (Young, 2012: 9). With the development of sophisticated applications, recreationists now have the ability to track complex data and to share the information with online communities. When writing about the fitness application STRAVA, Vanderbilt (2013) reported that access to instant cycling performance data can lead to risky behaviours and push individuals beyond their capable limits. This, in itself, changes the outdoor recreation experience.

Overall, our interest is in how digital technology users exercise agency through their use of their devices. We draw upon or critique a range of theoretical concepts designed to examine agency, including individualised control (Campbell and Park, 2008; Bull, 2005), technological determinism (Ewert and Shultis, 1999) and ANT (Latour, 2005) to analyse how recreationists alter or transform their experiences of the Port Hills through their digital devices.

The Port Hills and its outdoor recreationists

The Port Hills of Christchurch comprise a peri-urban zone where urban and rural activities are juxtaposed. On the west side of the Port Hills is the city of Christchurch, the most populous city in New Zealand's South Island, and on the north, east and south sides is the ocean and smaller settlements of the Banks Peninsula. The Port Hills area draws many of its recreational uses from these surrounding localities, all of which are currently experiencing considerable demographic change in the aftermath of the major earthquakes that affected the Christchurch and Canterbury area in 2010/2011. An increased migrant population (including young workers arriving for the rebuild of Christchurch) (Statistics

New Zealand, 2013), alongside more gradual shifts in the New Zealand population profile, such as an ageing population and increasing urbanisation, has put pressure on recreation areas such as those found in the Port Hills (Dignan and Cessford, 2009).

Access to the Port Hills is possible via a paved road system and through an extensive track network including more than 40 protected reserves, the vast majority of which are managed by the Christchurch City Council (CCC) for recreation and scenic amenity purposes. The last Port Hills recreation strategy conducted in 2004 reported that the most common recreational uses included walking, mountain biking, running and sightseeing. Since European settlement of the region 160 years ago, the Port Hills area has undergone significant modification to its biodiversity, with the complete removal of forest cover in the early days to make room for agriculture (Ogilvie, 2000). In more recent decades, the CCC and other public agencies have acquired large areas of land on the Port Hills, securing public access and initiating conservation measures. Notwithstanding substantial historic land-use changes, the area has remained natural with a strong rural character and limited built infrastructure. The extensive track network, regenerating native bush areas and historic heritage values appeal to locals and visitors alike.

Researching technology use in the Port Hills

In order to explore the contemporary recreational use of the Port Hills, and to gain an understanding of how digital technologies might influence outdoor experiences, this study adopted a mixed-method approach, including an intercept survey ($N=520$) and semi-structured in-depth interviews ($n=30$). The quantitative survey data collection took place over one year where Port Hills recreationists aged 13 years and over were intercepted and asked to complete a survey during their outdoor recreation activity. The survey method was used to gain an overall understanding of Port Hill users, which (if any) digital devices were used during the activity and for what purposes these devices were used. At the point of intercept, recreationists were given the option of completing the survey on a tablet, or on a personal device as close as possible to the end of their activity. When choosing to complete the survey on a personal device, research participants were handed in a research card with an online link and a Quick Response (QR) code to access the survey and asked to complete the survey by the end of the day on which the activity took place. In total, 520 surveys were completed, just over half of which were answered on the tablet at the time of intercept, and the remainder were completed using a personal device. During fieldwork, 1128 recreationists were intercepted resulting in a response rate of 55.4 per cent. According to Babbie (2013), this response rate is good for analysis and reporting. Carefully planned sample parameters were put in place to capture a group of participants that closely represented the overall population. Table 5.1 summarises the sample by activity. The most popular activities performed by research participants were walking (43 per cent) and mountain biking (33 per cent).

Table 5.1 Activity types of research sample

Activity	Sample
Walking	43% (*n*=225)
Mountain biking	33% (*n*=172)
Running	11% (*n*=55)
Rock climbing	10% (*n*=51)
Others	3% (*n*=17)
Total	100% (*n*=520)

As well as the intercept survey, qualitative interviews were completed with 30 recreationists who use the Port Hills. One of the purposes of qualitative research methods is to examine human behaviour in the social context in which it occurs (Salkind, 2012). In the research, this was achieved by seeking to understand digital technology use behaviour in the social context of the natural environment through the semi-structured interviews. As their primary activity, nine walkers, four runners, 13 mountain bikers and four rock climbers completed interviews. The majority of interview participants were selected from the pool of survey participants who indicated a willingness to be interviewed on the research topic. A planned effort was made to match the age groups, gender and activity types of the interview participant sample to the survey participant sample. In order to achieve a closer match of samples, the researcher recruited six interview participants from outside of the survey pool. Each interview took between 40 and 90 minutes to complete and was recorded. All interviews were transcribed and analysed for thematic findings by coding the data through the software NVivo.

Negotiating the use of digital technology in the natural environment

In terms of the survey sample profile, most respondents (84 per cent) came from Christchurch and were aged between 18 and 54 years (80 per cent). Male respondents outnumbered females by a ratio of 3:2. The study found that 87 per cent of research participants carried some form of digital technology with them when experiencing the Port Hills (Table 5.2). On average, each recreationist carried 1.25 devices with a variance from 0 to 5 devices with minimal difference by gender. The most commonly reported device was the mobile phone (smart or basic) with 80 per cent of participants carrying a phone. Since the majority carried a phone while recreating and few carried other devices such as tablets and heart rate monitors, a limitation of the study was to report findings on the less used devices. When looking at gender differences however, men were more likely than women to report carrying (and using) point-of-views cameras, digital cameras and devices to record fitness data (e.g. GPS, cycle-computers and heart rate monitors).

58 C. Dépatie et al.

Table 5.2 Digital devices carried by recreationists

Digital devices	n	% per n = 520
Smartphone	357	68.7
Basic phone	58	11.2
Digital watch	58	11.2
Digital camera	32	6.2
Cycle computer	28	5.4
Global positioning system (GPS)	27	5.2
Heart rate monitor	18	3.5
Digital music player	16	3.1
Other	16	3.1
iPod	13	2.5
Point-of-view camera	13	2.5
Tablet	3	0.6
	n = 639	
	1.25 devices per participant	
No digital devices	68	13.1
	Total responses	
	n = 707	

Survey respondents were asked about their reasons for carrying particular devices. Among the responses offered for carrying a smartphone, most said they carried it 'for safety' (80 per cent) and 'communicating with friends and family' (76 per cent), while some said they carried a smartphone so that they could 'communicate with work' (17 per cent). Beyond the main reasons for carrying smartphones during their activities, recreationists reported using them to check the time (50 per cent), call or text (41 per cent), take photos (40 per cent), collect fitness data (22 per cent), listen to music (16 per cent) and access information, such as trail status and/or the weather (15 per cent).

The interviews revealed how the devices used during the activity either altered or enhanced their experiences. For example, participants who listened to music on their phones or digital music players agreed that music increased their motivation to exercise, enhanced the enjoyment of the activity and made them feel 'in their own worlds'. As one mountain biker commented:

> I only would listen to music if I was going to go mountain biking by myself. I find that it adds to the experience. It has a psychological benefit especially going uphill. It keeps you going.
>
> (Mountain Biker 8)

Another mountain biker emphasised the way her experience had been enhanced by using technology through using the phone application STRAVA to self-track fitness data:

> In some ways it enhances the experience. It pushes you to do more because each time you are loading it [STRAVA] up and you can see that you have

gone further, you have done X amount more climbing or you have gone faster on a track than you did before. When you come home, it is always a cool thing to see what you have done. If you have ridden with other friends, you can see where they are in comparison.

(Mountain Biker 1)

When asked if she followed other STRAVA users and compared her mountain bike performance to others, the same respondent said:

Yes, that is quite fun and shows my competitive side. If you know there are a few friends, you see that you have beaten them on this section; it is quite cool. You can also look over the course of one year and see what you have done and keep track of it.

(Mountain Biker 1)

Some participants reported an increased dependence on carrying their phones in the Port Hills since the 2010 and 2011 Christchurch earthquakes. However, they were also aware that carrying a phone provided a false sense of security, since it was possible that wireless systems might not function during a high-magnitude earthquake or other catastrophic event. As one runner commented:

The interesting thing is that the phone did not even work anyway [referring to the February 2011 earthquake], I could not get hold of my husband but I had friends texting me so I could communicate via them but I could not get hold of my husband. I am holding on to this phone just in case but it will not do anything.

(Runner 2)

While some participants felt that carrying a device altered or enhanced their experience, some were uncomfortable using devices while recreating. A rock climber indicated being conflicted about the use of devices while climbing: 'I am absolutely conflicted and wonder where you draw the line' (Rock Climber 4). Drawing a line became a recurrent theme when interviewees discussed the use of phones when recreating alone or when recreating with others. As one runner revealed:

If I was by myself, I might have a texting conversation or ring somebody up. If I was doing it socially I wouldn't unless I was expecting something; or, if I was doing something relatively extreme like running down one of the steeper tracks. For instance, I do carry it to Packhorse Hut and back and places like that, particularly if I'm running by myself.

(Runner 4)

This participant negotiated the use of his phone use depending if he was recreating alone or not and depending on the difficulty of the terrain he was on. Another participant, while giving an example of when she would leave her phone at home, said: 'I was running and walking with a friend so chose to enjoy her company instead' (Runner 2). This suggests that while recreating with others the participant deliberately decided to leave her phone behind, as it represented a potential disruption to her social experience.

Audio listening (e.g. music, radio, podcast, e-books) was another area where recreationists negotiated the use of their digital devices depending on the social setting and, at times, the type of terrain. Within the survey sample, 91 (17.5 per cent) respondents indicated audio listening with a smartphone, an iPod or a digital music device. When listening to an e-book, a walker mentioned that he negotiated the use of his device according to the type of terrain and the length of the activity:

> It gets a bit boring because it is a long way. But as soon as I get to the top and the views start widening out and I get to the point where I can have a view or look back to the city and it looks awesome then I will turn it off. After a couple of hours of course, I am getting tired by then so as you get back down again and the views go away then I will switch back to the book. Just to make it more fun on the way back.
>
> (Walker 2)

In addition, some reported that the use of technological devices made the environment feel more familiar and contributed to the experience feeling 'less risky'. For two participants:

> It seems as if technology makes the environment feel safer, like you have your GPS there or you have your cell phone with music. It makes the environment feel more familiar even though it isn't necessarily.
>
> (Mountain Biker 10)

> I find myself when I am climbing outdoors with a group of people where you have lots of technology it feels more and more like an indoor experience. It makes you feel like safety isn't such an issue.
>
> (Rock Climber 4)

Since most respondents lived in the Christchurch area, recreating in the Port Hills was within close proximity for them and fitted easily into their regular schedules, so carrying portable technology did not appear to deviate from their normal urban technological habits. One participant indicated that where you recreate perhaps impacts upon the use of devices and that the 'further you go hopefully the less people will have that feeling of needing to stay connected. But if you're somewhere like the Port Hills then because you're so close it feels okay to stay connected' (Rock Climber 1).

Experiencing outdoor recreation in the digital technology age in a peri-urban setting

While Shultis (2012) argued that several researchers writing on the use of technology in wilderness settings assume a determinist stance, the interview data in this study suggest very little in the way of technological determinism. Participants instead described making very deliberate decisions about when and how to use their digital devices based on their motivations and the setting. These findings are consistent with Campbell and Park's (2008) and Bull's (2005) arguments that mobile phones and iPods allow users to experience individualised control. While most participants in this study carried a mobile phone, they used the device in very different ways, which allowed them to produce very particular experiences unique to each individual. A few participants described feeling conflicted about carrying devices in a natural environment, echoing concerns raised by Pergams and Zaradic (2006) and Louv (2005) that the unique experience of visiting a natural setting to escape normal life is being eroded by technology. However, most negotiated their use (or non-use) of such devices in order to create a particular experience. In some cases this involved music that created a personal world quite separate from the surrounding physical environment. For others it involved socialising or a deliberate disconnection from socialising, while other participants used STRAVA to facilitate their recreation becoming a competitive pursuit. In the peri-urban setting of the Port Hills, their technological devices allowed the tailoring of the recreation experience to suit each individual and provided each participant with personalised control.

This tailoring, or personalised control (Campbell and Park, 2008), is particularly well illustrated through the concept of solitude. Wiley (2005) raises the concern that the use of technology in wilderness and natural settings may threaten the solitude that is commonly prized as existing in those environments (Wray et al., 2010). By contrast, in this study, recreationists described how they deliberately did not use their phones if they sought solitude and vice versa, tailoring their use of the device to their particular preferences. Digital devices were not seen as eroding solitude but as a way to potentially enhance the overall experience, such as through listening to music to increase motivation during the activity. These findings relate to Bull's (2005) study of iPod use in the urban environment, where participants were found to use their iPods to purposely create solitude when in the midst of an urban crowd.

The consistency of behaviour between the peri-urban setting in this study and the urban settings of other studies suggests that even though the Port Hills may be considered a 'natural' environment, participants do not change their urban habits upon entering the environment. While in the Port Hills, recreationists stayed in their urban frame and maintained the behaviour of being digitally connected (Beedie and Hudson, 2003). As a rock climber previously remarked, this may be due to the proximity of the Port Hills to the city of Christchurch, with the hills being only minutes away from the central business district. Therefore, in contrast with a wilderness environment where recreationists need to set aside considerable time to reach their destinations, recreationists in Christchurch are able to spend time in the Port Hills without a significant spatial or conceptual shift. The concept that participants value the opportunity to visit the Port Hills without it taking too much time is confirmed by the survey revealing that most recreationists spend between 30 minutes and four hours in the Port Hills in a single trip. It is therefore not surprising that individuals may extend their urban behaviour to the Port Hills, as it can be a part of their daily routine rather than a separately planned excursion.

The finding that recreationists' behaviour may be similar to those in urban environments confirms Shultis' (2012) argument that researchers examining the use of technology in natural environments could benefit from utilising ideas from more mainstream technology literature, as currently the two areas include very little overlap. Connections between outdoor recreation and urban literature were particularly apparent through the theme of safety. As described above, recreationists in this study often carried their phones in order to increase their sense of safey. For example, one participant who had injured her ankle while walking with her baby on a Port Hills track described having to use her phone to contact emergency services to rescue her. This is consistent with findings in the outdoor recreation literature (Ewert and Shultis, 1999; Holden, 2002; Shultis, 2001) and with studies based in more urban environments (Foley et al., 2007; Pain et al., 2005). As in these studies, the carrying of phones increased the perception of safety, yet at the same time was a false sense of security, as the phone is limited in its ability to act to save an individual. Concerns were raised about limited battery life, breakability and network coverage, more so during natural disasters.

The respondents' comments about the phone and safety illustrate Latour's (2005) notion that technology can act as either an intermediary or a mediator. As an intermediary, technology can facilitate action, while as a mediator, it prevents action. In the case of the mobile phone as discussed above, recreationists revealed awareness that the phone could 'act' in either way. It could potentially ensure personal safety, such as in the case of the recreationist with the injured ankle where it facilitated contact with emergency services, but it could also act to prevent safety through breaking or not functioning. The recreationists appeared to consider both of these possibilities in their decision to carry a mobile phone and it illustrates the concept that technology is neither inherently negative/threatening nor entirely positive (Shultis, 2012).

The awareness of the recreationists of the potential for their devices to act in particular ways, together with their descriptions of how they individually choose to use their devices to produce a particular experience, connects strongly with the ANT perspective that agency is held by neither humans nor non-humans, but by the entity that is produced when the two combine together. Latour (2009) famously uses the example of the 'citizen-gun' to illustrate the notion that it is neither humans nor guns that kill people, but the combination of the two working together that produces action. In this study, we similarly found that it was the combination of the individual humans together with their devices that produced particular effects of a sense of safety or the alleviation of boredom.

To extend the ANT argument further, while the above paragraph discusses a hybrid relationship of a single human and single digital device, the core of the ANT approach is the concept of the network. In ANT terms, Latour (2005, 2009) defines the network as all encompassing, and consisting of all the varied components that make up a particular entity. To apply this notion to this study, we cannot consider the recreationists and the digital device as the sole points of interest; instead it is also necessary to include consideration of the physical environment. As the recreationists noted, the closeness of the Port Hills to the city of Christchurch (with the Port Hills remaining within the urban frame) was a factor in influencing their decisions to use their devices. To add the dimension of temporality to the spatial, some also acknowledged that the relatively recent nature of the Christchurch earthquakes was a significant reason for their choice to carry a mobile phone with them at all times. Within digital leisure cultures, this resonated with Bull's (2005) work on the notions of control and isolation given by technology where Port Hills users employed their digital devices to massage their individual recreational experiences of space and time.

Conclusion

The peri-urban setting is unique in combining the natural and the urban, and in this study recreationists' use of digital devices reflected this juxtaposition. Some participants felt the same awkwardness and disinterest in using technology due to its potential to erode their experience of the natural setting as identified in prior wilderness studies. But more commonly, they adopted similar behaviours as identified by previous studies set in urban environments. Further, participants utilised terms like 'enhance' to describe the influence of their devices, suggesting that technology facilitated a more positive rather than negative experience. At the same time, the study found that participants were extremely varied in their use of technologies, in line with Campbell and Park's (2008) notion of people using technology to individualise and personalise their experience to their own personal preferences.

These findings are significant for a number of reasons. First, the individualised usage found here suggests that recreation policy-makers could benefit from offering varied technological options for recreationists rather than considering policies that restrict the use of technology. Second, the similarity of behaviour observed between individuals in the urban and peri-urban environments suggests that recreationists in peri-urban environments could more easily be understood through utilising ideas from research in an urban environment rather than drawing on wilderness literature, despite the natural setting. Finally, the emphasis which participants placed on the ability of technology to enhance or add to the experience, rather than eroding it, confirms Shultis' (2012) argument that outdoor recreation literature could benefit from moving away from the view of technology as detrimental to the outdoor recreation experience. Although this study was completed in a New Zealand context, the findings relate to the wider urban and/or peri-urban outdoor recreation community.

References

Babbie, E.R. (2013) *The Practice of Social Research* (13th edn). Belmont, CA: Wadsworth Cengage Learning

Beedie, P. and Hudson, S. (2003) Emergence of Mountain-based Adventure Tourism. *Annals of Tourism Research*, 3(3): 625–643.

Bull, M. (2005) No Dead Air! The iPod and the Culture of Mobile Listening. *Leisure Studies*, 24(4): 343–355.

Campbell, S. and Park, Y.J. (2008) Social Implications of Mobile Technology: The Rise of Personal Communication Society. *Sociology Compass*, 2(2): 371–387.

Creeber, G. and Martin, B. (2009) *Digital Cultures. Understanding New Media.* New York: McGraw Hill.

Devlin, P.J. (1993) Outdoor Recreation and Environment. In H. Perkins and G. Cushman (eds) *Towards an Understanding of the Use of the Outdoors in New Zealand* (pp. 84–98). Auckland, NZ: Longman Paul.

Devlin, P.J., Corbett, R.A. and Peebles, C.J. (1995) *Outdoor Recreation in New Zealand.* Wellington, NZ: Joint publication of the Department of Conservation and Lincoln University.

Dignan, A. and Cessford, G. (2009) *Outdoor Recreation Participation and Incidents in New Zealand. A Scoping Study Relating Incidents to Participation Levels.* New Zealand: Mountain Safety Council.

Douglas, I. (2006) Peri-urban Ecosystems and Societies' Transitional Zones and Contrasting Calues. In D. McGregor, D. Simon and D. Thompson (eds) *Peri-urban Interface: Approaches to Sustainable Natural and Human Resource Use* (pp. 18–29). London: Earthscan Publications.

Driver, B. (1998) The Benefits are Endless ... But Why? *Parks and Recreation*, 33(2): 26.

Ewert, A. and Shultis, J. (1999) Technology and Backcountry Recreation. *JOPERD: The Journal of Physical Education, Recreation and Dance*, 70(8): 23.

Field, A., Oliver, M., Mackie, H., Arcus, K., Dale-Gandar, L. and Hanham, G. (2013) *Opportunities and Challenges for Peri-urban Recreation in New Zealand's Fastest Growing Cities.* Auckland, NZ: Synergia.

Foley, C., Holzman, C. and Wearing, S. (2007) Moving Beyond Conspicuous Leisure Consumption: Adolescent Women, Mobile Phones and Public Space. *Leisure Studies*, 26(2): 179–192.

Gere, R. (2008) *Digital Culture.* London: Reaktion Books.

Holden, T. (2002) Making Tough Calls from the Field: Cellular and Satellite Technology Used in the Backcountry. *Association of Outdoor Recreation and Education Conference Proceedings*: 97–101.

Latour, B. (2005) *Reassembling the Social: An Introduction to Actor-network-theory.* Oxford: Oxford University Press.

Latour, B. (2009) A Collection of Humans and Non-humans: Following Deadalus's Labyrinth. In D.M. Kaplan (ed.) *Reading the Philosophy of Technology* (pp. 156–157). Plymouth: Rowman & Littlefield.

Liu, J., Wang, R. and Chen, T. (2010) Factors of Spatial Distribution of Recreation Areas in Peri-urban Beijing. *Journal of Geographical Sciences*, 20(5): 741–756.

Louv, R. (2005) *Last Child in the Woods.* New York: Algonquin Books of Chapel Hill.

Louv, R. (2009) Children and Nature Deficit Disorder. *Countryside Recreation*, 17(2): 3–6.

Louv, R. (2011a) *The Nature Principle.* New York: Algonquin Books of Chapel Hill.

Louv, R. (2011b) Reconnecting to Nature in the Age of Technology. *The Futurist*, November–December: 41–45.

Manning, R. (2011) *Studies in Outdoor Recreation. Search and Research for Satisfaction.* (3rd edn). Corvallis: Oregon State University Press.

Matthewman, S. (2011) *Technology and Social Theory.* Basingstoke: Palgrave Macmillan.

Miller, G. and Spoolman, C. (2009) *Living in the Evironment.* Belmont, CA: Cengage Learning.

Ogilvie, G. (2000) *Enjoying the Port Hills, Christchurch.* Christchurch, NZ: Caxton Press.

Pain, R., Grundy, S., Gill, S., Towner, E., Sparks, G. and Hughes, K. (2005) 'So Long as I Take my Mobile': Mobile Phones, Urban Life and Geographies of Young People's Safety. *International Journal of Urban and Regional Research*, 29(4): 814–830.

Pergams, O.R.W. and Zaradic, P.A. (2006) Is Love of Nature in the US Becoming Love of Electronic Media? 16-year Downtrend in National Park Visits Explained by Watching Movies, Playing Video Games, Internet Use, and Oil Prices. *Journal of Environmental Management*, 80(4): 387–393.

Pigram, J.J. and Jenkins, J.M. (2006) *Outdoor Recreation Management* (2nd edn). London: Routledge.

Plummer, R. (2009) *Outdoor Recreation: An Introduction.* New York: Routledge.

Salkind, N.J. (2012) *Exploring Research.* New Jersey: Pearson.

Shultis, J. (2001) Consuming Nature: The Uneasy Relationship between Technology, Outdoor Recreation and Protected Areas. *The George Wright Forum*, 18(1): 56–66.

Shultis, J. (2012) The Impact of Technology on the Wilderness Experience: A Review of Common Themes and Approaches in Three Bodies of Literature. *USDA Forest Service Proceedings.*

Statistics New Zealand. (2013) 2013 Census QuickStats about Greater Christchurch. Available at: www.stats.govt.nz/Census/2013-census/profile-and-summary-reports/quickstats-about greater-chch.aspx.

Vanderbilt, T. (2013) How STRAVA is Changing the Way we Ride? *Outside Magazine.*

VanLoon, J. (2002) *Risk and Technological Culture. Towards a Sociology of Virulance.* London: Routledge.

Wiley, S.B.C. (2005) Repositioning the Wilderness: Mobile Communication Technologies and the Transformation of Wild Space. Paper presented at the Conference on Communication and the Environment, Jekyll Island, Georgia.

Wray, K., Espiner, S. and Perkins, H.C.P. (2010) Cultural Clash: Interpreting Established Use and New Tourism Activities in Protected Natural Areas. *Scandinavian Journal of Hospitality and Tourism*, 10(3): 272–290.

Young, N. (2012) *The Virtual Self: How Our Digital Lives are Altering the World Around Us.* Toronto: McClelland & Stewart.

6 GoPro panopticon

Performing in the surveyed leisure experience

Anja Dinhopl and Ulrike Gretzel

Introduction

Wearable cameras have become popular for recording adventure sports and leisure activities, and take many forms. While most are mounted on helmets or put on chest harnesses to film from point-of-view perspectives or mounted on sports equipment to film oneself, others are integrated as clip-on jewellery or sunglasses that house cameras in their nose-bridges. While some are more easily visible and others are completely hidden, all of them make it close to impossible to know whether they are recording or not. They no longer have viewfinders and almost none feature digital screens to look through or at when filming, representing aspects that are actively promoted by manufacturers as design innovations. Many offer automated visual documentation, taking photos at pre-specified time intervals (Bosker, 2014; Rettberg, 2014), while other models do not even feature an on/off button, but turn on when detecting movement.

Such 'invisible' cameras – that is, cameras that are either not easily distinguishable or that do not make it obvious when they are recording – necessitate a different understanding of performing for photos and videos during leisure experiences. Photography is considered a staged performance in tourism (Crang, 1997; Edensor, 2000) – a moment that is somehow outside of or external to the tourist experience. Such a perspective assumes that tourists know when they are being recorded, and that they opt to participate in the performance of photography by posing for pictures or modifying their behaviour in some other form. Emerging digital technologies undermine this perspective as wearable cameras do not require participants to hold them in their hands, signifying filming to others, and automatic visual documentation does not even inform the wearer of the camera when photos or video are being taken. Performing for the camera in the traditional sense as delineated moments of performance therefore does not offer a sufficient theoretical foundation.

The marketing of wearable cameras suggests that such invisibility and uncertainty about recording will free up participants to fully immerse themselves in their experiences and forget about being filmed. From this perspective, performing for the camera would disappear as a distinct element of leisure experiences. This chapter argues that rather than becoming diminished, such performances

Performing in surveyed leisure experience 67

become more prolonged and integrated as part of the overall experience with emerging digital technologies (Dinhopl and Gretzel, 2015) and that performances for photo- and video-recording moments must be considered to be much more deeply embedded in the experience rather than less. This argument builds on Foucault's (1977) use of the panopticon, a watchtower in prison, as a model to explain the effects of candid surveillance. The panopticon allows the observation from a single vantage point without the observed knowing whether they are being observed or not, leading them to believe they are being watched at all times. From this perspective, participants' uncertainty about being recorded will lead them to behave as though they are being recorded at all times. As a result, it may be assumed that performances are no longer confined to acts of photo taking or video recording, but rather span the entire leisure experience.

This chapter explores in particular how lifestyle sports enthusiasts in the snowboarding community participate in recording with 'invisible' cameras – that is, cameras that are either not easily distinguishable from equipment or that do not make it obvious when they are recording. The chapter is organised at the start with a theoretical section to build on existing foundations for understanding performing in tourist photography/videography as well as the importance of authenticity in lifestyle sports. Snowboarding is introduced as the case study context to highlight how leisure sports enthusiasts integrate video recording with wearable cameras into their experiences, and how the 'invisibility' of wearable cameras further enhances snowboarders' tendencies to 'be authentic'. The results of the case study are first presented and then discussed in relation to the theoretical arguments outlined, and the chapter concludes with implications for future research.

Authenticity in leisure experiences and lifestyle sports

The quest for authentic experiences is a long-standing concept in tourism and leisure studies (MacCannell, 1973). It builds on Goffman's (1959) classification of social life as a performance with differences between 'frontstage', where one is concerned with performing for one's audience, and 'backstage', where one is able to act authentically. MacCannell (1973) argues that tourist experiences are staged in order to give tourists the impression that they are participating in authentic experiences. Such object-related authenticity fails to explain many experiences found in tourism (Wang, 1999) and activity-related authenticity may be better suited to explain the participation in leisure experiences: 'people feel that they are themselves much more authentic and more freely self-expressed than they are in everyday life ... because they are engaging in non-everyday activities, free from the constraints of daily life' (Wang, 2000: 50).

Understanding authenticity as linked to tourists themselves allows for understanding intra- and interpersonal authenticity concerns (Pearce and Moscardo, 1986; Wang, 1999). This means that tourists are 'not merely searching for authenticity of the Other. They also search for the authenticity of, and between, *themselves*' (Wang, 1999: 364, emphasis in original). Tourists travel in search of themselves, which they may do by searching for others to reaffirm their own identity and participating in alternative lifestyles or identities outside of their everyday lives (Moscardo et al., 2014). Through this lens, Kim and Jamal (2007) explored how tourists perceive their participation in a renaissance fair as authentic, and find that tourists' experiences mapped on to Wang's (1999) notion of intra- and interpersonal notions of authenticity.

Adventure activities provide tourists with opportunities to engage in quests for authentic experiences (Vester, 1987). In this context, intra-personal authenticity is conceptualised as comprising both bodily pleasures as well as 'self-making' or identity processes that are facilitated by tourists' participation in non-routine experiences (Wang, 1999). Interpersonal authenticity is conceptualised in this context as aiming to create community (Wang, 1999; Kim and Jamal, 2007). In the context of snowboarding, being authentic is both an intra-personal value allowing snowboarders to engage in sense-making of the self as well as an interpersonal value that aids in maintaining one's status and membership within the community (Wheaton and Beal, 2003). Being authentic is therefore both the objective of participation in snowboarding as well as the means of achieving it.

In lifestyle and extreme sports, social processes related to participants' identity are more important than in other sports (Celsi et al., 1993; Thorpe, 2008, 2012; Wheaton, 2004). Being authentic is particularly important for status, membership and participation in lifestyle sports such as snowboarding (Wheaton, 2000), so much so that authenticity becomes something participants seek actively to achieve (Barker, 2000). Lifestyle sports participants use media such as video sharing sites to receive and display notions of their understandings of authenticity, which in turn helps them understand their status and position in their lifestyle sport community (Wheaton and Beal, 2003). Visual documentation is thus integral to this quest for authenticity and status by providing lifestyle sports participants with the answer to the 'fundamental phenomenological challenge' of 'how can one know that one is looking cool without being able to see oneself?' (Woermann, 2012: 625).

Visual documentation as performance in lifestyle sports

Technologies of visual documentation are therefore central to allowing lifestyle sports participants to communicate aspects of their identity and are closely related to participants' authentic participation in the lifestyle sport. The recording of lifestyle activities becomes equally part of the experience (Krotz, 2009; Thorpe and Rinehart, 2010). Lifestyle practices evolve through recording, viewing and sharing videos (Thorpe, 2008; Woermann, 2012). A study on the BASE-jumping community – another high-risk, counterculture-oriented lifestyle activity – finds that recording alters 'the experience and meaning of jumping itself' (Ferrell et al., 2001: 186), because the visual record renders the existence of an illicit activity tangible, thereby making it more meaningful to its participants. In these communities, visual documentation and lifestyle practice are therefore impossible to distinguish.

The visual documentation of leisure experiences has to contend with various layers of performance and authenticity. Photography is considered a staged performance within the tourist or leisure experience (Coleman and Crang, 2002; Edensor, 2000) which, by definition, cannot be considered as authentic. Within this staged performance, tourists are engaged in performativity. Performativity is the act of communicating an identity via discourse (Butler, 1990). Related to tourist photography, this means that tourists participate in tourist photography to communicate something about themselves related to their identity (Larsen, 2005). A family hugging in a picture shows loving familial relations – the family must love each other because they are hugging in this picture (Haldrup and Larsen, 2003; Larsen, 2005). How tourists participate in the performance of tourist photography is performativity. In the context of lifestyle sports, performing authenticity is a central element of participants' identity (Baker, 2000). As a result, they also have to perform authenticity in the visual documentation of their experiences.

In lifestyle sports, performative spaces overlap. On the one hand, participation in lifestyle sports is considered a liminal space (Graburn, 1983) where participants seek to achieve existential authenticity through their participation (Wang, 1999). On the other hand, participation in lifestyle sports is also concerned with the portrayal of authenticity to others (Wheaton and Beal, 2003), making the participation in lifestyle sports a performance of authenticity. The participation in snowboarding is then both a quest to be authentic and a quest to portray authenticity. In addition, the visual documentation of lifestyle sports is closely tied to the experience of participating in them. This creates another performative space, in which lifestyle sports participants are again concerned with enacting and portraying authenticity. The performativity in lifestyle sports is therefore linked to authenticity and encompasses how snowboarders want to see and portray themselves. The layering of performative spaces and the quest for authenticity in lifestyle sports is sufficiently complicated already in situations where snowboarders know that they are being recorded. They are aware of both performative spaces. The following section explores how snowboarders navigate performing authenticity when they may not be aware that they are being recorded.

Wearable cameras as panoptic tools

Foucault (1977) uses the panopticon, a watchtower in a prison, as a model to explain surveillance and the panoptic gaze. It allows the observation from a single vantage point without the observed knowing whether they are being observed or not, leading them to believe they are being watched at all times. For Foucault, this model explained how the potential of surveillance as a threat made the observed internalise the control imposed upon them and discipline their own behaviour:

> There is no need for arms, physical violence, material constraints. Just a gaze. An inspecting gaze, a gaze which each individual under its weight will

end by interiorising to the point that he is his own overseer, each individual thus exercising this surveillance over, and against, himself.

(Foucault, 1980: 155)

To be suitable to explain leisure experiences for which the recording and sharing of video is integral, the notion of the panopticon needs to be expanded. In addition to the disciplining notion of Foucault's panopticon, the filming of leisure experiences also brings participants joy. In consumer research, Kozinets *et al.* (2004: 659) reinterpret Foucault's notion of the panopticon to introduce the obverse panopticon, where 'surveillance is not oppressive but actually desired and libidinously charged'. Further, the panopticon is also constituted of online audiences, with which videos will be shared, which is a consideration for tourists, as Lo and McKercher (2015) suggest. Such notions of the panopticon provide grounding for how snowboarders navigate the uncertainty over being recorded.

Researching lifestyle sport practices

The snowboarding community was chosen as a study context, because it has been considered from its inception as an alternative, high-risk and counterculture-oriented sport (Thorpe, 2011), which places it alongside leisure practices that are considered lifestyle activities (e.g. mountain biking, skateboarding, surfing) in which video recording is integral to the activity (Woermann, 2012). Second, it is being aggressively marketed by wearable camera manufacturers, which makes it a market segment where there is both likely to be a higher adoption of participants using wearable cameras as well as a wider range of length of use by participants allowing for information-rich insights (Patton, 1990). Third, the lead author has been an active snowboarder for more than ten years, with familiarity of the community.

Ethnographic visits were chosen as the suitable method for exploring visual documentation practices with wearable cameras because of the inherent complexity in gathering data about something that participants may find difficult to verbalise. Further complicating this is the fact that wearable cameras are specifically designed to make users unaware of their recording with the marketing premise that the experience will not be disrupted as it is with conventional photo/video equipment. Therefore, snowboarders cannot possibly be expected to reflect reliably on their experiences. Combining participant observation with interviews allowed the observation of their actions, but also allowed an understanding of how they talk, think and present those actions, and allowed an identification of discrepancies between statements and actions. This method has previously provided rich insights into the snowboarding community (Thorpe, 2011).

The research involved visiting three different ski resorts in the Western United States of America (Boreal Mountain Resort and Squaw Valley Resort in California, and Jackson Hole Mountain Resort in Wyoming) and two connected ski resorts in Austria (Bad Hofgastein-Angertal and Sportgastein) between

Performing in surveyed leisure experience 71

December 2013 and March 2015. Each visit lasted from a minimum of two days to three weeks. In each of these resorts, in-depth interviews and participant observation with snowboarders and skiers (32 interviews in total) who use wearable cameras were conducted. The interviewees were all between 18 and 30 years of age, with the majority being male and college students. Experiences with snowboarding and length of time filming with wearable cameras were varied. Participants were approached through convenience sampling, with the behavioural criterion that they had to use wearable cameras and had to be snowboarding with at least one other person. Participants were approached either at ski lifts or in restaurants or ski shops in the various resorts, and not during snowboarding. We started by identifying ourselves as researchers interested in learning more about how snowboarders use wearable cameras. Permission from ski resorts was not obtained and participants were not filmed by the researchers. Sometimes participants volunteered to show videos to help them explain specific situations.

Pseudonyms are used to protect participants' confidentiality. Fieldnotes for observational data and notes from interviews were analysed at the end of each interview or at the end of the day snowboarding with participants following the analytic framework of grounded theory (Glaser and Strauss, 1967). Interviews were transcribed at the end of each ethnographic visit, rather than at the end of the day. A research journal was kept to keep track of immediate reflective thoughts. The data were first open coded and then grouped into categories to connect codes from participant observation and interviews. Surveillance, authenticity and performativity served as sensitising concepts (Glaser and Strauss, 1967). With data collection and analysis occurring simultaneously, theoretical foundations were identified iteratively. Data were integrated into the concepts of intra-personal and interpersonal authenticity (Wang, 1999), similar to authentic experiences in the performative space of a renaissance fair (Kim and Jamal, 2007). Several important themes related to surveillance via wearable cameras, performing for invisible audiences and the quest to portray authenticity as part of managing one's snowboarding identity emerged from the data.

Wearable cameras as panopticon

Roxy (female, age 27) describes what it is like for her when she goes snowboarding with a group of people who use wearable cameras to film. She is aware of when others have wearable cameras with them, but she is not sure whether they are recording at any point:

> They wanted me to not know [that they're recording]. Like, they'd click it [the record button], and I wouldn't know 'cos it's only red at the top. If it's on their chest, they're seeing it, but I don't see that they're filming. So I don't always know.... I would forget, because I'd be in the moment, and then I was like 'Crap, he is video-recording me' and then I'd be like [makes stopping sound] ... so, inhibitions, right? You drink, and you forget them,

and then you're fine. But it's when you sober up, right? So the same, thing, reality hits, and you're like – I'm being recorded, crap.

Being in situations like the one Roxy described happens so often that snowboarders assume that the cameras are on even when they may not be. They assume that when someone has a camera with them that it may be recording. RP (male, age 29) says:

> I mean, most people just assume it's on, especially when we're riding through good runs, like tree runs.... Most time I see someone with a camera, you know, I mean, it could be on, it couldn't be on, I mean, who knows.

Chelsea (female, age 26) said she expects to be recorded at all times: 'Because it's our culture, you can't do anything without someone video recording or taking a picture. So, the assumption that it's gonna happen is very high.'

Recording and staging authentic experiences

With the practice of snowboarding so closely tied to wanting to be perceived as authentic, the quest for authenticity also extends to the visual recordings. Snowboarders want to record authentic moments. Recording inauthentic moments will lack the emotional aspects of the experience that are important to them. Travis' (male, age 19) answer shows just how important it is for him to film authentic encounters:

> It does happen, but then we may go back, like in climbing, that is possible, but it's never the same, because it's not authentic. You're like, okay, I'm doing it for the second time now, 'cos you wanna catch the emotion and the try-hard. And the try-hard is still there, but ... I wanna see the first ascent, I wanna see them doing it for the first time. It's like watching your kid, I don't have a kid, but it's like watching your kid take his first steps and then you're like, wait, do it again, we're gonna put that on video. That's his second step, that's not his first step.

In order to film experiences that will look good on camera and contain the emotional qualities of authenticity that snowboarders seek, they participate in the staging of experiences. They do not consider the deliberate staging of entire sets of experiences as inauthentic. Conversations regarding the visual documentation of their experiences sometimes occur before the core experience starts. For instance, when sitting in the gondola and looking down on the ski slopes, snowboarders will talk about where there would be fresh snow or jumps that would be suitable for filming. As soon as they have decided what to film, there is no more conversation about filming until after the specific run or jump snowboarders were talking about is over. In addition, snowboarders talk about the specifics of filming – who is filming and what to film for which they often use media jargon

Performing in surveyed leisure experience 73

such as 'setting up shots'. However, they do so well in advance of filming rather than immediately before in order to allow them to experience the staged run as authentic, however staged or deliberately set up the authentic moment is. Snowboarders will use one run in the terrain park as what they call a 'recon' (reconnaissance) run, where they are trying to figure out how to link obstacles together so they can be filmed in sequence on the next run. Paul (male, age 21) confirms that filming is talked about prior to it taking place, but that the experience of it is supposed to look as 'natural' and 'unstaged' as possible. He remembered an instance of a snowboarding trip the previous year where he saw a sign about the dangers of snowboarding outside the resort boundaries. He saw that as a great opportunity to film himself and his friends, because the video would show others the dangers of snowboarding and, in turn, make him seem daring and 'cool'. In order to communicate those characteristics, he had to specifically stage the experience to make it look natural; it therefore had to occur at a different time than when he talked about it:

> It's usually talked about before. When we were in Utah last year, we were in this area, and it [the sign] said 'you're leaving the resort property, you can die', so when we were there, I said, let's do this run on the next run and I'll get it on film. So that's one way.

Denying performances, celebrating authenticity

On the run that is being filmed, snowboarders do not talk about filming. Part of snowboarders' performing for the camera necessitates acting as though it is an authentic experience and a spontaneous idea to cross the resorts' borders. Similar to findings from freeskiers, it is important not to pretend to want to be cool in order to be considered cool (Woermann, 2012). The previous examples show that snowboarders are not only interested in recording authentic experiences, but they are experienced in staging experiences and participating in them as though they are authentic when they are aware that the camera is on. They are aware that their performing for the camera as authentic is an element of snowboarding and have become used to performing authenticity. In the conversations after video recording, snowboarders go out of their way to emphasise that filming did not impact upon their leisure experience and try to deflect: 'We would've done everything we did today, whether we had the camera or not' (Ron, male, age 26). Findings from participant observation – from their 'recon' runs as well as their behaviour during runs they had agreed upon filming beforehand – contradict their statements.

With authenticity being such a high value for snowboarders, and with loss of authenticity associated with admitting that one is performing for the camera, snowboarders have created an environment where it is not possible to openly admit that one is performing for the camera without risking loss of status in the group. They believe that they are the only ones performing for the camera, and do not believe that others could be bothered by being recorded. As a result – and because they aim to record authentic experiences – snowboarders use wearable cameras to engage in unannounced recording. They believe that they are justified in doing so, as Jake (male, age 28) continued:

> I mean, that's kind of why you get a GoPro, so that you can film while you're snowboarding or whatever. It would be kinda weird for me to be like 'Hey guys, I'm gonna press record now!' Like, that would be silly!

The uncertainty over when wearable cameras are recording allows snowboarders to participate in unannounced recording. We noticed several times how this happens. In the coffee shop after snowboarding, we were sitting around a table talking about snowboarding, and we noticed one of the snowboarders secretively press the button to record with his GoPro, and then go back to engaging in the conversation as if nothing had happened. The longer people own and use their wearable cameras, the less they become concerned with the ethical dilemma of this practice and they no longer call it 'secret' recording. They know that others are doing it as well, so the practice becomes accepted. As a consequence, they are complacent in allowing surveillance to penetrate snowboarding culture.

Performativity–authenticity tension

In the same way that snowboarders use the uncertainty over knowing whether wearable cameras are recording to their advantage to film others who are not expecting it, they are also using it to their advantage when they are the ones being filmed. It gives them plausible deniability of performing for the camera. As a result – due to the uncertainty of knowing whether wearable cameras are recording – it is not only the filming itself, but the potential of being filmed that shapes participation in snowboarding. There is thus a lot of pressure to be 'authentic' and the 'true you', which is especially difficult in a sport that is so closely tied to identity management on its own. Unobtrusive equipment further accentuates that performance–authenticity tension. Snowboarders experience a lot of pressure to be their true selves and feel guilty for inauthenticity. Laine (female, age 20) feels guilt when she realises that she is changing her behaviour as a result of being recorded. She says it is difficult for her to be authentic:

> It's hard for me, because when the camera is on, even when it's not me holding it, I can still feel it, so it's not ... it's never really candid. You are playing up for the camera even just a little bit. I always know when it's on, so that's definitely something I have to get over.

It is very important for participants to be considered authentic rather than performing because their authenticity is tied to their status in the group (Wheaton and Beal, 2003).

By pretending not to notice that they are being recorded, snowboarders are able to perform the authentic version of themselves and for their friends. Most snowboarders we talked to, after some reflection, and some being more ashamed than others, admitted that they behave differently when they are being recorded. But they only felt comfortable doing so in private, without their friends hearing them. Bianca's (female, age 23) answers confirm that there are two layers to the surveyed leisure experience – participants are concerned not only with their immediate audience, but their perceived social media audience as well:

> If it's someone I don't know, if it's in a group, and somebody else films it, I just act totally normal. Unless it's like a friend of mine who will put it up on Facebook or whatever, I just totally act normal. But if it's a friend of mine, I can't help but play it up for the camera a little bit. A little bit more playful, or a little bit more conscientious of how I look. 'Cos more likely, I will see the video again, and they will put it up, and I will see it, so it becomes more real in my world and I treat that a little bit different.

I interject with 'So complicated, huh?' and Bianca continues: 'I know it is! Honestly, a lot of it is just intuitive; I don't think about it as much, it's just kind of an intuitive communication or world it seems.'

With the potential magnification of one's audience via social media, the notions of authenticity and performativity carry even more weight. Snowboarders tend to not only think about being recorded, but also the consequences of said recordings for their identity.

Discussion

The research raises important questions about performativity and authenticity as they relate to tourist and leisure experiences. Recording is a central part of leisure experiences, and especially of lifestyle sports such as snowboarding. Performing for recording is central as well. Performing for recording while pretending not to be performing is also not a surprise in lifestyle sports. The problem arises when the boundaries between when one is being recorded and when one is not being recorded can no longer be clearly distinguished because of the panopticon created by technologies and social practices. To some extent, leisure sports enthusiasts and tourists are faced with a choice. Because they are not certain whether they are being recorded, they could either assume that they are not being recorded or that they are being recorded. Whichever path they choose becomes the default status for their participation in a given experience. In the example of snowboarding, which is so intimately tied to identity and status within one's group (and the high likelihood of being among friends who have wearable cameras who could potentially record among the participants interviewed), the findings show that participants choose to assume that they are being recorded. They so choose to engage in performing authenticity beyond actual moments of recording.

This chapter has extended the notion of performativity in tourist photography and videography for emerging digital technologies, when participants may not always be aware whether they are being recorded or not. Due to participants' uncertainty over being recorded, their performativity is no longer bound by the moment of recording, but extended throughout the leisure experience. This finding is assumed to be transposable to other, more general areas of leisure and tourism once wearable cameras or increasingly invisible recording equipment become more common. The other extension to the current conceptualisation of performativity, namely the performativity–authenticity tension, is assumed to be more localised to lifestyle sports, such as snowboarding. For snowboarders, it is important for their community standing to be considered 'authentic'. They therefore feel pressure to not be regarded as though they are performing. As a result, they are not openly talking about how recording makes them feel as though they are performing and they feel tension when they are aware that they are performing. For other leisure sports enthusiasts and tourists more broadly, the performativity–authenticity tension is not expected to be present to the same extent.

Marketing efforts for emerging digital technologies aim to communicate the freedom which leisure sports enthusiasts will be able to experience by not having to worry about recording. The quasi-invisibility of the equipment and whether or not it is recording are considered innovative design features. Snowboarders use these design features to participate in new visual documentation practices of unannounced recording. They argue that one should expect to be recorded during one's experience. They want to be authentic and film experiences as they happen, but they are aware that they are performing at the same time. Because they experience uncertainty about being recorded (both due to the technologies' features as well as to the adopted practices of using them), snowboarders assume that they could be recorded at all times. The technology makes snowboarders more aware of their potential audiences. The camera becomes a more prominent – while at the same time hidden – part of the leisure experience with panoptic qualities. Advances in digital technologies make it difficult to know when one is being recorded. By not knowing whether one is being watched or recorded, snowboarders internalise the possibility that they could be recorded, and as a result will behave as though they are being recorded throughout their leisure experience. This is a relatively subtle exercise for them, as they are already participating in the quest for authenticity in the performative space of snowboarding. With unannounced recording, their performativity of authenticity spans the entire leisure experience.

Conclusion

For snowboarders, snowboarding provides the opportunity for intra- and interpersonal authenticity as part of a community where they can behave in the way they want to see themselves. Authenticity plays a central role in identity management; in order to be a cool snowboarder, one has to be authentic (Wheaton and Beal, 2003; Thorpe, 2008). Snowboarders thus take on a different aspect from their everyday life persona when they go snowboarding. Being in this performative space, similar to tourists participating in renaissance fairs (Kim and Jamal, 2007), tourists feel authentic. When snowboarders know that they are being recorded, they knowingly perform for the camera. Because visual documentation is so connected with their identity, performing authenticity for the camera is important. Recording becomes an accentuated identity performance. When snowboarders cannot be certain that they are being recorded, they will behave as though they are being recorded. This uncertainty creates pressure for snowboarders to perform for the camera during the entire leisure experience. The practical contribution of these findings is that such uncertainty and known performance during the experience may take away snowboarders' reason for participation in snowboarding. They participate in snowboarding to achieve authenticity. If they are not able to achieve authenticity, it is not clear whether they are able to fulfil their motivation for participating in snowboarding in the first place. This is further complicated by the fact that snowboarders themselves enjoy recording others without announcing that they are recording them. The findings suggest that it may be beneficial for snowboarders as well as camera manufacturers and tourist destinations to counteract the performativity–authenticity tension, by highlighting the positive elements of filming when filming is announced.

This study has provided insights from a new practice of unannounced recording. While it went into detail about what this means for performativity and authenticity of snowboarders' experiences, it did not touch on another vital point. There are ethical dimensions tied to such unannounced recording, namely that others do not have the opportunity to consent to such filming. While participants did not consider it to be the case, the opportunity to consent to one's image being taken should remain a right rather than a privilege or a sign of outdated technophobia. The silent acceptance of surveillance and voluntary giving up of privacy carry with them dangers far greater than this chapter is able to outline here. For participants, they bring with them the ability to use the recording as a way to discipline others into behaving appropriately or using the visual record as a way to shame them after they have done something wrong. This creates an environment where participants learn that it is the one being filmed without permission caught doing something wrong who deserves the blame rather than the person who filmed them without their permission. Future research needs to consider issues of privacy in relation to ubiquitous surveillance and what is considered ethical filming.

References

Barker, C. (2000) *Cultural Studies: Theory and Practice*. London: Sage

Bosker, B. (2014) Nice to meet you. I've already taken your picture. *Huffington Post*. Available at: www.huffingtonpost.com/2014/02/10/narrative-clip_n_4760580.

Bossewitch, J. and Sinnreich, A. (2013) The end of forgetting: Strategic agency beyond the panopticon. *New Media and Society*, 15(1): 224–242.

Butler, J. (1990) *Gender Trouble*. New York: Routledge.

Celsi, R.L., Rose, R.L. and Leigh, T.W. (1993) An exploration of high-risk leisure consumption through skydiving. *Journal of Consumer Research*, 20(1): 1–23.

Coleman, S. and Crang, M. (eds) (2002) *Tourism: Between Place and Performance*. Oxford: Berghahn.
Crang, M. (1997) Picturing practices: Research through the tourist gaze. *Progress in Human Geography*, 21(3): 359–373.
Dinhopl, A. and Gretzel, U. (2015) Conceptualizing tourist videography. *Information Technology and Tourism*. Doi: 10.1007/s40558-015-0039-7.
Edensor, T. (2000) Staging tourism: Tourists as performers. *Annals of Tourism Research*, 27(2): 322–344.
Ferrell, J., Milovanovic, D. and Lyng, S. (2001) Edgework, media practices, and the elongation of meaning: A theoretical ethnography of the bridge day event. *Theoretical Criminology*, 5(2): 177–202.
Foucault, M. (1977) *Discipline and Punish: The Birth of the Prison*. New York: Vintage Books.
Foucault, M. (1980) *Power/Knowledge: Selected Interviews and Other Writings, 1972–1977*. New York: Pantheon.
Glaser, B. and Strauss, A. (1967) *The Discovery of Grounded Theory: Strategies for Qualitative Research*. Chicago, IL: Aldin.
Goffman, E. (1959) *The Presentation of Self in Everyday Life*. Harmondsworth: Penguin Books.
Graburn, N.H. (1983) The anthropology of tourism. *Annals of Tourism Research*, 10(1): 9–33.
Haldrup, M. and Larsen, J. (2003) The family gaze. *Tourist Studies*, 3: 23–46.
Kim, H. and Jamal, T. (2007) Touristic quest for existential authenticity. *Annals of Tourism Research*, 34(1): 181–201.
Kozinets, R.V., Sherry, J.F., Storm, D., Duhachek, A., Nuttavuthisit, K. and DeBerry-Spence, B. (2004) Ludic agency and retail spectacle. *Journal of Consumer Research*, 31(3): 658–672.
Krotz, F. (2009) Mediatization: A concept with which to grasp media and societal change. In K. Lundby (ed.) *Mediatization: Concept, Changes, Consequences* (pp. 21–40). New York: Peter Lang.
Larsen, J. (2005) Families seen sightseeing: Performativity of tourist photographs. *Space and Culture*, 8(4): 416–434.
Lo, I.S. and McKercher, B. (2015) Ideal image in process: Online tourist photography and impression management. *Annals of Tourism Research*, 52: 104–116.
MacCannell, D. (1973) Staged authenticity: Arrangements of social space in tourist settings. *American Sociological Review*, 79(3): 589–603.
Moscardo, G., Dann, G. and McKercher, B. (2014) Do tourists travel for the discovery of 'self' or search for the 'other'? *Tourism Recreation Research*, 39(1): 81–106.
Patton, M.Q. (1990) *Qualitative Evaluation and Research Methods*. Thousand Oaks, CA: Sage.
Pearce, P.L. and Moscardo, G.M. (1986) The concept of authenticity in tourist experiences. *Journal of Sociology*, 22(1): 121–132.
Rettberg, J.W. (2014) *Seeing Ourselves through Technology: How We Use Selfies, Blogs and Wearable Devices to See and Shape Ourselves*. New York: Palgrave Macmillan.
Thorpe, H. (2008) Foucault, technologies of self, and the media: Discourses of femininity in snowboarding culture. *Journal of Sport and Social Issues*, 32(2): 199–229.
Thorpe, H. (2011) *Snowboarding Bodies in Theory and Practice*. New York: Palgrave Macmillan.
Thorpe, H. (2012) Transnational mobilities in snowboarding culture: Travel, tourism and lifestyle migration. *Mobilities*, 7(2): 317–345.

Thorpe, H. and Rinehart, R. (2010) Alternative sport and affect: Non-representational theory examined. *Sport in Society*, 13(7–8): 1268–1291.

Vester, H.G. (1987) Adventure as a form of leisure. *Leisure Studies*, 6(3): 237–249.

Wang, N. (1999) Rethinking authenticity in tourism experience. *Annals of Tourism Research*, 26(2): 349–370.

Wang, N. (2000) *Tourism and Modernity: A Sociological Analysis*. Oxford: Pergamon Press.

Wheaton, B. (2000) 'Just do it': Consumption, commitment, and identity in the windsurfing subculture. *Sociology of Sport Journal*, 17(3): 254–274.

Wheaton, B. (ed.) (2004) *Understanding Lifestyle Sport: Consumption, Identity and Difference*. London: Routledge.

Wheaton, B. and Beal, B. (2003) 'Keeping it real': Subcultural media and the discourses of authenticity in alternative sport. *International Review for the Sociology of Sport*, 38(2): 155–176.

Woermann, N. (2012) On the slope is on the screen: Prosumption, social media practices, and scopic systems in the freeskiing subculture. *American Behavioral Scientist*, 56(4): 618–640.

7 Serious leisure, prosumption and the digital sport media economy
A case study of ice hockey blogging

Mark Norman

Introduction: ice hockey blogging and serious leisure

The emergence and widespread adoption of digital media technologies has had a profound impact on the ways in which professional sport is produced and consumed. One major change brought by this new 'networked media sport' (Hutchins and Rowe, 2012: 5) is the proliferation of sport blogs, many of which are produced by amateur fans rather than by professional journalists. Although sport fan-produced media, such as football 'fanzines' (Haynes, 1995), have a history pre-dating widespread adoption of the internet, sport blogs are unique in their ease of production and distribution to a potentially global audience. Scholars have analysed sport blogs from a variety of angles, from their role in the media production of sport mega-events (Dart, 2009; Hutchins and Mikosza, 2010; Hutchins and Rowe, 2012) to their representation of gender and race (Antunovic and Hardin, 2013; McGovern, 2015). This chapter builds on existing analyses of sport blogging by situating it as a serious leisure practice (Stebbins, 1992, 2007), an approach that sheds light on both the dedication of amateur bloggers and the complex intersection of new media, social issues and sport fandom.

This chapter uses the case study of bloggers who write about the sport of ice hockey (hereafter hockey), and specifically the National Hockey League (NHL) and its Canadian and American teams. In North America, hockey is deeply intertwined with issues of national and regional identity, commercialism, race and gender (Gruneau and Whitson, 1993). Hockey bloggers operate within these complex intersections, sometimes helping to re-create problematic aspects of hockey culture and other times challenging them (cf. Norman, 2014; Norman *et al.*, 2015). As such, their blogging is not neutral and must be understood in its wider context. While the scope and complexity of these issues is too great to adequately address in this chapter, some of them are discussed in more depth as they relate to hockey blogging as a serious leisure practice.

Following a brief introduction to the serious leisure framework (Stebbins, 1992, 2007), this chapter discusses the methods and case study employed in this research. The bulk of the chapter is devoted to an analysis of hockey blogging as a serious leisure practice, drawing upon the framework developed by Stebbins (1992) to explore important characteristics of the activity. It then engages briefly in a discussion of the political economy of hockey blogging and its status as both a popular leisure practice and a potentially exploitative component of the digital sport media landscape (Dart, 2014; Hutchins and Rowe, 2012), drawing for analysis upon Ritzer and Jurgenson's (2010) conceptualisation of 'prosumption' as an accelerating feature of the online economy. The chapter then concludes by suggesting future areas for research on sports blogging and serious leisure.

Serious leisure

Serious leisure is a concept developed by Robert Stebbins and refined by him and numerous other leisure scholars (e.g. Elkington, 2013; Rojek, 1997; Stebbins, 1992, 2007). In short, serious leisure is understood as 'the systematic pursuit of an amateur, hobbyist, or volunteer activity that is sufficiently substantial and interesting for the participant to find a career there in the acquisition of its special skills and knowledge' (Stebbins, 1992: 3). Stebbins (2007: 6) further breaks down serious leisure into three categories: 'amateur pursuits, hobbyist activities, and career volunteering'. While individuals involved in amateur pursuits may receive remuneration for their output, they are differentiated from professionals in that they do not derive their primary livelihood in whole or in part from the pursuit (Stebbins, 2007). Thus, while the experience of an amateur hockey blogger and a professional sport journalist may share some similar characteristics, they are categorically different because the latter derives his or her income from writing about sports and has additional professional duties not required of an amateur blogger.

Throughout its development, the serious leisure perspective has been refined through the effective adoption of certain sociological concepts (Stebbins, 2007). For this case study, hockey bloggers' individual motivations and the formation of a loose-knit 'hockey blogosphere' community are explored in greater depth through blending serious leisure with an analysis of sport new media's political economy (Dart, 2014) and the uncertain relationship between the digital economy and capitalism (Ritzer and Jurgenson, 2010). Research drawing from the serious leisure perspective has focused on sport practices (e.g. Stebbins, 1992, 1993) and sports fandom (Gibson *et al.*, 2002; Jones, 2000), and on blogging about topics such as food (Cox and Blake, 2011) and knitting (Orton-Johnson, 2014). However, I am not aware of any studies that situate sport blogging within the serious leisure framework. As such, this chapter offers a unique approach to understanding the serious leisure practice of sport blogging while situating this activity within broader social and economic structures.

Methods and case study of hockey blogging

This chapter draws upon data collected from an ongoing study, started four years ago, which examines the social and political significance of new media use by fans of North American hockey. My multi-method research has included virtual ethnography (Hine, 2008) in an online 'electronic tribe' of hockey fans (Norman,

2014), participant observation of Twitter use in reaction to televised hockey broadcasts (Norman, 2012), and interviews with bloggers and content analysis of their online writing (Norman et al., 2015). I have also immersed myself ethnographically as a contributor to the hockey blogosphere, and have conducted informal discussions, both in person and online, with dozens of semi-professional and amateur hockey bloggers about their work. The data presented in this chapter are drawn from this ongoing ethnographic work, as well as interviews and content analysis of semi-professional and amateur hockey blogs. I use hockey blogging as a case study not only because of my own enmeshment in its online culture, but also because of the sport's unique history and cultural status in North America, and especially Canada, where it is heavily tied to structural issues concerning national identity, class, gender, race and the economy (Gruneau and Whitson, 1993). As such, it offers a rich site to explore issues relating to the media, hockey culture and sport fandom.

Hockey blogging as serious leisure

This section draws upon Stebbins' (1992: 6–7) six characteristics of serious leisure as a framework in which to situate hockey blogging as a digital leisure pursuit. These characteristics are: the development of careers in the leisure pursuit; perseverance through difficult circumstances; a large amount of effort and the development of specialised skills or knowledge; a variety of individual benefits; a strong identification with the activity; and the emergence of a unique ethos around the practice. Each of these characteristics of hockey blogging as serious leisure could be the subject of its own lengthy analysis, so this chapter presents a necessarily brief overview.

The development of careers in the leisure pursuit

Stebbins (1992: 68) describes a 'career' as 'the typical course, or passage, of certain types of amateur-professional practitioners into, and through, a work role'. Elaborating on this definition, he further notes that serious leisure careers pass through five overlapping stages: 'beginning, development, establishment, maintenance and [sometimes] decline' (Stebbins, 1992: 20). For hockey bloggers, the relative ease of publishing a blog means that thousands of hockey fans have passed through at least the first two stages of a leisure career. The wide array of new media platforms on which networked media sport (Hutchins and Rowe, 2012) is founded allow relatively unknown bloggers to establish their leisure careers by rapidly gaining readers and opportunities to write for more popular websites. This was the career path I followed in my fan blogging leisure career, as I used my own small blog to expose my writing before gaining a position with a much larger Vancouver Canucks blog (cf. Norman, 2014). Similarly, two bloggers I interviewed leveraged less-established blogging work into more prestigious writing positions with a widely read blog. This transition from development to establishment is common among hockey blogging devotees. Career maintenance occurs through regular blog posting once these bloggers are established with a well-known website or have developed a significant readership on their own websites.

For most hockey bloggers, their leisure career remains firmly within the sphere of amateurism and they receive little or no pay for their output. However, some bloggers have made the transition from serious leisure pursuit to a professional career as a direct result of their blogging work. For example, in 2011, a Vancouver Canucks blogger I wrote alongside relied on his entertaining blogging style and amusing Twitter posts to win a contest to be a paid writer for a new blog being launched by the *Vancouver Province* newspaper. Since leaving the unpaid blogging position to join the newspaper, he has diversified the outlets for which he writes to include other media sites and the official website for the Canucks. His online bio now describes him as 'a freelance writer who currently writes for The Province, Canucks Army, Canucks.com and Vancity Buzz' (VanCity Buzz n.d.). There are many other examples of individuals who have similarly shifted from blogging as a serious leisure pursuit into a professional or semi-professional writing career.

In much rarer cases, some serious leisure bloggers who have pioneered and promoted new ways of using statistics have been hired to the staffs of NHL teams. For example, in 2014 the Toronto Maple Leafs hired two hockey bloggers as part of their new analytics team (Johnston, 2014). Similarly, in 2015, the Carolina Hurricanes hired Eric Tulsky, a nanotechnology professional who did amateur hockey blogging, as a statistical analyst (Smith, 2015). Tulsky began blogging as a serious leisure pursuit before being hired to various part-time positions and, ultimately, a full-time professional job in the NHL:

> I found myself with time and interest and just started writing stuff.... It was generally well-received, and I found it being a bigger and bigger part of what I was doing.... I was putting more time into the analysis and eventually started to work with teams. It wasn't something I expected going in. It was just like, 'Hey, this looks like fun,' and here we are.
>
> (Quoted in Smith, 2015)

While some bloggers actively pursue such professional opportunities, it is interesting that others claim no interest in transitioning from the serious leisure pursuit to a related professional career. Instead, they prefer to maintain blogging solely as an amateur pursuit. Two statements from hockey bloggers, quoted below, typify this view. The first quotation is drawn from an interview and the second was posted in the comments section of a blog post about bloggers who transition into professional careers:

> [I was drawn to blogging] as a literary thing.... When I started reading [the blog I write for] I really liked it, it was informative, it was very funny.... So yeah, [blogging] is really a literary thing [for me].
>
> If the [commercial media] ever approached me I'd tell them to pound sand. I can't be reined in and forced to write [politically correct] articles.

Fuck that shit.... Plus, my regular job pays very well. I'd rather stick with this community right here. Because really that's what [this blog] is, and you don't get that anywhere else.

(Comment on Vancitydan, 2011)

Established career hockey bloggers are clearly aware of the possibility of shifting their serious leisure pursuit into a profession, especially given that a number of their peers have made such a transition. However, it appears that some bloggers are resistant to such a change, preferring to remain amateurs seriously pursuing a leisure practice than to become professionals working at a job.

Finally, hockey bloggers have gone through various forms of decline in their serious leisure careers. As discussed above, some exit the leisure pursuit of blogging by taking jobs in the hockey industry. Other blogging careers go into decline without the participant reaching the stage of establishment or maintenance, as numerous hockey blogs that have laid dormant for months or years attest. Yet other bloggers appear to, in Stebbins' words (2007: 20), 'reach a point of diminishing returns in the activity, getting out of it all that is available for them'. I have observed this in my experiences as part of blog-writing teams, as previously committed individuals will slowly spend less time blogging as they find it less fulfilling or find the time commitment too onerous. The changing online culture of hockey new media may also cause blogging to lose its appeal, as the 2012 'retirement' announcement of a prominent blogger made clear:

[Blogging has] lost the sense of fun that used to be there.... Now everyone just looks for another reason day after day to ... call people stupid, bad fans, or just gang up on them when they dare to have another opinion. I'm not okay being any part of that and frankly, it gives me some pretty massive anxiety.... Unfortunately the bad seriously outweighs the good at this point. I just need to unplug from all of this before I start hating the sound of the ice crunching under skates, pucks hitting the boards, or a pretty across the slot one timer.

(Travis Hair, 2012)

Clearly, while hockey bloggers find much enjoyment and fulfilment in this serious leisure pursuit, the activity has pitfalls that can lead some bloggers to disengage from this leisure career. Overall, however, many hockey bloggers appear to pass through the various career stages identified by Stebbins (1992) as they continue in their practice of serious leisure.

Perseverance through difficult circumstances

At a broad level, it may seem a stretch to say that the act of sport blogging gives rise to particularly difficult circumstances for participants, beyond perhaps receiving negative feedback on one's work or struggling to meet writing obligations. However, as the previously quoted 'retirement' announcement makes clear (Travis Hair, 2012), blogging can lead to anxiety when the online discussions concerning the blog become personal or insulting. Furthermore, fandom itself can present difficult circumstances that dedicated fans must endure. For example, a project about New York Islander bloggers (Norman *et al.*, 2015) found that these fans discovered personal solace and collective solidarity in blogging, despite having endured decades of the team's poor on-ice performance, bad ownership and fears of relocation. This finding suggests that dedicated sport fandom can require perseverance through challenging times, and that the serious leisure pursuit of blogging can be a means for coping with this characteristic of fandom. However, this section focuses on a particularly prominent and problematic challenge faced by some hockey bloggers: misogynistic online harassment directed towards women hockey bloggers.

Because professional sport is dominated by men and reflects male interests, it has been critiqued by scholars as a 'male preserve' (Kidd, 2013). This gendered structure has been reflected in sport journalism, where women journalists have faced sexism in various components of their professional careers (Hardin and Shain, 2005; Miller and Miller, 1995). The proliferation of blogs has seen many women gain prominent voices within the hockey blogosphere, some of whom have tackled social issues in hockey culture, such as online sexual harassment (Ramos, 2014) and the marginalisation of women's fandom (phylliskessel13, 2015). However, by publicly discussing these deeply ingrained features of North American hockey, women bloggers have drawn abuse from other fans in comment sections and on Twitter. Yet, in spite of these occurrences, many women bloggers continue to publish critical articles and even use their experiences of abuse and harassment to further critique hockey culture. Two excerpts from online pieces by women bloggers demonstrate this perseverance through extremely difficult circumstances:

> I've been harassed by two hockey writers by my count, and I know other women have been harassed numerous times, too. Plain and simple: being a hockey fan online isn't a safe space for women. In fact, it's downright frightening at times.
>
> (Ramos, 2014)

> I thought about quitting hockey altogether.... A hockey reporter I'd been casually chatting with as one fan to another sexually harassed me and I considered, in the days that followed, just deleting my Twitter account and being done with hockey. I thought about it again when my criticism aimed at another hockey reporter led to harassment from his followers on Twitter ... I manage. We all do. Sometimes I feel a bit like a goldfish swimming around in a bowl; in order to love this sport, I have to have a very short memory.
>
> (McIntyre, 2015)

While male bloggers may be forced to persevere through difficult circumstances, it is clear that women face particular challenges when entering and critiquing the masculine domain of hockey blogging. While many women persevere and continue to produce insightful and popular content, there may be others who decide to quit the leisure practice when faced with sexism and misogyny online.

The need for a large amount of effort and the development of specialised skills or knowledge

The application of specialised skills and knowledge in hockey blogging is variable. Certainly, a successful and rewarding leisure career in hockey blogging requires at least a basic level of knowledge about the sport, a solid grasp of the written word and some computer skills. Perhaps more importantly, it requires the digital literacy to navigate the online hockey blogosphere, reflecting concerns about the 'participation gap' that prevents some people from participating in online cultures (Jenkins, 2006). However, beyond these skills, hockey bloggers require no specialisation to pursue a serious leisure career. In fact, many bloggers write about the sport at a fairly basic level that many other fans could mimic.

Many hockey bloggers who enjoy long leisure careers do bring some unique skill to their practice, whether it be strong writing skills, a good sense of humour, technical proficiency, an ability to blend hockey and popular culture, or a curiosity to explore underreported aspects of the sport. One notable example of bloggers deploying highly specialised skills is in statistical analysis. The rise of 'advanced stats' in hockey has been accompanied by a proliferation of blogs devoted to developing and analysing various statistical techniques, and bloggers on these sites thus require specialised mathematical knowledge that other writers may not possess. As another example, the academic bent of my own blog, *Hockey in Society*, means that its 12 writers all possess or are working on Master's or PhD degrees in relevant fields. Hockey bloggers may therefore develop or possess particular skills that enable them to produce specialised writing. However, writing ability, competency in online environments and some knowledge of hockey are the only entry requirements to pursuing a serious leisure career in hockey blogging.

A variety of individual benefits

Stebbins (1992: 94) argues that 'although occasional costs may be endured by ... amateurs in the conduct of their pastime, in the end, these costs are substantially offset by the rewards found therein'. Some of the costs and difficult circumstances that can face hockey bloggers have been discussed already. That numerous bloggers persevere through these circumstances is a testament to Stebbins' assertion that the rewarding aspects of a serious leisure pursuit outweigh the negative ones. Among the rewards identified by Stebbins (1992) are self-actualisation, self-enrichment and self-expression; recreation; social interaction; and enduring material products.

In hockey blogging careers in which financial remuneration is limited or non-existent, many bloggers nonetheless accrue individual benefits that make the leisure pursuit worthwhile and enjoyable. The opportunities for social interaction offered by 'electronic tribes' of hockey fans (Norman, 2015), discussed in the following section, are one benefit offered to amateur bloggers. Meanwhile, for many bloggers, the opportunity to write about a sport they love is an important form of self-expression and a substantial reward of the leisure pursuit. For example, one interview participant explained:

> I consider writing my first passion, and I thought [hockey blogging] would be a good way, while holding down a full-time job, to force myself to write every day outside of my regular work.

Hockey bloggers may also receive non-financial material rewards that contribute to their positive view of the leisure practice. For example, a notable perk for some bloggers is the opportunity to gain press credentials, allowing them a chance to attend games at no cost and to interview the players they usually cheer for. This is demonstrated by the writing of a Vancouver Canucks blogger, who was granted a press pass to the 2011 Stanley Cup Finals championship series and thus given a once-in-a-lifetime opportunity to attend games, interview players and rub shoulders with hockey media personnel. Before the series, he expressed his excitement to the blog's readership:

> [The blog] Nucks Misconduct is proud to announce that we will be there, representing all of you ... at the Stanley Cup Finals. Right in the press scrums. News almost nearly as fast as those media guys.... Now that I've actually had a chance to stop hyperventilating, I am thrilled to tell you I have been chosen to represent Nucks Misconduct at all home games during the Finals.
>
> (Basky, 2011)

These examples demonstrate some of the ways in which hockey bloggers gain various individual benefits from their pursuit of the serious leisure practice. The next section considers in more depth how the activity facilitates the development of social relationships among fan bloggers.

The emergence of a unique ethos around an activity

For Stebbins (2007: 12), a unique ethos is 'the spirit of the community of serious leisure participants, as manifested in shared attitudes, practices, values, beliefs, goals, and so on'. Because so many hockey bloggers are also fans, and because these identities are frequently blurred in their writing, it is difficult to distinguish a unique blogging ethos separate from that of hockey fandom more broadly. That being said, there is evidence that hockey blogs can be the sites for the formation of loosely affiliated 'electronic tribes', with their own social worlds that develop online based on a shared fandom (Norman, 2014). Furthermore, some hockey bloggers understand their leisure practices to be motivated by the development of fan communities, consisting of bloggers and their active readerships. For example, a New York Islanders blogger explained that, as a fan residing far from New York, the opportunity to build relationships with like-minded fans is a big driver in his serious leisure practice:

> The community that has developed around the site has kept it rewarding for me.... Being a long-distance fan, I don't run into people everyday that say 'How 'bout them Isles?'

Reflecting this emphasis on community, fan bloggers have coined creative nicknames for the blogs and active readerships devoted to specific NHL clubs. These names recognise the specific focus of these collections of blogs, but also suggest the possibility that they possess a unique ethos. Bloggers of the Vancouver Canucks, for example, coined the term 'Smylosphere' in reference to former player Stan Smyl to describe 'the Canucks online community' (Basky, 2012). Other fan groups have created similar labels for the collection of blogs devoted to a particular team. The creation of these terms, and their explicit attempts to link together otherwise unique websites under one label, suggest that some bloggers desire to situate their work within a distinct group with its own ethos. However, these terms are often deployed without context and provide little evidence that such an ethos actually exists.

More broadly, many bloggers regularly use the term 'hockey blogosphere' in a similar fashion. Like the team-specific nicknames, this term suggests a unique ethos or subculture built around hockey blogs without offering concrete evidence of its existence. The term is most commonly used as a marker to distinguish blogs from commercial (or 'mainstream') hockey media, as in this quotation from a blog post:

> At times it seems the hockey blogosphere and hockey's mainstream media are bitter enemies destined to fight it out until the end of time.
>
> (Dangle, 2014)

Used in this way, the term 'hockey blogosphere' more directly suggests a unique ethos, albeit one defined relationally to the mainstream media. There is some merit to this relational identity, as hockey bloggers frequently take journalists to task for what they consider poor reporting or ignored narratives. Furthermore, the tone and style of blog posts can be markedly different from mainstream media articles. Sometimes blogs are much more casual and personal, while other times they are in-depth and highly analytical. In my observational experience, however, the development of a unique ethos in hockey blogging is limited and the idea of hockey blogs as sites for building community is overstated (cf. Norman, 2014). Nonetheless, it is clear that for some bloggers the development of social relations is a critical part of their leisure experience, even if it is difficult to identify a widespread ethos that characterises the 'hockey blogosphere'.

A strong identification with the leisure activity

The social relationships and conceptualisations of community developed by hockey bloggers lead into the final characteristic of serious leisure, which is a strong identification with the activity (Stebbins, 1992). This may be amplified in sports blogging, as it is often an extension of an already significant identification as a fan, which itself can be a form of serious leisure (Gibson *et al.*, 2002; Jones, 2000). Stebbins (1992: 7) suggests that the strong identification with serious leisure practices is reflected in participants' daily social interactions, in which they 'are inclined to speak proudly, excitedly, and frequently about [their serious leisure pursuits] to other people'. Hockey bloggers' proud identification with the activity is frequently on display in online environments, in which they may publicly represent themselves in biographies on blogs and other new media, such as Twitter. For example, a regular hockey blogger at SB Nation has the following Twitter biography, which places blogging for various hockey websites (identified, using the '@' symbol, by their Twitter handles) as a central component of her online identity:

> @SBNationNHL news desk. Metro Division editor, credentialed Flyers reporter @AlongTheBoards. Contributor @TodaysSlapshot. Penn State grad. Geek girl.
>
> (Clarke, n.d.)

This is a typical biography for a hockey blogger, and it places the practice of blogging as a central feature of an online identity *and* serves as a public expression of identification with the serious leisure pursuit. Thus, for many hockey bloggers, the practice appears to provide a significant point of identification, consistent with that of participants in a wide variety of serious leisure pursuits (Stebbins, 1992).

Hockey blogging, leisure and prosumption

The leisure practice of hockey blogging is enmeshed in the broader 'media sport content economy', in which there has been 'a fundamental shift in relations of [sport] media production from "broadcast scarcity" to "digital plenitude"' (Hutchins and Rowe, 2012: 9). Furthermore, while new media such as blogs and Twitter may suggest the possibility of alternative ways of consuming and producing sport (Norman, 2012), Dart (2014) highlights the ways in which these new media – and their user-generated content – are incorporated by powerful media companies to generate increased profits. This political economy argument provides an important nuance to understand hockey blogging as serious leisure, since it suggests that this practice is a form of free labour exploited by media corporations. As such, this chapter concludes by discussing blogging as a form of prosumption, a term used by Ritzer and Jurgenson (2010) to describe and analyse the duality within capitalism of production and consumption in online environments.

As Ritzer and Jurgenson (2010) outline, the rapid adoption of the internet and prominence of user-generated content has accelerated the social significance of prosumption and significantly impacted upon the operation of capitalism. Many prominent internet platforms rely on prosumers for their very existence; for example, Twitter requires its users to produce a massive volume of tweets to ensure its effectiveness and relevance. Ritzer and Jurgenson (2010) further highlight four unique features of online prosumer capitalism: the challenges for capitalists of controlling users; a complicated understanding of whether prosumers are exploited; the possible development of a new economic model based on the free provision of services and unpaid labour; and an abundance, rather than scarcity, of resources that leads to an emphasis on quality rather than efficiency of output. Bloggers may be usefully understood as prosumers. They are certainly active consumers of hockey, as they follow the sport through television broadcasts, newspapers and various new media platforms. However, blogging is also an inherently productive act that results in the creation of a piece of writing. Many of the characteristics of prosumption are reflected in the serious leisure practice of hockey blogging.

Ritzer and Jurgenson (2010: 21–22) write: 'the idea that prosumers are exploited is contradicted by, among other things, the fact that prosumers seem to enjoy what they are doing and are willing to devote long hours to it for no pay'. This dovetails with the characterisation of hockey blogging as serious leisure, which is undertaken for little or no remuneration. For, while the argument could certainly be made that bloggers' unpaid work is exploited if companies profit from its production and consumption, hockey bloggers clearly derive enjoyment and meaning from their devotion to the practice. Meanwhile, Ritzer and Jurgenson's (2010: 22) characterisation of 'prosumer capitalism online [as] increasingly a world of abundance' aligns with Hutchins and Rowe's (2012) characterisation of a new 'digital plenitude' in sport media. The rapid proliferation of hockey blogs, offering fans a wide variety of channels through which to consume the sport, is a vivid example of this digital plenitude. Furthermore, the digital economy, including blogs, has impacted upon local media reportage of hockey in many NHL markets as media outlets have slashed budgets and fired reporters (Wyshynski, 2008). Hockey blogs have continued to proliferate and most newspapers in NHL cities now include blogs among their online coverage. While this situation may not represent the new 'free' economy suggested as a possibility by Ritzer and Jurgenson (2010), blogs have nonetheless clearly reshaped the hockey media landscape in significant ways and the ways in which the sport is consumed and produced.

Conclusion

By situating North American hockey blogging as a form of serious leisure (Stebbins, 1992), this chapter has explored individual motivations and rewards of this activity and, using the concept of prosumption (Ritzer and Jurgenson, 2010), problematised its place in the broader political economy of contemporary sport media (Dart, 2014; Hutchins and Rowe, 2012). This chapter represents an initial exploration of sports blogging as both serious leisure and prosumption, and is far from comprehensive. Future research on sports blogging could fruitfully delve more deeply into the different characteristics of serious leisure outlined by Stebbins (1992), employ deeper use of interviews to understand the meaning of sports blogging to fans, and unpack more fully the tensions between sports blogging as a leisure pursuit and a growing feature of the networked media sport economy (Hutchins and Rowe 2012). Furthermore, this chapter is limited by its focus only on bloggers who write about North American hockey. Given the high popularity of ice hockey in Europe and its growth in popularity in countries like China and Australia, it would behove researchers to expand the field beyond North American hockey and adopt a broader global focus. This chapter creates a foundation for a deeper discussion of these and other critical questions about the leisure practice of sports blogging.

References

Antunovic, D. and Hardin, M. (2013) Women bloggers: Identity and the conceptualization of sports. *New Media and Society*, 15(8): 1374–1392.

Basky, K. [Kent Basky] (2011) Live from Vancouver … it's Saturday night… coffee? *Nucks Misconduct*, 28 May. Available at: www.nucksmisconduct.com/2011/5/28/2195411/live-from-vancouver-its-saturday-night-coffee (accessed 29 May 2011).

Basky, K. [Kent Basky] (2012) Canuck brunch – Embracing the hate more than ever. *Nucks Misconduct*, 15 February. Available at: www.nucksmisconduct.com/2012/2/15/2799924/canuck-brunch-embracing-the-hate-more-than-ever (accessed 25 August 2015).

Clarke, M. [marycclarke] (n.d.) Profile [Twitter]. Available at: http://twitter.com/marycclarke (accessed 23 November 2015).

Cox, A.M. and Blake, M.K. (2011) Information and food blogging as serious leisure. *Aslib Proceedings*, 63(2/3): 204–220.

Dangle, S. [Steve Dangle] (2014) Hockey wars: The blogosphere vs the mainstream media. *Pension Plan Puppets*, 21 August. Available at: www.pensionplanpuppets.com/2014/8/21/6051989/hockey-wars-the-blogosphere-vs-mainstream-media (accessed 25 August 2015).

Dart, J. (2009) Blogging the 2006 FIFA World Cup Finals. *Sociology of Sport Journal*, 26(1): 107–126.

Dart, J. (2014) New media, professional sport and political economy. *Journal of Sport and Social Issues*, 38(6): 528–547.

Elkington, S. (2013) Sites of serious leisure. In S. Elkington and S. Gammon, (eds) *Contemporary Perspectives in Leisure: Meanings, Motives and Lifelong Learning* (pp. 93–111). New York: Routledge.

Gibson, H., Willming, C. and Holdnak, A. (2002) 'We're Gators … not just Gator fans': Serious leisure and University of Florida football. *Journal of Leisure Research*, 34(4): 397–425.

Gruneau, R. and Whitson, D. (1993) *Hockey Night in Canada: Sport, Identities and Cultural Politics*. Toronto: Garamond Press.

Hair, T. [Travis Hair] (2012) Bye everyone! Five for Howling now under new management. *Five for Howling*, 27 December. Available at: www.fiveforhowling.com/2012/12/27/3809768/bye-everyone-five-for-howling-now-under-new-management (accessed 24 August 2015).

Hardin, M. and Shain, S. (2005) Strength in numbers? The experiences and attitudes of women in sports media careers. *Journalism and Mass Communication Quarterly*, 82(4): 804–819.

Haynes, R. (1995) *The Football Imagination: The Rise of Football Fanzine Culture*. Aldershot: Arena.

Hine, C. (2008) Virtual ethnography: Modes, variations, affordances. In N. Fielding, R.M. Lee and G. Blank (eds) *The SAGE Handbook of Online Research Methods* (pp. 257–270). London: Sage.

Hutchins, B. and Mikosza, J. (2010) The Web 2.0 Olympics: Athlete blogging, social networking and policy contradictions at the 2008 Beijing Games. *Convergence*, 16(3): 279–297.

Hutchins, B. and Rowe, D. (2012) *Sport beyond Television: The Internet, Digital Media and the Rise of Networked Media Sport*. New York: Routledge.

Jenkins, H. (2006) *Convergence Culture: Where Old and New Media Collide*. New York: New York University Press.

Johnston, C. (2014) Leafs hire bloggers for new analytics unit. *Sportsnet*, 19 August. Available at: www.sportsnet.ca/hockey/nhl/toronto-maple-leafs-set-to-create-new-analytics-department-with-darryl-metcalf-cam-charron/ (accessed 21 August 2015).

Jones, I. (2000) A model of serious leisure identification: The case of football fandom. *Leisure Studies*, 19(4): 283–298.

Kidd, B. (2013) Sports and masculinity. *Sport in Society*, 16(4): 553–564.

McGovern, J. (2015) Does race belong on sports blogs? Solidarity and racial discourse in online baseball fan forums. *Communication and Sport*. doi: 10.1177/2167479515577382.

McIntyre, T. (2015) Loving hockey isn't easy. *The Riveter*, 10 August. Available at: www.therivetermagazine.com/loving-hockey-isnt-easy/ (accessed 11 August 2015).

Miller, P. and Miller, R. (1995) The invisible woman: Female sports journalists in the workplace. *Journalism and Mass Communication Quarterly*, 72(4): 883–889.

Norman, M. (2012) Saturday night's alright for tweeting: Cultural citizenship, collective discussion, and the new media consumption/production of *Hockey Day in Canada*. *Sociology of Sport Journal*, 29(3): 306–324.

Norman, M. (2014) Online community or electronic tribe? Exploring the social characteristics and spatial production of an internet hockey fan culture. *Journal of Sport and Social Issues*, 38(5): 395–414.

Norman, M., Ventresca, M., Szto, C. and Darnell, S.D. (2015) Driving to the 'Net: Blogs, frames and politics in the New York Islanders stadium saga. *Journal of Sport and Social Issues*, 39(1): 19–39.

Orton-Johnson, K. (2014) Knit, purl and upload: New technologies, digital mediations and the experience of leisure. *Leisure Studies*, 33(3): 305–321.

phylliskessel13 (2015) Studying gender and sports fandom. *Pension Plan Puppets*, 3 June. Available at: www.pensionplanpuppets.com/2015/6/3/8702021/studying-gender-and-sports-fandom (accessed 25 August 2015).

Ramos, J.M. [Jen Mac Ramos] (2014) Female hockey fandom and the good ol' boys' club. *Fear the Fin*, 26 August. Available at: www.fearthefin.com/2014/8/16/6022719/Female-hockey-fandom-and-the-good-ol-boys-club (accessed 25 August 2015).

Ritzer, G. and Jurgenson, N. (2010) Production, consumption, prosumption: The nature of capitalism in the age of the digital 'prosumer'. *Journal of Consumer Culture*, 10(1): 13–36.

Rojek, C. (1997) Leisure theory: Retrospect and prospect. *Loisir et société/Society and Leisure*, 20(2): 383–400.

Rowe, D. (2004) *Sport, Culture and Media*. Berkshire: Open University Press.

Smith, M. (2015) Inside the mind of Eric Tulsky. *Tracking the Storm*, 24 August. Available at: http://hurricanes.nhl.com/club/news.htm?id=777511. (accessed 26 August 2015).

Stebbins, R.A. (1992) *Amateurs, Professionals, and Serious Leisure*. Montreal: McGill-Queen's Press.

Stebbins, R.A. (1993) *Canadian Football: The View from the Helmet*. Toronto: Canadian Scholars Press.

Stebbins, R.A. (2007) *Serious Leisure: A Perspective for Our Time*. New Brunswick, NJ: Transaction Publishers.

VanCity Buzz (n.d.) Posts by Wyatt Arndt. Available at: www.vancitybuzz.com/author/wyatt-arndt/ (accessed 20 August 2015).

Vancitydan (2011) Flames at Canucks recap; Woke up laughing (5–1W). *Nucks Misconduct*, 5 December. Available at: www.nucksmisconduct.com/2011/12/4/2611631/flames-at-canucks-recap-woke-up-laughing-5-1w (accessed 1 September 2015).

Wyshynski, G. (2008) Why your local newspaper chooses not to cover the NHL. *Puck Daddy*, 30 September. Available at: http://sports.yahoo.com/nhl/blog/puck_daddy/post/Why-your-local-newspaper-chooses-not-to-cover-th?urn=nhl,111634 (accessed 1 September 2015).

8 The (in)visibility of older adults in digital leisure cultures

Shannon Hebblethwaite

Introduction

Over the past 25 years, technology has transformed the world in which we live. The sheer speed and ease of transmission of information has altered how we communicate and interact, both on- and offline. Political and journalistic rhetoric suggests that the world has become an information village in which people are connected to each other in a global network society (Castells, 2010). Older adults, however, have been rendered invisible in this discourse. Until very recently, limited research has focused on understanding the technology needs of older adults. Even less work has examined technology in the context of leisure for older adults. This chapter presents an interdisciplinary approach to understanding older adults' experiences of emerging technologies and the digital leisure culture, drawing upon literature from leisure studies, critical gerontology, and communication and media studies. Situated broadly within critical theory, this work will be used to interrogate ageist assumptions in relation to leisure and digital media use (or non-use). Rather than assuming that older adults are incapable of learning and engaging with new technologies, I examine how older adults are agentic in their choices around media use and explore their meanings associated with digitally mediated leisure. By considering how 'digital ageism' (the individual and systemic biases that create forms of inclusion and exclusion that are age-related) operates in subtle ways, I will explore how communication is connected to social practices and shared rituals that constitute leisure experiences. The chapter provides two supportive case studies that highlight the importance of understanding digital leisure from the perspective of older adults: (1) MemorySpace, a digital literacy initiative that illustrates the potential for actively engaging older adults in the discourses around digital leisure, digital literacy and lifelong learning; and (2) Grannies on the Net, an exploratory case study of Canadian and Romanian grandmothers which illustrates the critical approach that grandmothers take in using social media.

Media and mediatisation

Although often associated with modern digital technologies, 'media' dates back to cave paintings at least 10,000 years ago. In its simplest form, media are ways in which we communicate with one another (Creeber and Martin, 2009). 'New media' reflects a shift that occurred in the 1980s from print and analogue communication to digital technology. What is deemed 'new media', however, has shifted over time. These new media forms originally included the internet, digital television and cinema, personal computers, DVDs, CDs, portable media players (e.g. MP3s), mobile phones and video games. These technologies were accessible in the 1990s when personal computers became affordable (Creeber and Martin, 2009). More recently, terminology such as Web 2.0 reflects the shift post-2001 to media that include a social element, allowing users to generate and distribute media content (e.g. social networking sites, wikis, blogs).

Lundby (2009) suggests that this shift in technologies reflects an increased 'mediatisation', whereby everyday practices and social relations are shaped by mediating technologies and media organisations. This process affects almost all areas of social and cultural life, including work, family, leisure, politics, health, learning and culture. Although often studied in the context of youth cultures, these effects are seen across the life course. We are privy today to an astonishing range of new cultural spaces involving social activism, electronic blogs and social networking, third-age niche magazines, senior-oriented cable TV networks and performance groups. For example, many viewers of YouTube have become enamoured with octogenarian rock groups such as Britain's Zimmers and the US's Young@Heart, who belt out songs by Out-Kast and Nirvana and transform The Clash's 'Should I Stay or Should I Go' into a drama about life and death. Miller (2011), in his ethnographic presentation *Tales from Facebook*, recounts the story of a 60-year-old man in Trinidad who used Facebook to decrease social isolation and 'give new life where there had been little hope' (p. 32).

So far-reaching are the effects of mediatisation that Krotz (2009) argues that it is a key meta-process that shapes modernity, along with individualisation, commercialisation and globalisation. Important here is that mediatisation is not a passive process. Rather, it is transformational in that it shapes society and culture. Communication is an important element of the set of practices whereby we construct our environment and ourselves, developing our identities and making sense of our lives. By changing communication and the core of human action, mediatisation influences the relationship that individual and institutional participants have with their environment and with one another (Silverstone, 2005). Mediatisation has far-reaching impacts on everyday practices and social relations. It can contribute to political mobilisation, extend social relationships across distance and time, and facilitate our decisions about our leisure engagement, to name a few.

Digital leisure practices

Media, therefore, have become increasingly relevant for the social construction of humankind generally and leisure more specifically. Media influence leisure through individual and collective identities as well as the sense and meaning that we construct through leisure practices. Communication is connected to social practices and shared rituals that constitute leisure experiences. Digital leisure has allowed us to reap a variety of benefits, many of which are outlined in this volume. Children with autism can develop meaningful relationships, fine motor skills and critical thinking abilities by playing video games (Finke *et al.*, 2015). Digital games have contributed to the cohesion and persistence of community (Taylor, 2006). More specifically, Delamere (2011) found that participation in Second Life enhanced social capital for individuals with disabilities and allowed them to leave behind the stigmatised components of their identity.

When we consider older adults and their use of ICTs, we assume that the majority of this involvement relates to their health and the use of assistive technologies (e.g. home sensors for people with dementia, blood sugar testers, CCTV for the hearing impaired). Although health certainly plays a role in older adults' ICT use, a much broader range of uses exist that mainly encompass social and leisure-based use. For example, older adults use the internet as an instrument for learning, planning or purchasing leisure services (Nimrod, 2009) and to enhance their tourism experiences (Patterson *et al.*, 2011). Internet and email use is positively associated with recreation participation and leadership for older adults (Koopman-Boyden and Reid, 2009). Studies also show the importance of online communities for older adults. These communities can provide an opportunity to have 'fun on line', give and gain social support, contribute to self-preservation, and serve as an opportunity for self-discovery and growth (Nimrod, 2010). Older immigrants use the internet in order to enjoy leisure and maintain and extend social networks (Khvorostianov *et al.*, 2012). Older adults also use the internet to play, despite limited online games designed with their age cohort in mind (Nimrod, 2011). Email and social networking sites (SNS) are also important to older adults, contributing to enhanced communication with both family and friends (Bosch and Currin, 2015) and to strengthen family ties between grandparents and grandchildren (Cornejo *et al.*, 2013). Digital literacy programs that are participatory in nature and actively engage older adults in determining the direction and content of the programs can contribute to enhanced leisure skills for participants (see Box 8.1).

Box 8.1 MemorySpace: a participatory digital literacy initiative with older adults

How do we remember and commemorate the history of a neighbourhood? How might the personal memories of a location, captured in the home or family photograph, intersect with public place?

These are questions that guided a participatory digital literacy initiative between Montreal's Atwater Library and Computer Centre (ALCC) and researchers at Concordia University. During the summer of 2012, members of Concordia's Mobile Media Lab collaborated with a community of older adults at the ALCC. This creative, interactive exhibit of their photographs was called 'MemorySpace: Private Memories, Public Histories' (http://memoryspace.mobilities.ca).

> In the MemorySpace project, personal memory and public history intersected in an exhibition of photographs, collectively curated. At night, a selection of these photographs was projected through the large windows of the Library. The collection was exhibited during the daytime on a large-format interactive touchscreen located on the ground floor of the Library. Original photographs and documents from the collections were on display in the glass cases also located on the main floor of the ALCC. The older adults took great pride in sharing their histories through photography and in developing their skills to preserve their photographs in digital format. They were co-creators of the exhibit, which contributed to a sense of empowerment with digital media.
>
> The MemorySpace project illustrates the importance of collaboration and consultation. Rather than asking what older people have to learn about digital media, or communications, this project emphasises important questions we can ask such as: What might leisure, media, communications and cultural studies learn about the digital world from the perspective of older adults who have lived through successive generations of media? How might we take their experiences of media into account? How can we better understand older adults' technology needs and motivations? What can we do to work more collaboratively with older adults to help them engage in a meaningful way with technologies that can enhance their well-being?

Despite the benefits of technology and digitally mediated leisure, the rapid evolution of media and the increased complexity of technologies create an uneasiness that cannot be ignored. We must acknowledge that some actors and agents have more power than others in this digital world. The MemorySpace example is a case in point. Taking, uploading, editing and producing digital photographs may seem second nature to younger generations. Yet it provided an important opportunity for the ALCC to participate in a digital literacy initiative *with* (as opposed to *for*) older adults who had identified digital photography as an interest. This participatory approach allowed older adults to feel comfortable and in control of their media learning, rather than outdated and obsolete as they often felt when asking for help from their families.

Creeber and Martin assert that new media is not only 'unequal in its geographical and social accessibility, but includes an obsession with triviality and consumerism' (2009: 6), and potentially undermines civil society through the expanded reach of pornography, hackers, religious and political fanaticism, and the oppression of civil rights. The role of ideology in the evolution of technology is usually portrayed as negative and the seductive effect of new technology is seen as one to be profoundly distrusted (Aarseth, 2004). Despite benefits associated with gaming for people with disabilities (see Delamere, 2011; Finke *et al.*, 2015), video games have regularly been vilified for contributing to the 'obesity epidemic' in North America, with opponents often advocating for more time outdoors engaging in physical activity. Interestingly, like much of the scholarship on gaming, this discourse has been highly youth focused and has ignored the possibility that older adults engage in online gaming. Leisure scholars have been slow to take up the study of digital media, despite the breadth of opportunities for digital leisure as illustrated throughout this volume.

When studying older adults' experiences of digital media, they remind us that they have been exposed to a multitude of new technologies imbued with promises that these technologies would change the way they live. Their scepticism of digital media is not surprising in light of media historians' (Marvin, 1988; Carey, 1988) assertions that the 'current media rhetoric closely follows its historical precedents, the discourse of the telegraph, telephone, and electricity, to the point that the "revolution" seems to be a permanent trend of the last 200 years' (Aarseth, 2004: 417). I suggest, and explore in more depth later in this chapter, that older adults are not incapable of adapting to new technologies, but rather that they are critical consumers of our new digital world. Their decisions to engage (or not) with digital media are carefully considered in light of their long history with 'new' media across the life course and in light of the neoliberal discourse of ageing that privileges individualism and productivity over collective, agentic experiences that may be achieved through leisure.

Agency in ageing

The dominant discourse of ageing reflects a biologically deterministic view of ageing as a period of inevitable decline. This 'decline narrative' (Gullette, 1997) begins at middle age and continues relentlessly into old age and death. Ageism, a term coined by Butler (1975), reflects a 'process of collective stereotyping which emphasises the negative features of aging which are ultimately traced back to biomedical decline rather than the culturally determined value placed on later life' (Featherstone and Hepworth, 2009: 138). Butler goes so far as to call ageism a psychosocial disease. Ageing is portrayed as something to fear and to fight at all costs. Older adults are homogenised and lumped together under a limited range of social categories.

Nimrod (2013a), however, highlights important intersections that influence older adults' experience of digital leisure. Older adults experienced online communities differently based on self-reported health and subjective well-being. In addition, older adults were found to use online communities in different ways: (1) as information swappers; (2) ageing-oriented users; and (3) socialisers (Nimrod, 2013b). Psychological variables also influence older adults' ICT use, including cognitive age, technology anxiety and level of venturousness (Peral-Peral et al., 2015). Previous use, not chronological age, has been found to be the best predictor of ICT use in older adulthood (Loos and Mante-Meijer, 2012).

Despite efforts to fight ageism, it is still deeply encoded in our language and pervasively transmitted by our youth-enamoured media (Vesperi, 2008). This is particularly problematic today because greater exposure to television is associated with more negative stereotypes of ageing (Donlon et al., 2005). Critical gerontologists and policy-makers consistently fault Western welfare states for the construction of later life as a period of decline and dependency. They have attempted to shift these stereotypes by exploring ageing as an experience that occurs across the life course, rather than simply a stage at the end of life. They assert that ageing is a complex process of interaction between biological, psychological and social factors. Butler challenges us to:

> alter our deep-seated cultural sensibility and work to overcome our fear, our shunned responsibility, and the harmful avoidance and denial of age. We must help people deal with their fears of aging, dependency, and death, and develop a sense of the life course as a whole.
>
> (Butler, 2008: 58)

As leisure scholars and practitioners, we need to be mindful of our contribution to this discourse and think critically about our role in formulating leisure activities as a way to administer, calculate and codify leisure experiences as evidence of healthy ageing. Taking a more constructivist perspective, we can adopt a more agentic approach when we explore and incorporate opportunities for digital leisure for older adults. Particularly relevant to the discussion of leisure is the notion of activity as an antidote to decline and dependency. Activity is often promoted not only as a positive ideal but as a universal 'good'. This discourse positions activity as the 'positive' against which the 'negative' forces of dependency, illness and loneliness are arrayed (Katz, 2000). Our Memory-Space example is again illustrative of a critical approach to this perspective. Rather than trying to *solve* the older adults' challenges with digital literacy, the ALCC and the MemorySpace project focused on what the older adults identified as important to *them* as well as on the strengths and abilities they brought to the table themselves. By engaging with older adults in this way, the digital photography project resulted in a sense of ownership of, and commitment to, the process of learning a new media skill. Meaningful engagement through leisure contributed to agency among the older adults and led to a more successful experience engaging with new media.

This is indicative of Bandura's (2001) social cognitive theory of agency and suggests that the capacity to exercise control over the nature and quality of one's life is central to our identities. He outlines four core features of human agency: (1) intentionality – acting in a purposive way; (2) forethought – setting goals, anticipating consequences and selecting a course of action; (3) self-reactiveness – executing the selected course of action; (4) self-reflectiveness – reflecting upon oneself and evaluating the adequacy of one's thoughts and actions.

The dominant discourses surrounding older adults' experiences of digital cultures are often void of any reflection on the continuum between agency and structure and the thought that older adults might be exhibiting agency in the ageing process. At the structural end of the continuum, individuals are viewed as passive recipients with little control over the conditions that influence their identity development. Agency, on the other hand, considers individuals as agents in a continual process of negotiating and re-creating their identities based on the social practices and rituals of their everyday worlds. Individuals are viewed as social actors who both shape and are shaped by social structures. The idea that human agency can be exercised over how ageing will be expressed and experienced has emerged only in the late twentieth century (Gilleard and Higgs, 2000). In our quest to understand digital leisure cultures, we need to make visible the experiences of older adults and include them in the discourse. In doing so, we will be better equipped to understand their use (or non-use) of digital media through an agentic lens, viewing older adults as agents of experiences rather than simply undergoers of experiences of digital media. Rather than assuming that older adults are incapable of learning and engaging with new technologies, I suggest that older adults are agentic in their choices around media use and are critical consumers in today's digital world.

Grannies on the Net: the use of Facebook for family communication

Guided by this agentic view, I turn now to an exploratory case study of grandmothers and their use of social media. Ageing, Communication, Technologies (ACT) is a recent international, interdisciplinary collaborative initiative funded by the Social Sciences and Humanities Research Council of Canada. Our aim is to investigate the nexus between ageing and digitally mediated communications from the point of view, and experience, of older adults. Rather than asking what older people have to learn *about* digital media, researchers at our partner institutions ask the following questions: What might media, communications, leisure and cultural studies learn about the digital world from the perspective of older adults who have lived through successive generations of media? How might we take their experiences of media into account?

Grannies on the Net is an exploratory case study that is part of the larger ACT project and brings together research on social media use, specifically Facebook, in Romania and Canada in order to understand how grandmothers use Facebook in their leisure to communicate with grandchildren living abroad or at a distance. Hebblethwaite and Ivan (2015) conducted semi-structured interviews with five Canadian and five Romanian grandmothers aged 65 to 85 who used Facebook. We found that children and grandchildren are often the primary motivator for grandmothers' Facebook use. The ability to keep up-to-date with their grandchildren outweighed the negative aspects of Facebook, including privacy, 'oversharing' of information and targeted advertisements.

> I get to see that sweet little face. She [daughter] will put pictures of the children. That's the best thing ever, when I open Facebook and I see a little video when they're [grandchildren] all involved in something so serious. They're just so sweet and I don't get to see them enough. So the advantages far outweigh the disadvantages for Facebook.

Facebook allowed grandparents to stay connected and adhere to the 'norm of non-interference' (Cherlin and Furstenberg, 1986). This is one of the strongest norms associated with grandparenting behaviour. Grandparent input and authority into family relationships is contingent upon the request and/or sanctioning by the parent. By using Facebook, grandparents could maintain their connections to their grandchildren without being perceived as 'meddling' or 'burdensome' by their children.

Although Facebook allowed for more frequent contact with family members, it did not achieve the depth of connection that grandmothers' preferred. They used Facebook for updates with their families, but still preferred the more personal connection they found when talking on the phone to their families. They were effectively able to merge new and older technologies to meet their leisure needs.

> It kind of allows you to stay in touch, but it's not maybe the depth of personal connection. I can sit and talk on the phone to [daughter] for an hour and of course you get more out of that than you get from a text or email. So I still prefer actual contact. I still like to phone.

Finally, although grandmothers were aware of the privacy (or lack thereof) on Facebook, their Facebook use was influenced more by social norms of decency. They were more passive users of Facebook, often viewing, reading and sharing information posted by others. They rarely posted new information or photos of themselves. They tried to impart this norm to their grandchildren, teaching them to be more cautious about what information they shared in a public forum like Facebook.

> Well, what people are raising now is the privacy issues and that people are not circumspect when it comes to Facebook. It's so instantaneous. People can get really hysterical and angry on Facebook. I'm not such an introverted, extremely private person, but why would I do that [post pictures of myself]? It's like going around and putting pictures of myself in my car, and my workplace saying 'This is what I look like!' It's too much.

By engaging in a more in-depth exploration of grandmothers' Facebook use and their motivations, we have begun to develop a more nuanced understanding of the role of social media in the lives of older adults. These grandmothers made conscious decisions to join Facebook and were agentic in how they used the social media platform. They resisted 'oversharing' and chose not to post photos on Facebook because of concerns over privacy and ownership of their data. Further studies are needed to explore other (non-)uses of social media. For example, what are the factors that influence some older adults' choices to *not* engage on social media? Are there differences based on gender? How do race and class influence their choices? How is (dis)ability implicated with respect to new technologies? What do older adults need in order to engage with social media in a meaningful way? Social inequalities are a reality in the world of digital leisure. How can this case help us to explore this issue?

Inequalities: ageing and digital exclusion

The growth of the so-called 'Information Society' is undermined by the fact that the benefits of digital media are not flowing evenly within countries or across the world. Unequal access to technologies results in digital exclusion at both international and local levels (Cammaerts *et al.*, 2003). Ricci (2000) indicates that several groups within Western society are most vulnerable to this digital exclusion, including low-income communities, individuals with little formal education, individuals who are unemployed or underemployed, foreign or diasporic communities, women, and older adults.

Although some older adults may not have been early adopters of new media, generalising this as the experience of all older adults is misleading. Not all older adults reject technology. Indeed, a recent Pew study has found that 'older' people are the fastest-growing population to use social media (Madden, 2010). Canada has typically had lower rates of cellular adoption overall, largely explained by extensive and affordable landline services and some of the highest cellular rates worldwide (Canadian Wireless Telecommunications Association, 2011).

Ownership and access, however, do not necessarily translate to use in all cases. Nearly 50 per cent of older adults in Canada have reported using the internet at least once over the past 12 months (Blanche, 2015). Access also includes motivational access whereby people see a relevance or potential benefit in using ICTs, as well as having the skills to effectively use the technology, along with the ability to use the technology (e.g. the amount of usage time available to a person and the diversity of applications available for use) (Van Dijk, 2005). When marginalised groups do log on, there is often scarce content that applies to their lives and their communities.

Our Grannies on the Net case study illustrates these trends. Grandchildren were the primary motivator for grandmothers to use social media, yet grandmothers still like to keep in touch using the telephone because of the increased depth that the telephone provides. This is indicative of the problematic nature of the assumption that ICTs will automatically lead to a more harmonious and egalitarian society, or induce a social, economic, cultural or political transformation that is inherently positive or progressive which is also problematic (Cammaerts *et al.*, 2003). For example, the use of social networking sites (e.g. Facebook) has shown no significant correlation with indices of personal satisfaction, social capital or intergenerational relations. This linear, monocausal thinking obscures the multi-dimensional character of social exclusion and implies that older adults should adopt ICTs in order to guarantee social participation (Colombo *et al.*, 2015). Warschauer (2004) cautions that when we focus on providing hardware and software, we pay insufficient attention to the human and social systems that must also change for technology to make a difference. He suggests that a complex array of factors be taken into account if meaningful access to new technologies is to be provided, including: physical, digital and social resources and relationships; content and language; literacy and education, community and institutional structures. Similarly, Colombo and colleagues propose that the 'process of digital inclusion should aim to promote the "good use" (conscious, careful, thoughtful, moderate, unperturbing, relational contexts) of ICTs and not simply the diffusion of computers, tablets, and smartphones to deal (deterministically) with age-related problems' (Colombo *et al.*, 2015: 54). Our Grannies on the Net case study also supports these claims. Grandmothers were careful about how they used Facebook and used this shared leisure experience with their grandchildren to try to impart valuable life lessons about privacy and decency. This reflects the generative nature of shared leisure experiences that provides meaning and a sense of purpose to multiple generations (Hebblethwaite and Ivan, 2015).

Despite finding very competent Canadian grandmothers using Facebook, studies that focus on older adult users, for example, have tended to describe them in terms that accentuate their timidity or fear of technology: they are considered 'hesitant' (Charness and Boot, 2009; Ling, 2008) or refuse to 'adopt' (Katz, 2008). Older adults are described in a deficit model that measures their practices against those of more exuberant users (Sourbati, 2009). This perspective fails to account for the changing life conditions that older adults experience. For example, many seniors, and many senior women in particular, live on fixed incomes and were raised in different economic cultures with values that considered debts to be shameful and therefore avoided. The speed with which new devices become obsolete may impact upon older adults' decisions around learning new technologies and adopting new devices. In addition, issues of privacy and decency may be more salient for generations that did not share their private lives as widely as youth today. Current research needs to move beyond the extremely basic statistics that we currently have, such as the number of households with internet connection. We need to ask more informative questions such as: What factors influence acceptance or non-acceptance of specific ICT innovations? What do users actually do with ICTs in their everyday lives? Why do they do it (or don't do it)? What sustains their involvement? Studies that have been more respectful of seniors' use of these technologies have argued that their lower adoption rates must take these socio-cultural considerations into account (Horst and Miller, 2006; Sawchuk and Crow, 2010).

Conclusions

Contrary to the dominant discourse, older adults clearly have the ability to learn and adopt emerging technologies in their leisure lifestyles. We need to be mindful of mediatisation when attempting to understand how older adults experience digital leisure. A more agentic approach to ageing allows us to better understand how older adults make choices about new media. As Eubanks argues, they 'come to technology and social justice programs as knowledgeable and asset bearing rather than as deficient and needy' (2011: 34). This approach takes seriously people's everyday interactions with digital media, and uses these experiences to explore what it means to be a critical citizen in the information age in a process of collaborative knowledge creation.

Leisure scholars, practitioners and policy-makers could benefit from a more participatory approach to understanding digital leisure cultures for older adults. Including older adults as active agents and collaborators can help us develop more appropriate languages and practices to enhance inter- and intra-generational engagement. We cannot assume that there is one universal life course model. Ageing is not merely a biological state, but rather a lived experience embodied and affectively felt, and as intersubjective, occurring within specific contexts and material and social circumstances. Interrogating these persistent myths through a rigorous, multi-method analysis will help us develop more nuanced understanding of the complexities of the contemporary digitally mediated world. One grandmother expressed her wish to me like this:

> One thing that kind of bothers me about the new technology is the way, for instance, some of these people treat the older users. Just be a little more patient! Because I know I'm not a stupid person, you know, just tell me a simple way to do it.

References

Aarseth, E. (2004) Genre trouble: Narrativism and the art of stimulation. In N. Wardrip-Furin and P. Harrigan (eds) *First Person: New Media as Story, Performance and Game* (45–55). Cambridge, MA: The MIT Press.

Bandura, A. (2001) Social cognitive theory: An agentic perspective. *Annual Review of Psychology*, 52: 1–26.

Blanche, D. (2015) *Statistical Summary of Ageing and ICTs*. Available at: http://act-project.ca/wp-content/uploads/2015/05/Report_Stats_Ageing_ICT.pdf.

Bosch, T. and Currin, B. (2015) Uses and gratifications of computers in South African elderly people. *Comunicar: Media Education Research Journal*, 23(45): 9–17.

Butler, R.N. (1975) *Why Survive? Being Old in America*. New York: Harper & Row.

Butler, R.N. (2008) *The Longevity Revolution: The Benefits and Challenges of Living a Long Life*. New York: Public Affairs.

Cammaerts, B., Van Audenjove, L., Nulens, G. and Pauwals, C. (eds) (2003) *Beyond the Digital Divide: Reducing Exclusion, Fostering Inclusion*. Brussels, Belgium: Brussels University Press.

Canadian Wireless Telecommunications Association. (2011) *2011 Cell Phone Consumer Attitudes Study*. Available at: www.cwta.ca/CWTASite/english/facts_figures_downloads/Consumer2011.pdf.

Carey, J. (1988) Technology and ideology: The case of the telegraph. In *Communication as Culture: Essays on Media and Society* (201–230). Winchester, MA: Unwin Hyman.

Castells, M. (2010) *End of Millennium* (2nd edn). West Sussex: Wiley Blackwell.

Charness, N. and Boot, W.R. (2009) Aging and information technology use: Potential and barriers. *Current Directions in Psychological Science*, 18(5): 253–258.

Cherlin, A.J. and Furstenberg, F.F. (1986) *The New American Grandparent: A Place in the Family, A Life Apart*. New York: Basic Books.

Colombo, F., Aroldi, P. and Carlo, S. (2015) New elders, old divides: ICTs, inequalities and well-being amongst young elderly Italians. *Communicar*, 45(23): 47–55.

Cornejo, R., Tentori, M. and Favela, J. (2013) Enriching in-person encounters through social media: A study on family connectedness for the elderly. *International Journal of Human-Computer Studies*, 71(9): 889–899.
Creeber, G. and Martin, R. (eds) (2009) *Digital Cultures: Understanding New Media*. Berkshire: McGraw-Hill.
Delamere, F.M. (2011) Second Life as a digitally mediated third place: Social capital in virtual world communities. In G. Crawford, V.K. Gosling and B. Light (eds) *Online Gaming in Context: The Social and Cultural Significance of Online Games*. London: Routledge.
Donlon, M., Ashman, O. and Levy, B. (2005) Re-vision of older television characters: A stereotype-awareness intervention. *Journal of Social Issues*, 61(2): 307–319.
Eubanks, V. (2011) *Digital Dead End: Fighting for Social Justice in the Information Age*. Cambridge, MA: The MIT Press.
Featherstone, M. and Hepworth, M. (2009) Images of aging: Cultural representations of later life. In J. Sokolovsky (ed.) *The Cultural Context of Aging* (3rd edn) (134–144). Westport, CT: Praeger.
Finke, E.H., Hickerson, B. and McLaughlin, E. (2015) Parental intention to support video game play by children with autism spectrum disorder: An application of the theory of planned behavior. *Language Speech and Hearing Service in Schools*, 46(2): 154–165.
Gilleard, C.J. and Higgs, P. (2000) *Cultures of Ageing: Self, Citizen, and the Body*. New York: Pearson Education.
Gullette, M. (1997) *Declining to Decline: Cultural Combat and the Politics of the Midlife*. Charlottesville: University of Virginia Press.
Hebblethwaite, S. and Ivan, L. (2015) *Grannies on the Net: Facilitating Intergenerational Family Communication Through Facebook*. Poster presented at the International Association of Gerontology and Geriatrics, Dublin, Ireland.
Horst, H.A. and Miller, D. (2006) *The Cell Phone: An Anthropology of Communication*. Oxford: Berg.
Katz, J.E. (ed.) (2008) *Handbook of Mobile Communication Studies*. Cambridge, MA: The MIT Press.
Katz, S. (2000) Busy bodies: Activity, aging and the management of everyday life. *Journal of Aging Studies*, 14(2): 135–152.
Khvorostianov, N., Ellas, N. and Nimrod, G. (2012) 'Without it I am nothing': The internet in the lives of older immigrants. *New Media and Society*, 14(4): 583–599.
Koopman-Boyden, P.G. and Reid, S.L. (2009) Internet/e-mail usage and well-being among 65–84 year olds in New Zealand: Policy implications. *Educational Gerontology*, 35(11): 990–1007.
Krotz, F. (2009) Mediatization: A concept with which to grasp media and societal change. In K. Lundby (ed.) *Mediatization* (21–40). New York: Peter Lang.
Ling, R. (2008) Should we be concerned that the elderly don't text? *Information Society*, 24(5): 334–341.
Loos, E. and Mante-Meijer, E. (2012) Getting access to website health information: Does age really matter? In E. Loos, L. Haddon and E. Mante-Meijer (eds) *Generational Uses of New Media* (185–202). Aldershot: Ashgate.
Lundby, K. (2009) *Mediatization: Concept, Changes, Consequences*. New York: Peter Lang.
Madden, M. (2010) Older adults and social media. Pew Internet and American Life Project. Available at: www.pewinternet.org/Reports/2010/Older-Adults-and-Social-Media.aspx.
Marvin, C. (1988) *When Old Technologies Were New: Thinking about Electric Communication in the Late Nineteenth Century*. Oxford: Oxford University Press.

MemorySpace (2012) Available at: http://memoryspace.mobilities.ca.

Miller, D. (2011) *Tales from Facebook.* Cambridge: Polity Press.

Nimrod, G. (2009) The internet as a resource in older adult leisure. *International Journal on Disability and Human Development,* 8(3): 207–214.

Nimrod, G. (2010) Seniors' online communities: A quantitative content analysis. *The Gerontologist,* 50(3): 382–392.

Nimrod, G. (2011) The fun culture in seniors' online communities. *The Gerontologist,* 5(2): 226–237.

Nimrod, G. (2013a) Applying gerontographics in the study of older internet users. *Journal of Audience and Reception Studies,* 10(2): 46–64.

Nimrod, G. (2013b) Probing the audience of seniors' online communities. *Journals of Gerontology: Series B,* 68(5): 773–782.

Patterson, I., Pegg, I. and Lister, J. (2011) Grey nomads on tour: A revolution in travel and tourism for older adults. *Tourism Analysis,* 16(3): 283–294.

Peral-Peral, B., Arenas Gaitan, J. and Villarejo-Ramos, A.F. (2015) From digital divide to psycho-digital divide: Elders and online social networks. *Comunicar: Media Education Research Journal,* 23(45): 57–64.

Ricci, A. (2000) Measuring information society: Dynamics of European data on usage of information and communication technologies in Europe since 1995. *Telecatics and Informatics,* 17(1–2): 141–167.

Sawchuk, K. and Crow, B. (2010) Talking 'costs': Seniors, cell phones and the personal and political economies of telecommunications in Canada. *Telecommunications Journal of Australia,* 60(4): 55.1–55.11.

Sawchuk, K. and Crow, B. (2012) 'I'm G-Mom on the phone.' *Feminist Media Studies,* 12(4): 496–505.

Schradie, J. (2011) The digital production gap: The digital divide and Web 2.0 collide. *Poetics,* 39(2): 145–168.

Silverstone, R. (2005) *Media, Technology, and Everyday Life in Europe: From Information to Communication.* Farnham: Ashgate.

Sourbati, M. (2009) 'It could be useful, but not for me at the moment': Older people, internet access and e-public service provision. *New Media and Society,* 11(7): 1083–1100.

Taylor, T.L. (2006) *Play between Worlds: Exploring Online Game Culture.* Cambridge, MA: The MIT Press.

Van Dijk, J.A. (2005) *The Deepening Divide: Inequality in the Information Society.* Thousand Oaks, CA: Sage.

Vesperi, M.E. (2008) Evaluating imaging of aging in print and broadcast media. Boomer bust? In R. Hudson (ed.) *Economic and Political Dynamics of the Graying Society.* Westport, CT: Praeger.

Warschauer, M. (2004) *Technology and Social Inclusion: Rethinking the Digital Divide.* Boston, MA: The MIT Press.

Wilkie, R. (2011) *The Digital Condition: Class and Culture in the Information Network.* New York: Fordham University Press.

9 Demystifying digital divide and digital leisure

Massimo Ragnedda and Bruce Mutsvairo

Introduction

Of what significance is the digital divide insofar as analysing the gap, among digital users, in consuming leisure? This chapter moves from this core question, attempting to provide a theoretically assembled response. In an attempt to analyse the entertainment and leisure dimensions of the internet, this chapter will draw extensively upon scientific literature, focusing on the concept of the digital divide (Bonfadelli, 2002; Van Dijk, 2005), but also exploring concepts such as networks (Castells, 2001), liquidity (Bauman, 2000), communities, identity and social inequalities.

It aims to investigate, from a theoretical point of view, how the use of digital technologies is influencing the consumption of leisure, questioning further the extent to which the consumption of leisure and free production of online content may influence social inequalities. Our first step will be to define the digital divide, a term used to describe differences in access to and the use of information and communication technologies (ICTs) correlated mostly with several factors such as age (Soker, 2005), gender (Ono and Zavodny, 2008), race/ethnicity (Mesch and Talmud, 2011), education (Clark and Gorski, 2002) but also geographic (Chinn and Fairlie, 2007) and socio-economic dimensions (Ragnedda and Muschert, 2013). All these elements and features are the basis of social strata, present in any given society. The social strata and the process of social stratification provide the grounds for social and digital inequalities. Indeed, it has been proven that the digital divide not only exists between richer and poorer countries in the use of ICT (Shih *et al*., 2008), but also within countries (Ragnedda and Muschert, 2013). Digital divide and digital inequalities affect the leisure culture which in turn influences – and this is what we argue here – social and digital inequalities. Indeed, as elaborated later in this chapter, the widespread proliferation of digital communication has revolutionised the way in which traditional entertainment and leisure media are distributed and consumed, which in a postmodern society is a vital part of the identity formation process. In fact, one's sense of belonging to a community, which is vital in the creation of an identity, is increasingly based on consumption, sharing lifestyles and experiences in an online realm.

McGillivray rightly points out that 'increasingly ubiquitous, digital technologies are more accessible, affordable and powerful than ever before' (2013: 99). These new digital technologies have offered people living in contemporary societies several possibilities for leisure in an unprecedented fashion, briskly transforming practices and trends in leisure activities in that process. The segmentation, customisation, and diversification of a networked world heavily influence social and power relationships. To this end, ICTs have had a profound effect not only on how we spend our free time, but also on how we form communities and identities. Indeed, as Gergen (1991: 38) argues, 'Individuals now have the mobility and technology to maintain membership in numerous discrete communities in which they have unique identities and social relations'.

ICTs have also changed the relationship between labour and leisure. Leisure patterns, indeed, have gone through significant changes from their co-existence with labour to the acceptance of the Internet as a leisure space at least in the liberal sense. Leisure, in some way, has gained its importance throughout the course of the history. Indeed, Aristotle proclaimed that 'we labour in order to have leisure' (Rosenzweig, 1985: 31). However, leisure today goes beyond the idea of 'free' time (in which 'free' is seen as free time from labour). Leisure is defined by Meurs and Kalfs (2000: 128) as 'all the time a person does not devote to ensuring their [sic] future welfare in a broad sense'. The capacities, the skills but also the chances to 'modify' and adapt identity to the flux of society, is an added value in a flexible society. Thus, the citizens who are able to move fluently in the digital realm, being part of several communities, playing and producing online content, can more easily move seamlessly into the fragmented society (Ragnedda and Muschert, 2013). Identity, it may be argued, is like a dress that can be worn depending on the context, to maximise advantages and benefits. This is particularly true in a postmodern society, predominantly characterised by uncertainty, the decline of metanarratives, risks and the need for flexibility.

Consuming leisure in a postmodern society

The experience of consuming leisure in a postmodern society – dominated by the blurring of difference between high and low culture (Lyotard, 1979; Harvey, 1989; Jameson, 1990) – is increasingly important as a distinctive form of identity. In the postmodern era as suggested by Lyotard metanarratives are becoming a thing of the past. Indeed, during modernity the social condition was based on the Enlightenment's metanarratives, exemplified by truth, science, progress and reason, which provided the platform to form and forge collective identity. The postmodern era is, on the contrary, characterised by the collapse of these metanarratives and the consequent disintegration of certainties. The postmodern era is defined by increasing unpredictability, insecurity and precariousness affecting perceptions of life that were once predictable and well structured. Under the conditions of modernity citizens, generally speaking, not only had firm beliefs in the nature of things, but also about their identities and national boundaries. Indeed, one of the main features of modernity in Europe was the rise of the nation state, with elaborate national boundaries and national identity formations. The modern period in Western societies began approximately in the Renaissance, moving to the Enlightenment, before ending at the beginning of the twentieth century. During this period there was a tendency to consider the possibilities for improvement in any area of life (for instance, job security) and strict adherence to knowledge as a clear law, probably founded on the basis of growing and continuous progress fuelled by the ubiquity of scientific research.

In its simplest terms, modern time (at least the second phase of modernity) was influenced by an emphasis on production while consumption has epitomised the period of postmodernity. In the former, the principal markers of identity were based mainly on social class and nation, while in postmodern times identity is viewed as much more hybrid and fluid and comes from other sources, such as consumption, participation in online activities and virtual communities. More specifically, regarding media, the arrival of postmodernity was accompanied by the replacement of one-directional media traffic by a dualised version recognisable in Baudrillard's (1988) assertion that in a postmodern society images and appearances help formulate hyper-realities thanks to the ubiquity of communication and mass media. Many postmodern scholars (Lyotard, 1979; Harvey, 1989; Jameson, 1990) argue that the sense of relativism and uncertainty, the fragmentation of social life, the importance of consumerism, the scepticism towards 'absolutism', the disillusionment with the idea of progress and the incessant necessity to make a choice, has transformed people's social lives and their sense of individuality. People living in a postmodern era, it is argued, cannot rely on institutions to support their lives (such as the family) but are driven by the dominant culture to pursue a solitary path of realisation, where the self is free from the constraints of its associated groups (Bauman, 2000).

Castells has, rightly, noted that:

> after the transition from the predominance of primary relationships (embodied in families and communities) to secondary relationships (embodied in associations), the new, dominant pattern seems to be built on what could be called tertiary relationships, or what Wellman calls 'personalized communities', embodied in me-centred networks. It represents the privatization of sociability.
>
> (Castells, 1996: 128)

Although not all scholars agree on these viewpoints, in an era in which life seems to be less predictable, more fragmented and uncertain and less based on strong belief systems (such as Marxism), the importance of leisure culture increases and plays a more crucial key role in forging our identity and self-perception. Postmodern society and culture tend to forge 'a pliant self, a collage of fragments unceasing in its becoming, ever open to the new experience – these are just the psychological conditions suited to the short-term work experience, flexible institutions, and constant risk-taking' (Sennett, 1998: 133). On the basis of Sennett's claims, it may be argued that in the flexible and fragmented contemporary societies in which we are living, the process of self-creation (and re-creation) is a seemingly endless process, denoted by mass popular culture, consumerism and corporate capitalism. The outcome of this process is arguably a fragmented self, continually unstable and endless. Cultural cohesion, once coming from national symbols, now comes from sharing the same media content, going beyond national boundaries and national identities and face-to-face relationships. Participating in the convergence culture (Jenkins, 2006) helps in creating a new sense of identity and community that provides the foundation of our identity. We believe that postmodernity, with the collapse of truth and objectivity, and the growing sense of scepticism and uncertainty, is forging a new identity (or, one should say, new identities) that we can define as a light and flexible identity. Rejection of the Enlightenment's preoccupations, we conclude, means that certainty, truth, and reality are now viewed as provisional and relative. While different opinions have been propounded on this topic, we believe that mass popular culture and leisure culture(s) play a key role in shaping a new self, in which lifestyle is conceived as a matter of choice.

According to theorists associated with this line of argument, postmodern concepts of time have weakened the sense of community, transformed more into a light cloak (Bauman, 2000) rather than an iron cage (Weber, 1930). According to Bauman (2000: 169), 'all communities are postulated; projects rather than realities, something that comes after, not before the individual choice'. Leisure time and leisure culture play a key role in experiencing and creating new formations of communities, which are increasingly based in the leisure domain. These leisure communities are communities formed within leisure spaces such as games and sports (Kemp, 1999), raves and clubs (Trammachi, 2000), or built around vacation-based communities (Neuman, 1993). Citizens and consumers can make choices which are more meaningful and personal, and a sense of community no longer needs to be based on face-to-face interaction. The advent of ICT, and more specifically the internet, has changed the way in which we experience our identity along with the way we form communities. Indeed, thanks to the affordances of ICT, communities are not simply tied to a shared territory but also include communities formed in virtual spaces (Jones, 1998). This is why communities should not be seen in the same vein as a considered physical space but – as Bender (1978: 6) before the introduction of the internet pointed out – as an experience, wherein 'community is where community happens'. Community is increasingly established on the emotional qualities of closeness and proximity, rather than the need to share a physical place (McMillan and Chavis, 1986). The availability and use of new communication technologies has dramatically changed the pace and character of interaction within several communities (Castells, 2001; Norris, 2001). Others have focused on the role of ICTs in advancing their political knowledge (Elwood and Leszczynsk, 2013) while some have explored the relationship between new media technologies and education (Buckingham and Willet, 2013).

The materialisation of ICT technologies, and the internet in particular, has revolutionised the way citizens 'experience' leisure culture, both in terms of participation and consumption. McGillivray (2014: 99) states, the potential of digital tools and technologies to flatten hierarchies, enabling a wider range of citizens to participate in leisure cultures (particularly around mega sporting events), to subvert controlled narratives and created alternative, localised readings outside of established commercial media platforms.

The use of digital technologies influences the way in which citizens/users experience leisure culture. It also impacts upon the way in which we 'create' our identity and sense of belonging to a community or social class. Previously, one's sense of belonging was heavily influenced by occupation, education, income or national identities and symbols, while in postmodernity, the sense of identity and belonging is based more on consumption, online activities, and online communities that create fluid and innovative social relationships (Sennett, 1998). These features began to trace the advent of the 'fractured', 'decentred', 'postmodern' subject that is more uncertain and disenchanted than the 'modern' one. The new subject seems to be more progressively based on online activities and their 'virtual' communities. Thus, the participation, both in terms of 'production' and 'consumption', in the online realm (even if the difference between online and offline is blurring) influences the way in which we create our identity and our sense of belonging. As Jenkins and colleagues (2013: 137) have suggested, 'the Web has become a site of consumer participation'. Thus, we participate in a formation of culture by consuming and vice versa. We also consume by participating in the formation of cultural groups to which we belong. Furthermore, participation in online activities affects the formation of new forms of 'citizenship', based on belonging to a 'community'. In its classic definition, 'citizenship therefore represents a relationship between the individual and the state, in which the two are bound together by reciprocal rights and obligations' (Heywood, 1994: 155). Here, citizenship is defined as 'full membership of a community' (Marshall, 1950). However, Marshall's idea of citizenship does not distinguish 'between active and passive forms of citizenship' (Turner, 2000: 21). Extending this idea to the online communities, we can say that to be a recognisable member of a community, citizens/users must not only be a part of the (online) community (access to the digital realm) but also be active members of the aforementioned community (having digital skills). This is why, in order to consider the new form of inclusion/exclusion from the digital realm and its advantages/disadvantages, it is not enough to simply consider one's access to the internet, but also the capacity, the motivation, the purpose of engagement and skills in using digital devices. Indeed, access to the digital realm could simply reduce and mitigate the first level of the so-called digital divide, while exacerbating the second level (digital skills deficits). Securing greater internet penetration will not eliminate digital inequality on its own. Instead, it will create a new kind of inequality among people and groups, potentially shaping their life chances in multiple ways.

Beyond the digital divide binary

While the gap in access to the internet has over the years been minimised, strong differences or divides persist in terms of 'internet usage', 'digital literacies', 'cultural capital' and 'digital skills' (Van Dijk, 2005; Halford and Savage, 2010). All these factors influence the way in which people use and experience the internet and associated digital technologies. More importantly, each of these features influences the amount of benefit individuals and collectives accrue from their use of ICTs. Yet, it remains unclear how the use of ICT and the internet, also in terms of leisure, may reduce or increase social inequalities already existing in the offline realms. Different groups of people are more or less privileged in their *access to* digital technologies and platforms (digital divide) and their *use* (digital inequalities) of these spaces. This disparity in access and use of ICTs and the internet influences parts of the population in different ways. It may be argued that digital disparities affect disadvantaged groups without access to ICT. Indeed, these groups are further marginalised and their disadvantaged position is further emphasised.

Henceforth, digital inequalities are influenced by many factors and not simply by access, gender or age. This is true also for digital leisure, one reason why we need to go beyond the literature focusing on the gender-based digital divide which suggests that males spend more time gaming than females (Willoughby, 2008) or the idea that digital natives spend more time gaming than digital immigrants. If we look only at these interesting analyses we will have a one-sided perspective, skewing the whole picture. Indeed, we will see only the first pillar of the digital divide (based largely on access) and not the second level in which features such as skills, literacies and social and cultural capital play a key role (Hargittai, 2010). Therefore, there is a need to go beyond the gender digital gap and the generational gap (Lenhart *et al.*, 2008) in our attempts to analyse how digital inequalities based on education (Attewell, 2001), income (Witte and Mannon, 2010), skills and motivation (patterns at the base of social structure) influence the ways in which we consume leisure online. Experiencing and consuming leisure is a distinctive element of social inequalities that influence and exacerbate digital inequalities. Indeed, in its simplest form, citizens/users excluded from the digital realm are also excluded from the context in which identities, their sense of belonging and membership of communities are created. Citizens/users who do not have the opportunity to access the online environment are excluded from a socialising place, which potentially provides the grounds for learning social norms, obtaining information and sharing emotions and experiences. Furthermore, citizens who have digital access but do not have the abilities, skills, motivation, awareness or understanding of the online rules are further marginalised. At the same time, digital inequalities, as in a vicious circle, influence social inequalities already existing in the offline realm (Ragnedda and Muschert, 2016). This is true also for digital leisure. Indeed, being excluded, both in terms of accessibility and usage, from the digital realm in which to consume leisure could mean the exclusion from an environment in which users share experiences, values and rules and are part of a culture or 'emotional communities' (Maffesoli, 1996). One may conclude that communities are not only intense but also based on feeling, emotion and shared experience, rather than obligation and duties. Virtual and offline communities are intrinsically different, but at the same time strongly intertwined, impacting upon each other. Having the ability to access (be a passive member of a community) as well as creating and sharing content (being an active member) allow citizens/users to play a key role in promoting themselves and improving their life chances.

Indeed, using digital platforms (including social media, online-based social network forums or consumer forums) also means being part of a community. As a consequence, being out of this space means being digitally excluded, and this has broader social consequences. Digital and social exclusion are inseparable, reinforcing each other. Leisure culture on digital platforms is becoming gradually more important as a common space for citizens/users to meet up, share, discuss and, more importantly, forge their self and identity. This is partly because there are more leisure-related options for people to choose from. Snir and Harpaz (2002) show evidence that people are paying more attention to leisure, and researchers are paying more attention to the relationship between the growth of ICTs and the growing interest in leisure activities. Conceptually, leisure time is sometimes seen in opposition to more important activities such as studying, looking for a job or improving one's life chances. However, we contest this view, arguing that leisure culture cannot be seen as a simple 'wasting time activity' because of its formative and socialising qualities. However, not everyone with direct access to the internet understands its operating principles and predominant practices and gains 'social' advantages from it. Furthermore, the internet is expensive to access in some parts of the world, creating a potential geographical digital divide, with wider social consequences. At the same time, 'a cultural gap remains between those that are comfortable using mobile devices, social networks and other online environments to participate in civic life as consumers and citizens and those that are not' (McGillivray, 2014: 99). Indeed, it is not only a matter of access (digital divide), but a matter of use, engaging, understanding and taking advantage of the possibilities (digital inequalities) that matters. However, it would be an oversimplification to replace the term 'digital divide' with 'digital inequality' because they are vividly two separate but strongly interrelated issues influencing our society.

Digital inequalities and leisure time

Skills, motivation, age, income, gender, education and other elements at the base of social structure influence the way in which we access and use the digital devices and digital content available. At the same time, usage influences the formation of identities, sense of community and sense of belonging to a group, with real consequences for people's 'social lives'. The rich, in terms of skills, income and abilities, gain more advantages from the internet than poorly skilled users (DiMaggio et al., 2001; Gilbert, 2010). Indeed, it seems that pre-existing inequalities are amplified in the digital sphere (Helsper, 2012). Among the different usages that in some ways influence the lifestyle, the identity, the self-perception and the way in which we interact with peers, we can find free time for leisure activities. Internet and ICT use in terms of leisure may differ in relation to skills. Indeed, some scholars (e.g. Whitty and Mclaughlin, 2007) have shown how those with enhanced digital skills are more likely to spend time in online entertainment.

It would be an oversimplification to reduce leisure time simply to the time spent playing online and with other devices. Digital skills, literacies and cultural capital influence the ways in which we 'participate' in cultural production and media content: 'participating in media production is now an everyday leisure culture made possible by the availability of self-publishing platforms and its evolution, and future direction is in need of further critical exploration' (McGillivray, 2014: 99). Further critical explanation is needed in order to understand the nuances of online content production and its social and cultural consequences. One of the first criticisms of this everyday leisure culture is that it 'produces' online content that is labour intensive (Ritzer and Jurgenson, 2010). The production of online content is often a kind of 'free labour' used by the digital economy, increasing profit by exploiting this free labour. The tendency to exploit free labour in this way is not new, but has been amplified by the advent of the internet and ICT. Scholars have been studying the free production of content since the 1980s with Toffler (1980) who first introduced the concept of a prosumer economy, based on the neologism made by the union of production and consumption. This notion, which is now taken for granted, has been revolutionary in the way it managed to mix two activities often seen as antithetic, effectively triggering an upsurge of debate in several disciplines. For some scholars, postmodernity represented a shift away from production and towards culture, identities, economy and lifestyles based on consumption. In this vein, Huws (2003) introduces the notion of 'consumption work' enabled by ICT, while Bruns (2008) talks about the producer, and Kücklich (2005) introduces the notion of play labour, an activity that is not work but is also *not* not work. What is interesting about this neologism is that play labour is a leisure and a productive activity, although its products are immaterial (community, intellectual property and so on). These immaterial products, sometimes seen as valueless, make it difficult to reconcile with conventional conceptualisations of play and labour, blurring the difference between paid and unpaid workers. The value of play labour is inherent to its creation of social ties or being part of a social network in which to grow up, socialise and gain social status.

However, this discussion requires a 'sociology of prosumption' (Ritzer and Jurgenson, 2010), to analyse the rise of the prosumer capitalism, where the desire to co-create and co-produce is ever present. There is a need for this type of sociology because all 'classic' concepts studied by sociologists, such as society, individuality, identities, labour, leisure, community, exploitation and alienation, have been revolutionised by the advent of ICTs. As Scholz (2012: 1) suggests, the Internet has become a simple-to-join, anyone-can-play system where the sites and practices of work and play increasingly wield people and are source for economic amelioration by a handful of oligarchic owners.... These are new forms of labour but old forms of exploitation.

Thus, there is a need to further investigate these concepts from a different perspective, as well as further enquiry into the dynamics of leisure cultures in influencing digital inequalities. As we have seen, digital inequalities should be viewed not only in terms of production, but also in terms of participation frameworks. Access to the internet and new technologies of communication in order to 'consume' leisure gives individuals the right to be and feel part of communities. However, in order to be an active member of communities, users/consumers must have skills, capacities, educational capital, spare time and the motivation to turn the enjoyment into something more. The offline socio-economic status influences the way in which we acquire information and knowledge while we are online, and thus the gap between high socio-economic status and lower status will increase. This is valid also for digital leisure. Indeed, the way in which we consume leisure (passive or active, viewer or producer) is influenced also (but not only) by our socio-economic status and, in turn, influences our sense of belonging and identities, a vital part of social status. Indeed, while both statuses (high and low) will benefit from rich opportunities offered by new digital devices, those individuals and groups of highest status (in terms of income, education and skills) will gain more and sooner, thus widening the pre-existing gap.

Conclusion

This chapter has argued that digital inequalities go beyond the binary division of accessibility. Instead, to understand digital unevenness, one has to look at several factors, including age, gender, family structure, education, ethnicity, motivation, skills, cultural capital, among several issues. All these features are at the base of the social structure that in turn also influences digital inequalities. Therefore, it seems as though social and digital inequalities are inseparable and any analysis of the two should show this intrinsic off–online connection. Socio-economic status, in some way, influences the way in which citizens/users acquire, and use, information and knowledge. The consequence of this is that the pre-existing gap between those occupying the higher socio-economic strata and their lower strata counterparts will increase. Indeed, the more affluent segments of society in terms of skills, income and abilities gain more advantages from the internet than poorly skilled users. Furthermore, it would be impossible for people to see the benefits of digital technologies if they have not been educated on how to engage, use and adopt these new ICT technologies into their everyday lives. Literacy is, therefore, one of the key elements in ending technological inequalities or, at least, reducing differences. Moreover, technophobes may fear using new technologies due to lack of ICT skills. Again, this could hamper one's progress towards ensuring one's full integration into the digital society. Neither is addressing these issues an easy task. Lack of funding and different sets of priorities could deter some governments from investing towards completely eradicating digital inequalities and effectively bridging the digital disparity gap.

Better still, the concept of identity in our society is changing thanks to the introduction of new ICTs and different conceptions of space and time. Technology consumption has become more important in a postmodern system dominated by inequalities. At the same time, access to these technologies has become somewhat more personalised and, in many ways, is clearly a stepping stone in defining one's identity. Unlike in the past, identity has departed from its synchronised relationship with the nation/state concept, becoming close to the 'virtual' world as digital natives parade their preferences on social media platforms such as Facebook or Twitter. Moreover, spending time engaging in leisure cultures is no longer just about 'consuming' but also about 'producing' free content. The global focus on a high technology and knowledge economy has led to contested understandings of a knowledge work leading to the inevitable introduction of Fuchs' notions (2010) of free internet labour and the commodification of free time along with the exploitation of leisure as discussed in this chapter. Ultimately, not everyone can spend resources and time playing games online, indispensably showing how social class even influences the way we play online along with the way we experience leisure time. Being excluded from the leisure culture and leisure 'context', both for socio-economic and educational reasons, may have consequences in terms of full participation in virtual communities. This form of digital inequality, in turn, may influence wider social inequalities, since citizens digitally excluded from a culture have less chance to gain status. Furthermore, since digital and offline communities are increasingly tied and the difference is blurring, exclusions or passive participation in one of these communities inevitably influence the other community.

References

Attewell, P. (2001) The first and second digital divides. *Sociology of Education*, 74(3): 252–259.
Baudrillard, J. (1987) *The Ecstasy of Communication*. New York: Semiotexte.
Bauman, Z. (2000) *Liquid Modernity*. Cambridge: Polity Press.
Bender, T. (1978) *Community and Social Change in America*. Baltimore, MD: Johns Hopkins University Press.
Blurton, C. (1999) *New Directions in ICT-use in Education*. Paris: UNESCO.
Bonfadelli, H. (2002) The Internet and knowledge gaps: A theoretical and empirical investigation. *European Journal of Communication*, 17: 65–84.
Bruns, A. (2008) *Blogs, Wikipedia, Second Life and Beyond: From Production to Produsage*. New York: Peter Lang.
Buckingham, D. and Willet, R. (eds) (2013) *Digital Generations: Children, Young People, and the New Media*. London: Routledge.
Castells, M. (1996) *The Rise of the Network Society*. Cambridge, MA: Blackwell.

Castells, M. (2001) *The Internet Galaxy: Reflections on the Internet, Business and Society*. Oxford: Oxford University Press.

Chinn, M.D. and Fairlie, R.W. (2007) The determinants of the global digital divide: A cross-country analysis of computer and internet penetration. *Oxford Economic Papers*, 59(1): 16–44.

Clark, C. and Gorski, P. (2002) Multicultural education and the digital divide: Focus on socioeconomic class background. *Multicultural Perspectives*, 4(3): 25–36.

Deery, J. (2003) TV.com: Participatory viewing on the web. *Journal of Popular Culture*, 37(2): 161–183.

DiMaggio, P., Hargittai, E., Russell Neuman, W. and Robinson, J.P. (2001) The social implications of the internet. *Annual Review of Sociology*, 27: 307–336.

Elwood, S. and Leszczynsk, A. (2013) New spatial media, new knowledge politics. *Transactions of the Institute of British Geographers*, 38(4): 544–559.

Fuchs, C. (2010) Labor in informational capitalism and on the internet. *The Information Society*, 26: 179–196.

Gergen, K. (1991) *The Saturated Self: Dilemmas of Identity in Contemporary Life*. New York: Basic Books.

Gilbert, M. (2010) Theorizing digital and urban inequalities. *Information, Communication and Society*, 13(7): 1000–1018.

Halford, S. and Savage, M. (2010) Reconceptualizing digital social inequality. *Information, Communication and Society*, 13(7): 937–955.

Hargittai, E. (2010) Digital na(t)ives? Variation in internet skills and uses among members of the 'Net Generation'. *Sociological Inquiry*, 80(1): 92–113.

Harvey, D. (1989) *The Condition of Postmodernity*. Cambridge, MA: Blackwell.

Helsper, E. (2012) A corresponding fields model for the links between social and digital exclusion. *Communication Theory*, 22(4): 403–426.

Heywood, A. (1994) *Political Ideas and Concepts. An Introduction*. New York: St Martin's Press.

Hiroshi, O. and Zavodny, M. (2003) Race, internet usage, and e-commerce. *The Review of Black Political Economy*, 30(3): 7–22.

Huws, U. (2003) *The Making of a Cybertariat*. London: Merlin.

Jameson, F. (1990) *Postmodernism, Or, the Cultural Logic of Late Capitalism*. Durham, NC: Duke University Press.

Jenkins, H. (2006) *Convergence Culture: Where Old and New Media Collide*. New York and London: New York University Press.

Jenkins, H., Ford, S. and Green, J. (2013) *Spreadable Media: Creating Value and Meaning in a Networked Culture*. New York: New York University Press.

Jones, S.G. (1998) *Cybersociety 2.0: Revisiting Computer-mediated Communication and Community*. Thousand Oaks, CA: Sage.

Kemp, S.F. (1999) Sled dog racing: The celebration of co-operation in a competitive sport. *Ethnology*, 38(1): 81–96.

Kücklich, J. (2005) Precarious playbour: Modders and the digital games industry. *The Fibreculture Journal*, 5: n.p.

Lenhart, A., Kahne, J., Middaugh, E., Macgill, A., Evans, C. and Vitak, J. (2008) Teens, video games, and civics. Pew Internet and American Life Project. Available at: www.pewinternet.org/Reports/2008/Teens-Video-Games-and-Civics.aspx (accessed 26 August 2015).

Losh, S.C. (2003) Gender and educational digital chasms in computer and internet access and use over time: 1983–2000. *IT and Society*, 1(4): 73–86.

Lyotard, F. (1979) *The Postmodern Condition*. Manchester: Manchester University Press.
Maffesoli, M. (1996) *The Time of the Tribes: The Decline of Individualism in Mass Society*. London: Sage.
Marshall, T.H. (1950) *Citizenship and Social Class and Other Essays*. Cambridge: University of Cambridge Press.
McGillivray, D. (2014) Digital cultures, acceleration and mega sporting event narratives. *Leisure Studies*, 33(1): 96–109.
McMillan, D.W. and Chavis, D.M. (1986) Sense of community: A definition and theory. *Journal of Community Psychology*, 14: 6–23.
Mesch, G.S. and Talmud, I. (2011) Ethnic differences in internet access: The role of occupation and exposure. *Information, Communication and Society*, 14: 445–472.
Meurs, H. and Kalfs, N. (2000) Leisure and vacation: A forgotten travel market? In *Transport and Leisure, Report of the Hundred and Eleventh Round Table on Transport Economics on Transport and Leisure*. Paris: European Conference of Ministers of Transport.
Neumann, M. (1993) Living on tortoise time: Alternative travel as the pursuit of lifestyle. *Symbolic Interaction*, 16(3): 201–235.
Norris, P. (2001) *Digital Divide: Civic Engagement, Information Poverty, and the Internet Worldwide*. New York: Cambridge University Press.
Ono, H. and Zavodny, M. (2008) Gender and the internet. *Social Science Quarterly*, 84: 111–121.
Ragnedda, M. and Muschert, G.W. (2013) *The Digital Divide: The Internet and Social Inequality in International Perspective*. London: Routledge Advances in Sociology.
Ragnedda, M. and Muschert, G.W. (2016) Theorizing digital divides and digital inequalities. In J. Servaes and T Oyedemi (eds) *Social Inequalities, Media, and Communication: Theory and Roots*. Baltimore, MD: Rowman & Littlefield.
Ritzer, G. and Jurgenson, N. (2010) Production, consumption, prosumption: The nature of capitalism in the age of the digital 'prosumer'. *Journal of Consumer Culture*, 10: 13–36.
Rosenzweig, R. (1985) *Eight Hours for What We Will: Workers and Leisure in an Industrial City, 1870–1920*. Cambridge: Cambridge University Press.
Scholz, T. (2012) *Digital Labor: The Internet as Playground and Factor*. New York and London: Routledge.
Sennett, R. (1998) *The Spaces of Democracy, Raoul Wallenberg Lectures, 1998*. University of Michigan, Ann Arbor.
Shih, E., Kraemer, K.L. and Dedrick, J. (2008) IT diffusion in developing countries: Policy issues and recommendations. *Communications of the ACM*, 51(2): 43–48.
Snir, R. and Harpaz, I. (2002) Work–leisure relations: Leisure orientation and the meaning of work. *Journal of Leisure Research*, 34(2): 178–203.
Soker, Z. (2005) Age, gender, ethnicity and the digital divide: University students' use of web based instruction. *Electronic Journal of Sociology*. Available at: www.sociology.org/content/2005/tier1/soker.html (accessed 20 July 2015).
Toffler, A. (1980) *The Third Wave*. New York: Bentham Books.
Tramacchi, D. (2000) Field tripping: Psychedelic communitas and ritual in the Australian Bush. *Journal of Contemporary Religion*, 15(2): 201–214.
Turner, B.S. (2000) Liberal citizenship and cosmopolitan virtue. In A. Vandenberg (ed.) *Citizenship and Democracy in a Global Era*. London: Macmillan.
Van Dijk, J. (2005) *The Deepening Divide: Inequality in the Information Society*. Thousand Oaks, CA: Sage.
Van Dijk, J. and Hacker, K. (2003) The digital divide as a complex and dynamic phenomenon. *Information Society*, 19(4): 315–327.

Whitty, M.T. and Mclaughlin, D. (2007) Online recreation: The relationship between loneliness, internet self-efficacy and the use of the internet for entertainment purposes. *Computers in Human Behavior*, 23(3): 1435–1446.

Willoughby, T. (2008) A short-term longitudinal study of internet and computer game use by adolescent boys and girls: Prevalence, frequency of use, and psychosocial predictors. *Developmental Psychology*, 44(1): 195–204.

Witte, J.C. and Mannon, S.E. (2010) *The Internet and Social Inequalities*. New York: Routledge.

10 Understanding cyber-enabled abuse in sport

Emma Kavanagh and Ian Jones

Introduction

> I think at the beginning when I would see mean, hurtful messages, it would really hurt my feelings because I wasn't used to it. I wouldn't remember any of the good comments; I'd just remember that one bad one ... I've had people threatening to kill me and kill my family, wishing that I get cancer and die a slow, painful death. Horrible words I couldn't even think up in my head to be that mean.
>
> (Heather Watson, cited in Ward, 2015)

These words from tennis player Heather Watson demonstrate the confusion, anguish and upset an individual can experience as a result of vile and hateful abuse within social media environments. Watson encountered this through Twitter during the 2015 Wimbledon finals, and highlighted the personal distress and worry resulting from negative fan interaction. In cyber-space, people can communicate in an instantaneous, uncontrolled and often anonymous manner, and this makes policing or controlling such spaces extremely difficult. Online environments create an optimal climate for abuse and, as a result, social media sites are increasingly providing an outlet for a variety of types of hate to occur, and it is evident that such environments 'enable' abuse rather than act to prevent or control it. This chapter introduces the virtual environment and the nature of abuse within the online space. The justifications provided for the presence of cyber-enabled abuse alongside some of the potential impacts of being abused online are then presented. Finally, we consider some of the potential for research that will extend our understanding of these leisure spaces and human interaction within them.

Understanding virtual worlds

Online spaces are becoming increasingly significant as a medium for social interaction. Take yourself as the reader of this chapter; you may be viewing this online through a digital medium rather than reading it in print. While looking through the chapter, your thoughts may be distracted by an instant message from a friend or a post on Facebook. You may be multi-tasking; watching video content or listening to audio, streaming the latest music and keeping up-to-date with news and sport through a constant feed of real-time information. We shop online, communicate with others, update our knowledge, plan travel, conduct business and consume sport. The possibilities are endless and our use of these spaces is rapidly expanding and changing. Technology remains continually accessible through smartphones and personal computers; the internet has infiltrated our lives and the digital revolution permeates everyday interactions.

Barlow (1990, cited in Blakemore, 2012) created the term 'cyberspace' to refer to the present-day nexus of computer and information technology networks, a non-physical terrain created by computer systems. Such space may be used to simply describe the World Wide Web (WWW), the internet as a whole and also to include all global media and communication channels (Blakemore, 2012: 6). It is recognised as the essential communication and information medium within our society (Castells, 2010), and around 40 per cent of the world population has an internet connection (Hutchins and Rowe, 2013). In June 2014 it was recorded that there are over three billion internet users currently active (Internet Live Stats, 2015). Over three-quarters of adults used the internet every day, or almost every day, in Great Britain in 2015 (78 per cent, or 39.3 million). Social networking is one of the primary uses (Office for National Statistics, 2015) and it is behaviour within such online spaces that will be the focus of this chapter.

Social media

'Social media' is a term used to group internet-based applications that allow the creation and exchange of user-generated content (UGC) (Hanna *et al.*, 2011). These sites include applications that enable users to connect by creating and inviting others to have access to personal profiles. People correspond through emails, posting written or video content and sending instant messages. Currently there are hundreds of social media platforms available online, including social networking sites (e.g. Twitter, Facebook and Pinterest), text messaging, podcasts, wikis, blogs, online forums and discussion groups (Ferrara, 2015; Kaplan and Haenlein, 2010).

One area in which social media has had a significant impact is the way in which individuals consume and experience sport. Most professional sports organisations use social media platforms (primarily Facebook and Twitter) to keep fans abreast of news (Sanderson, 2011). Professional sports teams, athletes, journalists and sports media brands connect with audiences, creating a social media experience (Sanderson and Kassing, 2011; Sanderson, 2011). Although the rapid advancement of computer technology has allowed multiple social networks to proliferate (Hambrick *et al.*, 2010), Twitter appears to be the dominant social media platform adopted by sports organisations and athletes alike (Sanderson and Kassing, 2011). Gibbs and colleagues (2014) describe Twitter as a personal communication tool, a news distribution vehicle and a celebrity tracker all on one platform. This real-time information network connects users to the latest stories, ideas and opinions (Twitter, 2015) and allows them to share personal views. People communicate using tweets, limited to 140 characters. Tweets may include text, photo or video content. Individuals become followers of others or gain followers and interact through liking, re-tweeting or commenting on tweets. The hash tag feature allows individuals to assign a topic to a tweet and enables others to search and find trends in content. In 2015 Twitter boasted 316 million active users every month with over 500 million tweets being sent daily (Twitter, 2015). Twitter has been championed for the increased networking ability and global reach that it provides individuals. As such, it has had a 'profound effect' (Pegoraro, 2010: 501) on sport, specifically through allowing direct and immediate communication between fans and athletes (Hutchins, 2011), giving followers unprecedented access (Kassing and Sanderson, 2010), bringing fans 'closer to their sport heroes' (Pegoraro, 2010: 501), and giving them a look into their lives that they would be unlikely to receive via traditional mass-media broadcasts (Kassing and Sanderson, 2010). Crucially, and unlike other forms of mass media such as television (Boehmer, 2015), the nature of Twitter also allows fans the opportunity for 'parasocial interaction', or the illusion of an actual interpersonal relationship with an athlete, especially where the disclosure of personal information from an athlete (for example, regarding their home or family life) may create a sense of intimacy with the follower (Marwick and Boyd, 2011). Although parasocial interactions are – in many cases – positive, the nature of social media also makes it a rich environment for less desirable parasocial interaction. It is to this concept, that of 'maladaptive parasocial interaction' (Sanderson and Truax, 2014: 337), that we turn, specifically through the idea of online abuse.

Abuse on social media

Online abuse in sport is becoming increasingly significant as a social problem. A recent study by anti-racism in the football group *Kick It Out* exploring social media abuse of English Premier League players revealed that it was widespread on these platforms. Approximately 134,000 discriminatory posts were present between August 2014 and March 2015. This equates to an average of almost 17,000 abusive posts per month, or over 500 per day. Abuse directly targeted a range of areas, including race (28 per cent), gender (25 per cent), sexual orientation (19 per cent), disability (11 per cent) and anti-Semitism (9 per cent). Other forms of discrimination accounted for 8 per cent of the abusive content (Roan, 2015). The top five Premier League clubs who received the most discriminatory abuse were Chelsea, Liverpool, Arsenal, Manchester United and Manchester City, and the professional player most abused on social media during the study was Liverpool striker Mario Balotelli. Balotelli was sent more than 8000 discriminatory posts on social media, of which more than half were racist in nature. Other studies have reinforced the extent of the issue. Sanderson nd Truax (2014) have identified an increasing trend of fans attacking athletes via social media platforms, due to the development of maladaptive parasocial interactions. Their study examined tweets directed at Cade Foster, a University of Alabama place-kicker, finding that behaviour manifested in a variety of ways, including belittling, mocking, sarcasm and threats. Farrington and colleagues (2015) have identified social media as a prime platform for facilitating racial abuse in a number of sports, including cricket, football and boxing, in the United Kingdom. They believe that social media are providing an outlet for the mass publication and sharing of racist views and abuse; magnifying the problem both inside and outside of sport.

Despite its apparent pervasiveness, research into the nature and prevalence of cyber-enabled abuse, commonly referred to as 'cyberbullying', is relatively recent (Kowalski and Limber, 2013) and has predominantly examined abuse against children. Yet this literature fails to increase our understanding of abuse on social media. Bullying includes behaviour, which is generally persistent, systematic and ongoing, and occurs without provocation from the victim. An incident cannot be categorised as bullying unless there is a power gradient, perceived or actual, between individuals involved and the behaviour is repeated over a prolonged period of time involving the same individuals (Simons and Mawn, 2010; Zapf and Gross, 2000). With this in mind, the concept of cyberbullying is too narrow to truly help understand negative interaction in online environments and all cyber-enabled abuse. Although there is an emerging body of literature that does explore the nature of online abuse against adults (Kavanagh and Jones, 2014) this literature has been clouded by a lack of conceptual clarity concerning the types of behaviour that constitute abuse and variations in definitions of it. Kavanagh and Jones (2014) sought to address this problem through their conceptualisation of a typology of virtual maltreatment. They argue for the need for context-specific typologies that accurately reflect the nature of the phenomenon but which may also be used as a tool with which to analyse such behaviour. They use the term 'virtual maltreatment' to encompass the variety of cyber-enabled abuses that can manifest in virtual environments, and define it as:

> Direct or non-direct online communication that is stated in an aggressive, exploitative, manipulative, threatening or lewd manner and is designed to elicit fear, emotional or psychological upset, distress, alarm or feelings of inferiority.
> (Kavanagh and Jones, 2014: 36)

Abuse online is likely to occur within virtual relationships and is enabled by the instantaneous access and global reach that the internet affords the perpetrator. Virtual relationships include the follower-to-athlete (coach or official) or athlete-to-athlete relationship, and abuse may be experienced directly or indirectly within such relationships. *Direct* refers to those incidents where a message is directly sent to a recipient or includes a hashtag (#) as an identifier or link to the subject of the abuse adopting their user name (@Twitteruser). *Non-direct* refers to cases whereby a message is not sent to the actual subject of the message, but the content would make reference to them perhaps through the use of a hashtag or descriptor. Non-direct abuse can become direct abuse through the process of re-tweeting or through media uptake or coverage of the abuse. In this instance, the subject of the abuse could become a direct recipient of it. Athletes, coaches, officials, fans and other stakeholders all have the potential to become both victims and perpetrators of abuse in online environments.

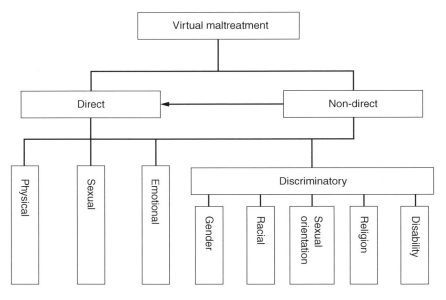

Figure 10.1 A typology of virtual maltreatment in sport (source: Kavanagh and Jones (2014: 37)).

Four types of abuse may be experienced either directly or indirectly within virtual relationships (see Figure 10.1). These are physical, sexual, emotional and discriminatory, of which the final type can be further categorised into discrimination based on gender, race, sexual orientation, religion and/or disability. We will provide a brief overview of each type.

Although virtual environments would, at first, seem to exclude the possibility of physical abuse, abuse based on physical characteristics is still evident. Virtual physical abuse may include threats of physical violence and/or focus on an individual's physical attributes. Comments may be stated in an aggressive, exploitative, manipulative or threatening manner and may be designed to elicit fear, emotional or psychological upset and distress, alarm and/or inferiority. Examples of direct and indirect physical abuse may be seen in messages to the Premiership footballer Wayne Rooney, and Olympic gymnast Beth Tweddle:

@WayneRooney cheers Wayne you fat ugly wanker

@SkySportsNews #Sportswomen Beth Tweddle on a scale of 1/10 how pig ugly would you class yourself?

Abuse may extend from comments about physical appearance to threats of physical violence, demonstrating how this can escalate in severity. The following are examples of indirect physical abuse towards tennis players Marion Bartoli and Andy Murray, and footballer Raheem Stirling:

> If Bartoli fist pumps one more time I'm gonna knock her out the slag.

> I hope Andy Murray loses, breaks an arm and never plays tennis again, cunt.

> I still hope to see Sterling in a red kit again. Not playing for Liverpool, but his City kit being soaked in his own blood. That'd be nice.

It is clear that even in a virtual environment the physical safety of athletes can be threatened, albeit in the form of focusing on physical attributes, through a threat of physical violence or willing an individual to come to harm.

Virtual sexual abuse may include threats of rape and sexual assault or sexual acts to which the adult would not consent, or comments regarding sexual behaviour with or of an individual. Data retrieved during the 2013 Wimbledon Women's Final demonstrate how both athletes competing in this event were subject to abuse of a sexual nature:

> Sabine Lisicki – I'd definitely let her sit on my face. Not a great face but those legs are amaze, body ain't too shabby either #wimbledon

> Bartoli wouldn't get raped let alone fucked #wimbledon

The use of the #Wimbledon tag here is interesting, as this provides a descriptor to the tweet and demonstrates how an indirect comment could be linked to an individual or viewed beyond the followers of the individual tweeting.

Virtual emotional abuse includes comments designed to elicit a negative emotional and/or psychological reaction, and may include rumour spreading, ridiculing, terrorising, humiliating, isolating, belittling and scapegoating. Emotionally abusive content is a common form of abuse present within online environments; at a basic level, tweets may simply be designed to humiliate and belittle athletes, for example:

> Raheem Stirling is a cunt and a waste of space @MCFC enjoy and good riddance.

> Fuck u @shelveyJ. Do us LFC supporters a favour and just leave LFC. Or do everyone a favour and just stop playing football.

Emotionally abusive tweets may also be intended to cause upset and distress. Football referee Mark Halsey was subject to abusive tweets in 2012 in the aftermath of a game between Manchester United and Liverpool where fans were unhappy with decisions he made. The abuse focused on a previous illness and demonstrates the hateful content that sports figures can receive from followers:

> I hope Mark Halsey gets cancer again and dies

> Mark Halsey should've died of cancer

More recently he has reported being the recipient of vile abuse threatening his family and linked to both his and his wife's battle with cancer (Wheatstone, 2015). The content demonstrates how online commentary can extend far beyond a sports field and emotionally target individuals.

Finally, virtual discriminatory abuse is more far-reaching and may include comments that negatively refer to an individual's membership of a social group based on gender, race, religion, nationality, disability and/or sexual orientation. Examples of gender discrimination are illustrated by a direct tweet to the female American racing driver Dana Patrick and an indirect tweet linked to Australian Cricketer Ellyse Perry:

> @DanicaPatrick you will never win a race they only got you in the sport because you look good now go back to the kitchen

> She must have a really long chain to reach a cricket pitch, still don't understand why she is out of the kitchen

These tweets demonstrate sexist and misogynistic undertones that permeate commentary concerning women's sport. Clearly, this content has little to do with the sport or the sportswomen's athleticism. Two highly publicised tweets, reported widely in the press, demonstrated blatant racial discrimination, both directly sent to the recipient:

> @anton_ferdinand RT this you fucking black c***

> @louissaha08 go back to France ya fuckin nigger

In 2012, Fabrice Muamba, a footballer for Bolton Wanderers, collapsed and had a cardiac arrest on the pitch. A student, Liam Stacey, tweeted racist and hateful content concerning the episode on Twitter:

> LOL. Fuck Muamba. He's dead!!! #haha

After further negative interaction between Stacey and other fans he was arrested and charged under the Racially Aggravated s4A Public Order Act 1986 (Farrington et al., 2015). Tweets that are overtly racist have perhaps been easier to police and identify than other types of discriminatory abuse but, as Farrington et al. (2015) note, only a small fraction of the race-related incidents appearing on social media even draw police attention, and the problem persists.

Discrimination based on sexual orientation is evident in terms of male and female sexuality. Female weightlifter Zoe Smith received homophobic tweets surrounding the London Olympic Games branding her a lesbian due to the sport in which she takes part. Similarly, the former athlete and athletics presenter on the BBC, Colin Jackson, was subject to a variety of messages regarding his sexual orientation:

> 2 gays involved in tonight's Olympic coverage … Justin Gay … and Colin Jackson #100mfinal

Homophobic language is common in tweets and may be used to abuse people regardless of their actual sexual orientation. In the case of Jackson, this may be seen as speculative or rumour mongering rather than being based on fact, yet it has clear homophobic undertones. Conversely, overt homophobia may also be witnessed within online spaces, as was demonstrated when rugby player Gareth Thomas was targeted after coming out.

> I wouldn't want the bed next to Gareth Thomas #padlockmyarse

Such behaviour demonstrates how homonegative opinions are expressed within online spaces, allowing social media to provide an outlet for the mass publication and sharing of discriminatory views. Interestingly, abuse on social media is not always discrete. One tweet can include multiple types of abuse, as may be seen within the examples provided above. In addition, it is not always the athlete who is the victim of abuse. Analysis of Twitter demonstrates how fans can in-fight and/or individuals come under attack by fans of opposing teams. Athletes are also not always innocent bystanders to abuse; they too post inflammatory or provocative tweets, fuelling negative interaction among Twitter users. What is clear is that abuse on social media is becoming more common and, as the examples presented above demonstrate, athletes and other key stakeholders can experience a variety of abusive or negative behaviours within virtual environments.

Understanding cyber-enabled abuse

To understand why social media is such fertile ground for abuse, the work of Suler (2004) is important in gaining an understanding of how the nature of the online environment leads to behaviours not normally encountered in face-to-face interaction. As he suggests, 'people say and do things in cyberspace that they wouldn't ordinarily say and do in the face-to-face world' (Suler, 2004: 321). Suler identifies six factors to explain this:

1 *Dissociative anonymity* – The online self becomes anonymous, and their identity becomes hidden, or manipulated to present an alternative identity.

Thus, what they post online cannot be linked with the 'real' person, the online self becomes compartmentalised, and thus any behaviour is not the behaviour of the 'real' person, but of the 'online person'.

2 *Invisibility* – This removes the opportunity for others to react, and for the perpetrator to experience the consequences of the behaviour such as observing reactions to a post, for example, in terms of body language.

3 *Asynchronicity* – Online interaction is not real-time interaction. People may post knowing that others will not read, or not be able to reply immediately. Thus, feedback that may reinforce certain behaviours or deter others is missing.

4 *Solipsistic introjection* – The lack of visual cues results in the individual assigning traits and characteristics to others with whom they are interacting, traits and characteristics that support their own worldview. Thus, a picture of the recipient is created that may not be accurate.

5 *Dissociative imagination* – This is the idea that the online environment is somehow 'not real', and as such the norms and values of 'real-life' interaction do not apply to the 'unreal' virtual environment.

6 *Minimization of status and authority* – Power relationships online are less apparent, with greater equality between those interacting. Thus, status becomes less important in terms of being able to influence behaviour.

Thus the online environment, through a combination of several or all of these factors, may be seen as a particularly dangerous one for potential abuse given its nature, and that it provides an environment whereby norms and values have less of a controlling influence upon behavior.

The potential impact of cyber-enabled abuse

Online maltreatment has a number of negative consequences, which can result in a lasting negative impact. Parry and colleagues (2015) highlight the fact that cyber-enabled abuse can have a significant effect upon all aspects of the victim's life – not just athletic performance. Based on anecdotal accounts from athletes in the media, the impact is extremely broad, and may include a range of psychological, behavioural and performance effects. Similar to the impact of abuse within face-to-face environments, abuse on social media can negatively affect an individual's self-esteem, and lead to performance anxiety, sleep disturbances and depressed mood states. Social media therefore provide another forum for abuse to present in sport. Some athletes are able to negotiate negative treatment, but for others the only way to cope is to stop using social media – or in some instances to retire from sport completely.

Personal accounts from athletes are increasingly commonplace, and elite athletes are now speaking up about their experiences of being abused online and the impact it has had upon them, yet this is failing to reduce the frequency of abusive incidents in online environments; if anything they are on the rise.

Rebecca Adlington highlighted the distress she experienced through receiving abuse on Twitter that targeted her personal appearance and weight:

> I suppose that social media in one sense is fantastic, but turned the wrong way round it is very, very personal and it destroys people's lives. So I think people should be much more careful about what they say.
>
> (Rebecca Adlington, cited in Meikle, 2012)

Adlington expressed concern that fans comment on more than her performance in the pool, demonstrating the helplessness that may be experienced when receiving hateful tweets.

In 2013, 22-year-old Canadian tennis player Rebecca Marino gave up the game, citing abuse on social media as the primary reason. She could no longer cope with the negative interaction and abuse on social media – this increased her performance anxiety and had a negative impact upon her mental well-being. She felt that fans were 'berating' her on social media and that this took a toll on her and her tennis. Sanderson and Truax (2014) highlight how the volume of messages received can be overwhelming and daunting for athletes. In their work studying high school athlete Cade Foster, they determined that he received over 12,000 messages over a 24-hour period. Both the volume and content of tweets can contribute to the significant emotional and psychological impact of online abuse. Sanderson and Truax highlight that while abuse on social media will not necessarily drive athletes from sport it may lead them to stop using social networks in order to avoid interaction with abusive fans. They contend that abusive behaviour will be impossible to eradicate, so the media training of athletes is integral to address coping.

Browning and Sanderson (2012) conducted semi-structured interviews with college athletes ($n=20$) competing in Division 1 of the NCAA in America. Interviews explored the athletes' perception/experience of receiving negative tweets. Some respondents reported that critical tweets had no impact upon them and explained how it is something you have to accept if you want to compete. Others adopted ignoring techniques to negotiate negative fan interaction or used it as a motivator. For others, critical tweets were deemed to have a significant negative impact, finding such interaction overwhelming and difficult to negotiate. Although a narrow sample, this demonstrates the broad impact abuse can have on athletes exposed to abuse on social media.

Justifying abuse: the case of Stan Collymore

In 2014, the *Guardian* newspaper reported how the former footballer Stan Collymore had been subject to an extensive range of abusive tweets (Riach, 2014). The abuse received high-profile media attention, and stimulated wide-ranging discussions including that regarding the extent to which such behaviour was justified. Using a 'netnographic' approach (Kozinets, 2010), two internet forums (from the *Guardian*, where the article was published, and Digital Spy, a more general discussion forum, were analysed (Jones and Kavanagh, 2014)). A key finding was that while many condemned the abuse, there were also a high number of individuals willing to support those abusing Collymore. Analysis of comments revealed that four types of justification were apparent.

Dissociative imagination

Suler (2004) identifies that a key characteristic of the virtual environment is that it is not seen as 'real', and norms and values of the 'real' world do not apply. This idea that such abuse was not real was highlighted by comments such as:

> Is this guy for real? I would imagine it is easier to just ignore a 'tweet' than a punch to the face.

> A threat on Twitter, or any other social media site, would be like getting a threat in a Christmas card. How can you take that seriously?

Cognitive distortions: 'it's just banter'

The second strategy, namely suggesting that online maltreatment is just 'banter' or harmless fun and denying any serious intent in terms of the content, was illustrated by comments such as:

> That's all it is, people taking the piss. Unfortunately what that gets interpreted as these days is 'vile abuse' or 'bullying'.

> It's just a bit of childish humour. I'm sorry you're so offended. You should stay off the internet probably.

Displacement of responsibility

This is a form of 'moral disengagement' which permits individuals to behave in a way that allows them to commit transgressions while maintaining a clear conscience (Hinrichs *et al.*, 2012). This form of moral disengagement focuses on the idea that such abuse is the fault of the medium itself, in this case Twitter:

> If you put yourself in the public eye then you make yourself a target on social networking sites. There is enough crime ... without the police having to monitor them. If you don't like being called names then either ignore it or stop reading it.

> In the old days one could go ex-directory, obtain a post-office-box, and live somewhere tucked away. SC has done the absolute opposite. He has created a forum around himself, and then quibbles when the odd bitter person sends a digital set of words to said forum. If you are so egotistical that you

encourage myriad persons to follow you, or make comments to you, then your sense of self is already at a dubious point. So, to complain that a few of the comments are unwelcome and offensive is kind of churlish.

Moral justification

The final justification identified was another moral disengagement strategy, in this case through attribution of blame, in that the victim, in this case Collymore, somehow 'deserved it' through reference to past misdemeanours, and thus abusers were morally justified:

> I think any minute of police time spent investigating 'twitter' abuse is completely pathetic and utterly incomparable to the physical abuse he has dished out in the past.

> Oh no! words on the internet! That must really upset a man who punches women in the face.

Thus, it is possible to identify a number of specific characteristics of virtual environments that, in this case, may be used to account for greater acceptance of such abuse than would certainly be the case for face-to-face abuse. It is, however, important to note that in the same way that abuse itself may not always just relate to a single category, justifications may also overlap. Thus we may see dissociative imagination and displacement of responsibility occurring concurrently, making the overall picture more complex. Although self-serving strategies are evident in many aspects of sport (sport performance, fandom and so on), these strategies add another element of understanding to the literature that examines what we could see as 'negative' behaviour within sport.

Conclusions

The nature and pervasiveness of cyberspace make it a particularly dangerous environment in terms of abusive behaviour. Although the benefits of social media are potentially widespread to the fan, athlete and sport organisations, it is clear that – through its very nature – it also provides the opportunity for a wide range of abusive behaviours towards the athlete, whether direct or indirect, behaviours that have the potential to negatively impact upon the athlete in a variety of ways. Certainly, fan interaction can span one-off hateful comments within the running commentary of sports consumption to far more targeted, systematic and pervasive examples of abuse. Abuse can sit anywhere on a spectrum from statements thought to be idle 'banter' or said in jest, to those that include threats of physical violence, and/or sexually degrading and demeaning content. The variety of behaviours and potential for impact on the individual make this an extremely diverse problem to classify and subsequently police.

While research has started to provide valuable insight into interaction in online spaces, as Frederick *et al.* (2012) note, the picture continues to be incomplete. The relatively recent emergence of the subject, especially within a sporting context, means that there are a number of rich areas for further exploration. The typology presented in this chapter certainly provides a starting point with which to identify and classify virtual maltreatment, yet it is acknowledged that more work is needed to truly understand abuse in this setting. It would be interesting for research to focus more closely on individual abuse types, such as discriminatory abuse and/or to provide a comparison across types. Research into the motivations towards cyber-enabled abuse is urgently needed. Further, understanding of the varied impact of abuse upon those targeted would provide a rich insight into experience, as well as – given its inevitability – the need for greater understanding of coping strategies for athletes of all levels who may experience its negative consequences. It is clear that social media is and will continue to be a central part of the sporting landscape, and as such, further exploration of cyber-enabled abuse is critical in terms of managing athletes' well-being.

References

Blakemore, B. (2012) Cyberspace, cyber crime and cyber terrorism. In B. Blakemore and A. Imran (eds) *Policing Cyber Hate, Cyber Threats and Cyber Terrorism* (pp. 5–20). London: Ashgate.

Boehmer, J. (2015) Does the game really change? How students consume mediated sports in the age of social media. *Communication and Sport* (published online before print). Doi: 10.1177/2167479515595500.

Browning, B. and Sanderson, J. (2012) The positives and negatives of twitter: Exploring how student athletes use Twitter and respond to critical tweets. *International Journal of Sport Communication*, 5: 503–521.

Castells, M. (2010) *The Rise of the Network Society*. Chichester: Wiley-Blackwell.

Chan, M. (2014) *Virtual Reality Representations in Contemporary Media*. London: Bloomsbury.

Clavio, G. and Kian, T. (2010) Uses and gratifications of a retired female athlete's Twitter followers. *International Journal of Sport Communication*, 3(1): 485–500.

Farrington, N., Hall, L., Kilvington, D., Price, J. and Saeed, A. (2015) *Sport, Racism and Social Media*. London: Routledge.

Ferrara, E. (2015) Manipulation and abuse on social media. *SIGWEB Spring Newsletter*, 12 March. Available at: http://arxiv.org/abs/1503.03752 (accessed 10 August 2015).

Frederick, E.L., Hoon Lim, C., Clvio, G. and Walsh, P. (2012) Why we follow: Examination of parasocial interaction and fan motivations for following athlete archetypes on twitter. *International Journal of Sport Communications*, 5: 481–502.

Gibbs, C., O'Reilly, N. and Brunette, M. (2014) Professional team sport and twitter: Gratifications sought and obtained by followers. *International Journal of Sport Communication*, 7: 188–213.

Hambrick, M., Simmons, J., Greenhalgh, G. and Greenwell, C. (2010) Understanding professional athletes' use of Twitter: A content analysis of athlete tweets. *International Journal of Sport Communication*, 3(1): 454–471.

Hanna, R., Rohm, A. and Crittenden, V.L. (2011) We're all connected: The power of the social media ecosystem. *Business Horizons*, 54(3): 265–273.

Hinrichs, K., Wang, L., Hinrichs, A. and Romero, E. (2012) Moral disengagement through displacement of responsibility: The role of leadership beliefs. *Journal of Applied Social Psychology*, 42(1): 62–80.

Hutchins, B. (2011) The acceleration of media sport culture. *Information, Communication and Society*, 14(2): 237–257.

Hutchins, B. and Rowe, D. (2013) *Digital Media Sport*. London: Routledge.

Internet Live Stats (2015) Internet users. *Internet Live Stats*. Available at: www.internetlivestats.com/internet-users/ (accessed 21 July 2015).

Jones, I. and Kavanagh, E.J. (2014) *It's Just Megabantz, Innit? LOL: Justifying Virtual Maltreatment in Sport*. Leisure Studies Association, University of the West of Scotland, 7–9 July.

Kaplan, A.M. and Haenlein, M. (2010) Users of the world, unite! The challenges and opportunities of social media. *Business Horizons*, 53: 59–68.

Kassing, J. W. and Sanderson, J. (2010) Fan–athlete interaction and Twitter: Tweeting through the Giro: A case study. *International Journal of Sport Communication*, 3(1): 113–128.

Kassing, J.W. and Sanderson, J. (2015) Playing in the new media game of riding the virtual bench: Confirming and disconfirming membership in the community sport. *Journal of Sport and Social Issues*, 39(1): 3–18.

Kavanagh, E.J. and Jones, I. (2014) #cyberviolence: Developing a typology for understanding virtual maltreatment in sport. In D. Rhind and C. Brackenridge (eds) *Researching and Enhancing Athlete Welfare* (pp. 34–43). London: Brunel University Press.

Kowalski, R. and Limber, S. (2013) Psychological, physical, and academic correlates of cyberbullying and traditional bullying. *Journal of Adolescent Health*, 53(1)(supplement): S13–S20.

Kozinets, R. (2010) *Netnography. Doing Ethnographic Research Online*. Thousand Oaks, CA: Sage.

Marwick, A. and Boyd, D. (2011) To see and be seen: Celebrity practice on Twitter. *Convergence: The International Journal of Research into New Media Technologies*, 17(2): 139–158.

Meikle, J. (2012) Teenager issued with harassment warnings over tweets sent to Tom Daley. *Guardian*, 31 July. Available at: www.theguardian.com/sport/2012/jul/31/teenager-arrested-tweets-tom-daley (accessed 28 July 2015).

Office for National Statistics (2015) Internet users 2015. *ONS* , 22 May. Available at: www.ons.gov.uk/ons/rel/rdit2/internet-access--households-and-individuals/2014/stb-ia-2014.html (accessed 28 July 2015).

Parry, K.D., Kavanagh, E. and Jones, I. (2015) Adoration and abuse: The impact of virtual maltreatment on athletes. *The Conversation*, 14 December. Available at: www.theconversation.com (accessed 27 April 2015)

Pegoraro, A. (2010) Look who's talking? – Athletes on Twitter: A case study. *International Journal of Sport Communication*, 3(4): 501–515.

Price, J., Farrington, N. and Hall, L. (2013) Changing the game? The impact of Twitter on relationships between football clubs, supporters and the sports media. *Soccer and Society*, 14(4): 446–461.

Riach, J. (2014). Stan Collymore attacks Twitter over abusive tweets. *Guardian*, 22 January. Available at: www.theguardian.com/technology/2014/jan/22/stan-collymore-attacks-twitter-abusive-tweets (accessed 1 August 2015).

Roan, B. (2015) Chelsea suffers most abuse from social media trolls. *BBC Sport*, 23 August. Available at: www.bbc.co.uk/sport/0/football/32327460 (accessed 23 August 2015).

Sanderson, J. (2011) To tweet or not to tweet: Exploring Division 1 athletic departments' social-media policies. *International Journal of Sport Communication*, 4: 492–513.

Sanderson, J. and Kassing, J.W. (2011) Tweets and blogs: Transformative, adversarial, and integrative developments in sports media. In A.C. Billings (ed.) *Sports Media: Transformation, Integration, Consumption* (pp. 114–127). New York: Idea Group Global.

Sanderson, J. and Truax, C. (2014) 'I hate you man!': Exploring maladaptive parasocial interaction expressions to college athletes via Twitter. *Journal of Issue in Intercollegiate Athletics*, 7: 333–351.

Simons, R.S. and Mawn, B. (2010) Bullying in the workplace: A qualitative study of newly licenced registered nurses. *American Association of Occupational Health Nurses Journal*, 58(7): 305–311.

Suler, J. (2004) The online disinhibition effect. *Cyber Psychology and Behavior*, 7(3): 321–326.

Twitter (2015) Twitter usage/company facts. *Twitter*. available at: https://about.twitter.com/company (accessed 1 August 2015).

Ward, V. (2015) Heather Watson: I won't let death threats wreck my chances at Wimbledon. *Telegraph*, 1 July. Available at: www.telegraph.co.uk/news/uknews/11710172/Heather-Watson-I-wont-let-death-threats-wreck-my-chances-at-Wimbledon.html (accessed 6 August 2015).

Wheatstone, R. (2015) Mark Halsey: Sick Twitter trolls threaten daughter of former referee with acid attack. *Mirror*, 4 March. Available at: www.mirror.co.uk/news/uk-news/mark-halsey-sick-twitter-trolls-5268976 (accessed 1 August 2015).

Zapf, D. and Gross, C. (2000) Conflict escalation and coping with workplace bullying: A replication and extension. *European Journal of Work and Organizational Psychology*, 10: 497–522.

11 Consuming authentic leisure in the virtual world of gaming

Young gamers' experience of imaginary play in second modernity

Michael Wearing

Introduction

> Year: 2004. Game: World of Warcraft. Played roughly 40+ hours straight (it got blurry towards the end). Forgot to eat, called in to work during that time, and fell over when I finally got up to hit the toilet. Not my finest moment.
> (Male, actual age unknown, online thread www.gamesradar.com/problems-being-obsessed-games/ (accessed 21 November 2014))

The commercialised imaginary worlds of online and console gaming are interlinked by the broader trajectories of Western society and cosmopolitan civil societies. These trajectories constitute new relations and transformations in youth (12–25 years) leisure cultures in late modernity (Giddens, 1990; Rojek, 1993). Since the 1970s the escalation of these new forms of socially governed leisure have broadly coincided with the neoliberal or capitalistic market imperatives of the age, including economic globalisation, market competitiveness and market-oriented governmental reforms that have been largely (de)regulated and enabled by the late modern state. I am particularly concerned with youths' quest for authentic leisure through the means of video gaming. Is it possible to find authenticity, and secure and stable identities in such imaginary play? In cultural terms the impact of virtual gaming raises new risks and creates ontological uncertainty for young people (Beck, 1992; Hutchins, 2008). These risks are designed and distributed through multinational corporations' dominance and governance of this online space as the consumer marketplace for games. Conventional parental and governmental wisdom, tainted by the knowledge of more violent games, is that role-play and multiple video gaming itself creates social and personal risks as well as significant financial outlays for young people in this global digital leisure activity

Nonetheless, the macro and global systems in which people are embedded in late modernity also promote resistance and activism. More recently, this has been characterised as a second modernity where reflexively knowing our past mistakes and the harm done creates a redemptive consciousness and a contrition ethic within capitalism itself (Beck and Grande, 2010). More than a quarter of a century ago, Giddens (1990: 149) emphasised the key feature of late modernity as social reflexivity, or the 'folding back' of social knowledge onto governments, communities and broader civil society, and equally important is Beck's revision to this understanding as 'reflexive modernisation' that includes unintended/ unaware consequences of second modernity (Beck, 1992). Under these new polyarchic systems many Western societies have entered second modernity and are experiencing the cosmopolitanism of social life defined by Beck as reflexive learning within the multiple maternities of second modernity (Beck, 2000). These multi-maternities in second modernity mean that different senses of time, space, leisure and so on may be experienced within and across social groups and social classes internal to a nation state as well as across national boundaries. The use of the internet and video gaming has moved beyond first modernity's leisure privations such as book reading or painting into something more like both the knowledge-based and unintended/unaware consequences created in the social reflexivity of a second modernity (Beck, 1999; Hutchins, 2008). In this second modernity there is a new consciousness and awareness of play as affecting sociality and possible activism among gamers – perhaps what Beck's analysis would call 'a sub-politics of gaming'.

Other authors have demonstrated that much of global gaming technology and marketing reinforces oppressive hegemonic representations of gender and race (Dunlop, 2007). Binary categories of 'us' and 'them' based around race and gender are pre-set within the dominant markets of gaming and these representations need to be challenged by gamers and designers themselves (Harrell, 2010). This theorising of a 'sub-politics' can open up possibilities of communities of resistance and self-representation against such categorisations of sexist and racist norms. Gamers cannot only work individually but also collectively against the digital and in-game 'normalising' and stigmatising representations. While this may seem somewhat utopian, several authors have pointed to such resistance around challenging racist and sexist conversations, gamer aggression and 'chatter' in their studies (Dunlop, 2007; Gray, 2014).

Commodification, consumption and atomisation

In late 2013 Geek.wire.com reported that 1.2 billion people were playing computer and video games and that at any one time 700 million were active, with 54 per cent male and 46 per cent female (www.geekwire.com/2013/gaming-report-12-billion-people-playing-games-worldwide/). The impact of such online and computer gaming upon leisure cultures and lifestyles has wide- and far-reaching implications in terms of the identity and lived experience of gamers. Long-term gamers can take years and even decades to find a balance between real-world and virtual-world realities. I am particularly concerned with young people's (12–25 years) quest for authentic leisure in gaming based on their experiences. Understanding gamers' cultural and lived experience involves exploring how such leisure interacts with schooling, work and personal life. This chapter argues for a sociological analysis of video gaming to help understand the effects on visual imaginary in leisure consciousness in the current era of second modernity.

The chapter draws upon secondary data sources only from the literature and some online conversations that are readily available via online 'threads' for gamers' conversations on specific areas such as gaming addiction.

The broad issue addressed here is the commodification of everyday worlds captured by, and directly related to, an escalation in the commercialisation of youth technologies and social practices. The mega shift, or significant social change, in young people's authentic leisure experiences among affluent Western youth is analysed in this chapter as virtual leisure gaming. The term 'Western' will be used to embrace Said's (1995) use of the term and its implications for a 'double consciousness' to understand how non-Western and non-white youth might mimic and be complicit in gaming cultures despite the financial burden. The chapter is a conceptual reflection upon new leisure consciousness and, to a lesser extent, freedom of speech in gaming. Developing these issues could lead to more substantial research on imaginary and visual consciousness and sociability involving youth and gaming communities. There is a need to highlight positive effects of gaming in light of the size of the global gaming market and the risks and harms created by the commercialisation of identity in this market (Lin and Sun, 2015).

The main focus of this chapter is on how the consumption of gaming technology constructs the gamer's subjectivity and micro worlds as leisure in the private worlds of 'bedroom culture'. The rise of this youth leisure phenomenon, based in new technologies, was documented by sociologists more than a decade ago: 'this media rich bedroom culture represents a vital yet taken-for-granted aspect of ... (*youths'*) daily lives which significantly enriches the variety of leisure opportunities open to them' (Moira and Livingstone, 2001: 178). Second modernity and globalisation have created 'new worlds' for young people through the commodification of bedroom culture. This raises questions as to whether this consciousness is one-dimensional, a dominating culture with instrumental reason and formal rationality and therefore a kind of 'repressive tolerance' (see Marcuse, 1991) or whether it opens up possibilities for new personal horizons, leisure identities and personal freedoms. In the latter analysis, gaming communities can exercise some power from below in countering the dominant profit motives, instrumental reason and planned obsolescence of the global marketplace as fostered by large gaming companies, in particular. The global gaming marketplace is by no means static or a monopoly 'owned' by large companies, and there is some flexibility in opening up decommodifed experiences and social interactions in gaming. The growth of gaming companies both large and small has developed exponentially and globally with many breakaway companies in recent years. The rapidly changing technology in the area allows new companies to flourish, with developers migrating from older and larger companies. This new gaming economy has enabled companies to develop and distribute games quickly and secured increasing market share to smaller companies. This has advantages for consumers, in that they can trial free games and choose not to purchase or 'exit' brand loyalty if they are not satisfied with the quality of hardware or software.

Changes in the design, quality and type of technology affect leisure gaming identities and require further exploration by leisure theorists. For example, new gaming technologies using 3D headsets to create even more 'real' yet illusionary spaces of consciousness, sociality and relationship with others is an untapped area of social research. For researchers, questions are posed by such technology and its design in terms of the socio-cultural costs and impacts of such consumption upon the lives of young people. Issues are raised in this chapter about time distortion in gaming and whether this consciousness represents forms of 'online social oblivion' from real-world engagement. Does gaming also encourage lived personal freedoms and more stable inner mechanisms to cope with the stressors of second modernity? The macro focus here is on gaming as part of late Western capitalism's conspicuous consumption and second modernity's 'reflexive modernisation' given the now two decades of the escalation of the multiplayer and video gaming industry. South Korean society, for example, has been characterised as the commercialised gaming ideal where gaming culture permeates all levels of cultural activity (Jin, 2010). The rise in gaming cultures in many ways parallels the rise of consumption and the buying power of middle-class youth in South Korean culture with access to their own or their parents' disposable incomes and ready access to a global consciousness through the internet (Natkin, 2006). A brief overview of this new political economy of bedroom culture and gaming for youth will assist our understanding of the critical perspective used in this chapter.

Critical gaming studies and bedroom leisure cultures

Several key aspects of youth gaming culture include peer and broader youth competition to own the newest technologies, and participation in games that motivate gamers to consume ever-increasing upgrades and new games in the gaming distribution marketplace. These trends are associated with the globalisation of youth leisure cultures and an intensification of commoditised 'bedroom culture' in affluent Western countries. This has resulted in youth spending significantly more amounts of their leisure time, at least in terms of the statistics for affluent Western countries, connected to or living around new technologies such as computers and mobile phones rather than, say, watching TV or participating in sporting activities (Entertainment Software Association, 2015). New technologies enable young people to feel a sense of 'safe and secure' belonging in their own home or bedroom while maintaining a flow of online friendships and communication with others. Meaning is then given to the inner worlds of the gamer who is immediately connected via their computer-based bedroom culture with those in the 'outside world' and is often also grounded in other social media such as Snapchat, Facebook and Twitter. What is different today about this technologically generated mass leisure consumption is the amount of time young people and particularly teenagers spend immersing themselves in bedroom culture. Precise global statistics on young people who play multiplayer games, time use in leisure activities and who self-identify as gamers are not readily available. However, certain trends in the USA and elsewhere where surveys have been conducted indicate a broader shift in youth leisure culture (Sublette and Mullan, 2012). Statistics on 4000 US households in 2015 found that 56 per cent of gamers were under the age of 35 and 26 per cent were under 18, and 57 per cent of the overall sample were male and 43 per cent female. Also in this sample nearly 40 per cent of gamers said they were spending less time going to the movies or watching TV as a result of gaming (Entertainment Software Association, 2015: 5, 8).

It is my contention that gamers are entering a new age and phase of leisure consciousness driven by the forces of mass (hyper-)consumption and second modernity. Mead's (1934) work on the symbolic construction of identity, Levinas' (1987, 2006) work on 'the other' as difference or alterity and Gee's (2011) work on situated meaning in discourse (as conversational) participation help shape the conceptual background of this chapter. Briefly, gamers are involved in their own authentic meaning making in the discursive play of online communication. In creating this meaning system the identity of the gamer becomes immersed in virtual realities where a different sense of being or alterity is constructed. This theoretical frame on identity will help situate how authentic leisure identity is immersed and constructed in the role-plays, narratives and conversational play of the console game and multiplayer online environments. This concept of alterity can help illustrate the tensions between becoming hegemonic identities as mentioned earlier in racist and sexist categorisations counter-posed to different playful identities or otherness in virtual reality (Dunlop, 2007; Gray, 2014). Hegemonic identities either fit the norms of society as accepted category types, or 'fit into' (conform to) the dominant cultural apparatus. For example, this may be noticeable in gamers' performance within games of dominant masculinities such as aggressive competition and 'win at all cost'. Aggressive play of this sort disregards the impact upon and potential harm to others in the game. Giroux (2011) has linked corporate media in particular to the shaping of youth identity, and some of these ideas will be explored and critiqued below and extend to earlier work (Taylor and Cohen, 1992; Foucault, 1990; Rojek, 1993) on leisure as perceived freedom and even more so as virtual 'escape attempts' from everyday life. In online resistance to hegemonic identities there are also possibilities in virtual environments for non-conformist sociability, and social resistance to hegemonic meaning and dominant cultures through alternate identities and a freeing 'otherness' online.

Behind this in terms of macro-social forces driving the gaming industry are the ways in which multinational companies such as Sony and Microsoft and smaller country-based technology gaming companies reach into and embed their products for use in indoor leisure cultures. The cost of the new bedroom economy for gamers or their parents and social supports is reasonably high when compared to, say, going to the movies or local amateur sporting activities. In 2012 one US marketing survey found that the average weekly spend on gaming-related products had reached almost $100 per week, or $5000US a year. This spending is higher among boys, who average $124 per week, than girls, at $70 per week; and ranges from $56 per week for 12–13 year olds to $192 per week for 18–19 year olds.

(www.marketingmag.com.au/news-c/digital-teens-boys-shun-traditional-media-flock-to-gaming-and-social/ (accessed 9 August 2015))

The social and demographic characteristics of gamers and numbers of gamers on a global scale are significant. In the USA alone in 2007 gaming was a US$9.5 billion-a-year industry and by 2010 profits increased to US$25.8 billion. In addition, contrary to popular perception, about one-third to half of online gamers are females and there is a significant breadth of ages and cultural diversity across both sexes who play online and video games (Lin and Sun, 2015). The market orientation is strongly skewed to games designed for youth under 25 years (https://en.wikipedia.org/wiki/Video_game_industry (accessed 12 January 2016)). Space does not permit a full account of the histories of indigenous and global markets in creating the video industry over the past two decades. The financial cost to individuals of buying into the leisure activity of gaming is determined by a player's income and family circumstances (Wolf, 2015). It is noted, however, that gaming infrastructure including games themselves is readily available across developed and developing nations, notably countries such as South Korea, Singapore and China, at reasonable prices, at least for middle-class youth. There are various points of consumption for gaming, including how games are organised and sold, which are the main companies and who buys these games within countries. The large commercial producers such as Microsoft and Sony also spend considerable amounts on advertising, and global spending on video games will reportedly reach US$7.2 billion in 2016, an increase from US$3.1 billion in 2010 (http://venturebeat.com/2011/09/12/global-ad-spending-in-video-games-to-top-7-2b-in-2016/). Such heavily marketised and commercialised sociability and play is highly commodified in the branding and packaging of the product, notably through the aggressive marketing by large companies such as Microsoft (e.g. Xbox) and Sony (e.g. PlayStation).

Nonetheless, gamers are not confined always to 'bedroom culture', although for them this may be the most comfortable space. Recent studies show that mobile gamers worldwide play in various spaces: 'on the couch (69 per cent), while in transport (63 per cent), in bed (57 per cent), waiting for an appointment (55 per cent), in front of the TV (41 per cent) and on the john (34 per cent)' (www.geekwire.com/2013/gaming-report-1.2-billion-people-playing-games-worldwide/ (accessed 21 November 2014)). The lack of adult mediation, fewer 'real-world' friendships and isolation from 'real-world' local communities are some of the more negative consequences of the rise of video gaming and bedroom living (Calado et al., 2014; Brookes et al., 2016).

Central to this global consumption is how gamers and potential gamers are involved in identity formation and forms of resistance within games. The meaning of the spaces and cultures of these new techno-leisure activities is contested by young people themselves. Leisure spaces are created in this largely manufactured imaginary play for a new and potentially healthy engagement with lived realities and, as well as potentially healthy resistance from, normalising youth identities in society. The development of otherness or alterity can represent the gamer's authentic leisure quest over time – a quest that is potentially oppositional to authoritative and normalising youth identities.

These authentic leisure experiences are theorised here as a kind of spontaneous anarchism of ethical play that derives from the sociability and social capital of online play and, subsequently, affects leisure lived experience. It is also important not to forget that gamers are also playing and forming relationships with non-human forms within the games, which implies a different kind of human-to-non-human virtual sociability (Giddings, 2007). The real-world equivalence here is perhaps close to a child's relationship with family pets that encourages in the child feelings of care, protection and even love.

Youth leisure identities online

> An online gaming avatar is a lot like a mask. You can't tell anything about the real person who controls a character by looking at his or her representation in-game.
>
> (Culp, 2014: 29)

This quote implies that even anonymity has an authenticity in the online play and dramaturgy of virtual leisure cultures. The mask is no longer a person's face, as in our real, everyday 'face work' (Goffman, 1971), but a way of displacing the person to a different authentic self, online. It is one that plays out the individual and team-based role-play performances in secrecy whether as collaborative and/or competitive relationships. This represents a new 'global existentialism' of othering as anonymous selves and multinational gaming companies' commoditised and marketised designs on social identity (Levinas, 1987, 2006). The 'styles' of this culture are manufactured within the games without necessarily indicating any trace of a subculture and with a strong sense of belonging to the virtual community. Researchers have suggested that while 'subcultural' communities do emerge, allegiance to the norms of these 'subcultures' are weak or thin, and individualised modes of behaviour are predominant as part of gaming culture, despite team-based play (Pearce and Artemesia, 2009; Gray, 2014).

The social discourse and cultural representations that surround or inform popular understandings of gaming come from many media sources, including newspapers, television and social media that pander to the fears of parents and the broader population. In the broader context of second modernity, the construction of new internet risks offsets relations of trust to create a reflexive modernity of insuring against such risks (Giddens, 1990; Beck, 1992, 1999). 'Safety and protection' to counter the risks of the invisible other (the person behind the mask) become integral to the cultural globalising of the internet. We do not need to look very far to illustrate the safety awareness campaigns on the part of governments and citizens, and also the safety awareness literature that is springing up to set agendas for parental control and promote understanding of the real and perceived dangers and risk of gaming cultures. The Australian government, for example, has a Child eSafety Commissioner whose responsibilities include young people's as well as children's safe and enjoyable experiences online and a complaints system (see https://esafety.gov.au/about-the-office/role-of-the-office).

The societal issues that come out of multiplayer gaming are potentially significant, but their immediate implications are tentative and not at all clear today. The earlier concern introduced in this chapter for the 'reflexive modernisation of risk' in modern societies (Beck, 1992) is relevant here in that new leisure risks and uncertainties for young people have been created through gaming design and marketed by companies, including narratives of addiction and financial exploitation. Various authors have claimed both negative and positive consequences of gaming notably for young girls as included or excluded by such cultures, the levels of trust that might be compromised in such gaming and the need for anonymity to protect gamers from aggression and bullying within gaming worlds (McRobbie, 2008; Sublette and Mullan, 2012; Lundmark, 2015).

The sheer numbers of multiplayer gamers online in the world at any one time makes analysis of definitive cultures of gamers difficult for researchers to quantify (Yates and Littleton, 2001; Lin nd Sun, 2015). The global industry itself remains largely unregulated, unaccountable and complacent (if not unreflective) about the ethics and legality of designing and manufacturing such games. At the consumer level, the data indicate that young people use and identify with characters and less so with their team members in online gaming (Yu, 2009; Lundmark, 2015). The following section addresses gaming as sociability and authentic leisure. A critical perspective on 'gaming' as hyper-consumption is discussed in the final two sections as an indicative case study of how anxiety has been constructed and manufactured by experts and often with the (sometimes reluctant) complicity of parents or friends.

'Authentic leisure' as sociality and relational experience

A gamer usually plays anonymously and the gamer's consciousness is immersed within the virtual worlds of gaming. This creates a space for imaginary identity that can display authenticity and illusion. Players create their own situated language and meaning within the context of play (Gee, 2011). Simmel (1950) defined sociability as the joy and imagination of play in social life, and I have used this to define the leisure consciousness of gamers even within second modernity where reflexivity can overwhelm gamers with the financial, school, work-based and personal risk they take in pursuing gaming. This approach helps explore the development of sociability and social capital in online gaming from studying 'friendships' and character interaction in multiplayer games. Online threads and chats are readily available on the internet to show how gaming shapes young people's development and consciousness as leisure activity. A brief example is only possible in this chapter and is drawn again from secondary data sources.

Some gamers are now in their thirties and forties and have been playing these types of games in multi-gaming or console models for almost two decades, if the US 2015 survey reflects what is happening in most affluent societies (ESA, 2015). Online chat threads include confessions of 'online addicts' but also young people's testimonies and experiences of using certain games. These threads need further phenomenological research and socio-cultural interrogation to unpack their cultural and socially meanings. For example, consider the gender switching of identity undertaken by some male players in games:

> I thought like this for the longest time. I tried playing Skyrim as a female and when people said 'she' I wouldn't know who they talked about for minutes at a time. I recently tried running as a female in *Dark Souls 2*, and y'know what? It's not that bad. It's only really uncomfortable when I'm playing as a super sexualized bustier-than-life object of a juvenile mind. But I'm pretty sure they make women uncomfortable too.
> (A gamer quoted on 15 April 2014 at: http://tmi.kotaku.com/im-a-man-who-plays-as-a-woman-in-games-and-im-definite-1576592743)

This gender switching illustrates the way in which the anonymity and temporality of virtual cultures can alter the gamer's sense of otherness in these realities. This anonymous gender switching is only now possible with sophisticated computer technology, the internet and globalised online playing. The main reason for such gender switching in online gaming appears to be strategic in order to gain advantage over others and/or experience the sense of female otherness in a game (Martley et al., 2014).

Riding the hyper-consumptive gaming wave

The practice of gaming is framed in this section as global hyper-consumption in second modernity. Even within gaming itself players may be seen to undertake risky behaviour that leads to a sense of escape and greater leisure freedoms. Such risks in virtual reality can, however, shift into potential psychological and emotional harms for young people, notably through cyberbullying and possible addictions associated with gaming including potentially harmful effects on both physical and mental health. Equally tainted by the dominant consciousness is mainstream academic discourse, particularly in psychology and leisure studies, that can naively support gaming as a 'normal' rather than normalising leisure pursuit. I have argued for both the positive effects and potential harms that online gaming can bring about. Both aspects are part of the normalising effects of gaming cultures for young players. Nonetheless, issues such as cyberbullying and the creation of sexist and racist identities and cultures among gamers are also raised by such analysis.

The global gaming market deliberately encourages gamers to think it necessary to purchase the newest hardware and games or to go online constantly to keep up with consumer trends. The rapid rise of gaming in some Asian countries parallels their swift economic and social change over the past three decades with structures and social infrastructures that reflect what one South Korean sociologist (Kyung-Sup 2010) has argued is a 'compressed modernity', a process of modernisation that took place in Western Europe over two centuries or in Japan over 60 years. In countries with degrees of compressed modernity rather than second modernity such as South Korea (where industrialisation was rapid following the Korean War), Singapore and China, gaming may be experienced in heightened commodified form as an instrumental leisure experience where competition is spurred on by the cultural representations of defined celebrities and hierarchies of elite players akin to professional sport such as USA NBA basketball and similar to virtual-based world sports contests (Hutchins, 2008). This may also be seen as an instrumental aspect of these countries' new-found conspicuous hyper-consumption (Chang, 2010).

The experience of gaming is a process of entering a new world or what some writers term 'a magic circle' (Taylor, 2006). The individual here however needs to be located in my earlier arguments on the broad hyper-consumption processes orchestrated by the global gaming industry and the commodifying and marketing of this industry. Atomisation and individualisation of a youth's identity takes place in the isolation of bedroom cultures while sitting at the console. A brief description of this body–mind isolation will suffice to illustrate the process. At home in the room the gamer is content, moving the mouse and watching the basic narrative of the game unfold. Occasionally, the player is able to rest between the simulated performances of playing, shooting, running, jumping, chatting and so on. Time passes quickly but the gamers' will to succeed and achieve completion of a game at certain levels drives them on. The bedroom culture also gives the sense of timelessness or at least a 'slowing down of time'. Basic cognitive psychology relating to perception and 'divided attention' indicates that the receptors of the sensory system of the brain are distracted if not blocked by engaging in gaming (Riegler and Robinson, 2012: 110–111). In particular, gamers' highly focused vision and their auditory senses including sensing vibrations from amplified sound (while, say, using headsets in a darkened room) immerse the player in the phenomenology of role-play and the conversations in the game: the body and mind are immersed almost as one. These communicated actions may be theorised as both the phenomenological constructions of identity in virtual worlds and the use of a communicative interactional self to perform actions within the gaming world as agency (Levinas, 2006; Janack, 2012). The gaming experience is as much one of inner world or psyche reconfigurations in narrative and play of the gamer's identity as it is an observable or external change.

Despite the seeming passivity of these interactions – sitting in a chair, playing and chatting – they constitute new spaces for bodies and minds to pursue personal and inner freedoms through experiential and imaginative play, among other meaningful actions that may result. The gamer steps from the real into the virtual world with a password and a couple of clicks of the mouse. In this space the inner life of becoming an 'avatar' or virtual being takes over and drives the gamer forward from task to task and level to level of play. The quest is based partly in competition but also in the pleasures of immersion in an entirely constructed world which is not real but a fantasy of game designers and interpreted by gamers themselves. The enjoyment and pleasure of gaming comes as the gamer virtually role-plays, enters the journey narrative, and navigates and moves within these worlds (Sclater and Lafty, 2014). Such worlds are of course illusionary because the language and social division of the real world impinge upon such space: memory of the real world catches up. Broader socio-structural entities, institutions and social forces such as gender and race also orchestrate the situated practices of talk and communication on the net (Gray, 2014).

In the shift from the real to the virtual world the player is entering the 'magic circle' of fantasy play online. In this online world,

> we find people negotiating levels of self-disclosure and performance, multiple forms of embodiment, the integration of dual (or multiple) communities, webs of technologies, and the importance of meaningful online issues and values.
>
> (Taylor, 2006: 152)

The key aspect of the lived experience of gaming here is the degree of meaning attributed to an individual's immersion in gaming and the gaming culture itself. More broadly, some authors consider gaming as representative of the 'play turn' in global culture beyond the idea of a global village popularised during the 1960s and 1970s (Pearce and Artemesia, 2009: 279). Pearce and Artemesia's (2009) ethnographic account of entering the avatar virtual world of the game 'Uru' argues that new communities, identities and a sense of belonging are created by such virtual worlds. Such play, they argue, involves emergent communities created 'from below' or the grass roots of the gaming population and involves highly social and collaborative forms of association with others in these games.

Virtual world play as multi-game or console gaming is part of the process of cultural globalisation of a sense of 'community' as it is related to processes of economic and neoliberal globalisation. The community within any game is closer to the traditional notions of a small village where team-based, collaborative and competitive play form transient bonds between players. In this context individual and group identity are intertwined (Pearce and Artemesia, 2009). Gamers from this village perspective are forming friendships and player associations to continue in the game not only for months but sometimes for years. What gamers do online may differ by age and gender, in particular. Large studies of school-age children on the internet have shown that there are key differences across gender where boys are more likely to by bullied online and engage in excessive playing, going to bed hungry. Girls, on the other hand, are likely to become more isolated from family activities and real-world friendships (Brookes et al., 2016). These studies indicate some of the negative consequences of such sociality and living out leisure time in bedroom culture.

'Doing fun things': gaming spontaneity and time warps

One dimension that requires further research and exploration is how time is used and distorted by the gaming as alterity and leisure experience. Does immersion in gaming cultures alter a gamer's consciousness and perception of reality? Rigorous bio-psychological testing of the health and mental health consequences of gaming is still ambivalent on this question (Drummond and Sauer, 2014; Brookes *et al.*, 2016). From a sociological viewpoint I agree with Zygmunt Bauman that a fluid consciousness of pleasurable activities is part of modern liquid society (Bauman, 2000). An element of this theory posits that the heightened sense of ontological insecurity in second modernity has undermined trust and manufactured (real and perceived) risk to create greater anxieties and fears in the risk society (Beck and Lau, 2005; Wearing, 2015; Lundmark, 2015). The ontological insecurities of second modernity could potentially be ameliorated by a new leisure consciousness provided by gaming technology and relationships. There are, however, 'hidden hooks' in forming and spending time in relationships and the technology of gaming. For example, social anxieties and phobias such as 'shyness' may be overcome in working through this experience in gaming play. However, acute shyness can also be more broadly located in the new social relation of second modernity and, with youth taking virtual-world risks through belonging to a gaming community, they are also offsetting the real-world risks of relationships with others in real time (Hickinbottom-Brawn, 2013).

More affluent young people with greater leisure time and money in societies of second and compressed modernity arguably have greater access to such leisure consciousness and partly depend on the financial and social supports of parents they live with to gain such access. As Bauman (2000) reminds us, there are still the 'haves' and have nots' in liquid modernity and the 'haves' are usually the ones with access to a liquid and more reflexive consciousness as partly a product of online virtual realities and social media (i.e. quick and fleeting friendships and associations with others, constant entertainment running through young minds and an endless capacity for playback and rewind of material in gaming narrative journeying – just restart the game!). Such liquidity of consciousness is itself intensified by the emergence of hyper-consumption in affluent societies over the past few decades.

Bauman uses the example of shopping to show how individuality as consumers is constructed in modernity. This analysis may also apply to gaming as a 'soft' addiction but also a very time-consuming one. In a recent qualitative study, adolescents themselves saw gaming as an addiction, whereas young adults perceived it more as a way to improve cognitive and social communication skills (Calado *et al.*, 2014). The perceptions of young people in this study were that the underlying goal of gaming was winning and they believed that the pleasures of open competition were the main driver for games becoming compulsive and addictive. Gaming also provides 'cathartic effects' in game violence such as maiming and killing. Recent studies indicate that adolescents (12–18 years) are particularly vulnerable to gaming addiction due to leisure boredom and the leisure time they have at their disposal (Calado *et al.*, 2014). These then become some of the unintended harms and risks of the gaming environment and underpin cautionary tales on the web and elsewhere of the negative effects of gaming.

I argue here that gaming is contradictory in terms of agency and constraint on the individual in that both free will and control are experienced almost together in the highly commodified and globalised gaming industry. The issue of social constraints or social control as an aim of market strategies, and within gaming design and technology in such a commercialised for-profit industry, is complex. Whether or not it is an intentional part of companies' strategies is difficult to test empirically. Companies' marketing strategies and activities do however mean that individual players are highly exposed to the global market in their personal lives in, for example, their bedrooms and in other gaming spaces, including on mobile phones. Given the strategic marketing reach of such corporate big business in designing and marketing virtual leisure worlds, any decommodifed and authentic leisure experience is probably at best fleeting. I have used secondary data sources in this chapter to explore such possibilities. The perceived personal freedoms and self-representation of identity offered to players are manufactured and constrained within the design and marketing of the games themselves. On the one hand, gamers are immersed in the freedoms of communities of play and spontaneity (Pearce and Artemesia, 2009). On the other, gamers' identities are constrained by and within hyper-consumptive mechanical solidarity. Is this gaming leisure outside or inside compressions of time? This phenomenology of time in contemporary second modernity helps us understand how virtual belonging and relationships with others is constructed in gaming (Levinas, 1987, 2006; Janack, 2012). The reflexive leisure of this gaming is 'slowing down time' and perhaps allowing gamers to cope better generally with everyday anxieties and the modernities of the real-world 'risk society' (Beck, 1992). Anecdotal evidence appears to show that gamers, once immersed in major gaming cultures, will stay with the game for several years, building their confidence, competence and expertise within the game (ESA, 2015). Games like *World of Warcraft* (WWC) have been around for more than a decade and at one stage in the mid-2000s had over ten million players. Long-term players are building their gaming identity and also developing 'soft skills' for relationships in the real world. Nonetheless, they are also using up valuable time and energy in video-based and online activity that may have been better spent in terms of emotional and mental health on real-world leisure pursuits.

Another, darker dimension to this new leisure reality is anonymous immersion in the realms of prejudice and harassment of gaming conversations and communication. One of the important areas in the development of gaming is the gamer's apparent right to anonymous 'free speech' where a particularly extreme form is sometimes labelled 'trash talk'. This also raises questions about the dangers of virtual sociability in cyberbullying and harassment. These online conversations, Gray (2014) argues, effectively give pleasure to aberrant gamers by trash-talking others. Their conversations are commonly laced with homophobic, racist and sexist slurs within headset conversations taking place in gaming worlds. This darker side of gaming cultures perpetuates hegemonic oppressive views of social groupings from the wider realities of the non-virtual community (http://venturebeat.com/community/2011/05/12/how-to-survive-multiplayer-trash-talk/).

Questions are raised by this chapter as to whether young people are experiencing new forms of digital sociability and identity from those of first (industrial) modernity in affluent societies. Youth gaming as leisure activity is best explained in second (post-industrial) modernity as the creation of new social spaces and potential 'inner worlds' and personal journeys of youth. These youth immerse themselves in the narratives and fantasies of gaming role-plays in manufactured but nonetheless potentially liberating worlds of hyper-consumption. How identity is constructed in the intricate play and manufactured spontaneity of these games requires intensive research and analysis. More research is needed, for example, on the gendered nature of this gaming play (McRobbie, 2008). Space is created in this manufactured imaginary play for a new and potentially healthy engagement with (as well as potentially healthy resistance from) lived realities and normalising youth identities in society. Under these terms, the development of otherness or alterity can have some claim to being part of the gamer's authentic leisure quest over time. This quest is potentially oppositional to authoritative and normalising youth identities. This authentic leisure is theorised as a kind of spontaneous anarchism of authentic play in second modernity that derives from the sociability and social capital of online play and subsequently affects leisure biographies.

Conclusion

This chapter has outlined some of the dimensions of experiential consciousness in understanding gaming culture's embeddedness in second modernity. I have highlighted, in particular, how the spontaneity of gaming may help players find new 'inner' configurations of identity and forms of consciousness previously largely unknown on this scale to humankind. There is a balance here in such new leisure cultures between creating positive identities and new languages of self, and the negative consequences of boredom in everyday life leading to addictions and compulsivity. The new 'bedroom culture' invokes an inward-looking and inner-world othering within the visual–verbal–text-based spatial and time dimensions of play. Young people's gaming subjectivities become part of a different and emerging set of realities that make them 'other like' in authentic gaming leisure pursuits. Gaming is an enormous and expanding consumerist industry and a leisure culture that perhaps challenges our accepted notions of alienation and isolation for gamers themselves almost despite its manufacture within the hyper-consumptive world of second modernity.

Acknowledgement

I would like to thank my son Aron Wearing for his background knowledge on these games and his assistance in shaping this section of the chapter.

References

Bauman, Z. (2000) *Liquid Modernity*. Cambridge: Polity Press.
Beck, U. (1992) *The Risk Society*. London: Sage.
Beck, U. (1999) *World Risk Society*. Cambridge: Polity Press.
Beck, U. (2000) The cosmopolitan perspective: Sociology of the second age of modernity. *British Journal of Sociology*, 51(1): 79–105.
Beck, U. and Grande, E. (2010) The varieties of second modernity: The cosmopolitian turn in social and political theory research. *British Journal of Sociology*, 61(3): 409–443.
Beck, U. and Lau, C. (2005) Second modernity as a research agenda: Theoretical and empirical explorations in the 'meta-change' of modern society. *British Journal of Sociology*, 56(4): 525–557.
Brookes, F.M., Cester, K.L., Smeeton, N.C. and Spencer, N.H. (2016) Video gaming in adolescence: Factors associated with leisure time use. *Journal of Youth Studies*, 19(1): 36–54.
Calado, F., Alexandre, J. and Griffiths, M.D. (2014) Mom, Dad it's only a game! Perceived gambling and gaming behaviours among adolescents and young adults: An exploratory study. *International Journal of Mental Health Addiction*, 12: 772–794.
Chang, K. (2010) The second modern condition? Compressed modernity as internalized reflexive cosmopolitanization. *British Journal of Sociology*, 61(3): 444–464.
Culp, J. (2014) *Online Gaming: Safety and Privacy*. New York: Rosen Publishing Group.
Drummond, A. and Sauer, J.D. (2014) Video games do not negatively impact adolescent academic performance in science, mathematics or reading. *PLOS One* (online open access journal), 9(4): 5.
Dunlop, J.C. (2007) The U.S. video game industry: Analysing representation of gender and race. *International Journal of Technology and Human Interaction*, 312: 96–109.
ESA (Entertainment Software Association) (2015) *Essential Facts About the Computer and Video Game Industry*. Sales, Demographics and Usage Data. Available at: www.theesa.com/wp-content/uploads/2015/04/ESA-Essential-Facts-2015.pdf (accessed 21 January 2016).
Foucault, M. (1990) *The History of Sexuality, An Introduction: Volume* I. New York: Vintage.
Gee, J.P. (2011) *An Introduction to Discourse Analysis* (2nd edn). London: Routledge.
Giddens, A. (1990) *The Consequences of Modernity*. Cambridge: Polity Press.
Giddings, S. (2007) Playing with non-humans: Digital games as technocultural form. In S. de Castell and J. Jenson (eds) *Worlds in Play: International Perspectives on Digital Games Research*. New York: Peter Lang (pp. 115–128).
Giroux, H.A. (2011) How Disney magic and the corporate media shape youth identity in the digital age. *Truthout*, 21 August. Available at: http://truth-out.org) (accessed 12 May 2015).
Goffman, E. (1971) *The Presentation of Self in Everyday Life*. New York: Penguin Books.
Gray, K.L. (2014) *Race, Gender, and Deviance in Xbox Live*. Oxford: Anderson Publishing.
Harrell, D.F. (2010) Designing empowering and critical identities in social computing and gaming. *CoDesign: International Journal of Cocreation in Design and Art*, 6(4): 187–206.
Hebdidge, D. (1979) *Subculture – The Meaning of Style*. London: Routledge.
Hickinbottom-Brawn, S. (2013) Brand 'you': The emergence of social anxiety disorder in the age of enterprise. *Theory and Psychology*, 23(6): 732–751.
Hutchins, B. (2008) Signs of meta-change in second modernity: The growth of e-sport and the World Cyber Games. *New Media and Society*, 10(6): 851–869.
Janack, M. (2012) *What We Mean by Experience*. Stanford, CA: Stanford University Press.

Jin. D.Y. (2010) *Korea's Online Gaming Empire*. Cambridge, MA: The MIT Press.

Kyung-Sup, C. (2010) The second modern condition? Compressed modernity as internalized reflexive cosmopolitization. *British Journal of Sociology*, 61(3): 444–464.

Levinas, E. (1987) *Time and the Other*, trans. R. Cohen. Pittsburgh, PA: Duquesne University Press.

Levinas, E. (2006) *Humanism of the Other*, Introduction by R.A. Cohen, trans. N. Poller. Baltimore: University of Illinois Press.

Lin, H. and Sun, C. (2015) Massively multiplayer online role playing games (MMORPGs). In R. Mansell and P.H. Ang (eds) *The International Encyclopedia of Digital Communication and Society* (1st edn). London: John Wiley (pp. 1–7).

Lundmark, S. (2015) Gaming together: When an imaginary world affects generalised trust. *Journal of Information Technology and Politics*, 12: 54–73.

Marcuse, H. (1991) *One Dimensional Man* (2nd edn). London: Routledge.

Martley, M., Stromer-Galley, J., Banks, J., Wu, J. and Consalvo, M. (2014) The strategic female: Gender switching and player behaviour in online games. *Information Communication and Society*, 17(3): 286–300.

McRobbie, A. (2008) Young women and consumer culture: An intervention. *Cultural Studies*, 22(5): 531–550.

Mead, G.H. (1934) *Mind, Self and Society*. Chicago, IL: University of Chicago Press.

Moira, S. and Livingstone, M. (2001) Bedroom culture and the privatization of media use. In S. Moira and M. Livingstone (eds) *Children and their Changing Media Environment*. Englewood Cliffs, NJ: Lawrence Erlbaum (pp. 179–200).

Natkin, S. (2006) *Video Games and Interactive Media: A Glimpse of New Digital Entertainment*. Massachusetts: A.K. Peters.

Pearce, C. and Artemesia (2009) *Communities of Play: Emergent Cultures in Multiplayer Games and Virtual Worlds*. Cambridge: The MIT Press.

Robinson R.B. and Robinson Riegler, G. (2012) *Cognitive Psychology: Applying the Science of the Mind* (3rd edn). Boston, MA: Pearson.

Rojek, C. (1993) *Ways of Escape: Modern Transformations in Leisure and Travel*. London: Palgrave Macmillan.

Said, E. (1995) *Orientalism* (2nd edn). London: Palgrave. First published 1978.

Sclater, M. and Lafty, V. (2014) The realities of researching alongside virtual youth in late modernity creative practices and activity theory. *Journal of Youth Studies*, 17(1): 1–25.

Simmel, G. (1950) *The Sociology of Georg Simmel*. London: The Free Press.

Sublette, V.A. and Mullan, B. (2012) Consequences of play: A systematic review of the effects of online gaming. *International Journal of Mental Health and Addiction*, 10(1): 3–23.

Taylor, I. and Cohen, S. (1992) *Escape Attempts: The Theory and Practice of Resistance in Everyday Life*. London: Routledge.

Taylor, T.L. (2006) *Play between Worlds: Exploring Online Game Culture*. Cambridge, MA: MIT Press.

Walkerdine, V. (2007) *Children, Gender, Video Games: Towards a Relational Approach to Multi-media*. Basingstoke: Palgrave Macmillan.

Wearing, M.J. (2015) The experiential bond: The impact of research with at-risk youth – The relational and ethical challenges of qualitative research. In H.B. Holmarsdottir and S. Bastien (eds) *Youth at the Margins*. Rotterdam: Sense Publishers (pp. 65–86).

Wolf, M. (2015) Introduction. In M. Wolf (ed.) *Video Games Around the World*. Cambridge, MA: The MIT Press (pp. 1–16).

Yates, S. and Littleton, K. (2001) Understanding computer game cultures: A situated approach. In E. Green and A. Adam (eds) *Virtual Gender: Technology, Consumption and Identity*. London: Routledge (pp. 103–123).

Yu, T.W. (2009) Learning in the virtual world: The pedagogical potentials of massively multiplayer online role playing games. *International Educational Studies*, 2(1): 32–38.

12 *E'gao* as a networked digital leisure practice in China

Haiqing Yu and Jian Xu

Introduction

E'gao is a Chinese term for online spoofing. It literally means 'evil (*e*) doings (*gao*)'. The word is often linked to the Japanese *kuso*, which is translated into Chinese as *kewu* (repulsive, horrible). It is also compared to the Cantonese technique of 'wu li tou' ('mo lei tau' in Cantonese, meaning silly talk), made popular in China through Hong Kong comedy films such as those of Stephen Chow. The character 恶 (pronounced 'er') means evil and wicked. The character 搞 (pronounced 'gao') means to do/make/manage/get/organise and fuck (slang). It carries a sense of playfulness, tricks, mischief, deviance, double-dealing, unsettling, messing up and maliciousness. To Chinese speakers, the word *e'gao* invokes the spirit of humour, irony, satire and wicked fun.

E'gao is an online phenomenon that started in the early 2000s. It can be a clever wordplay or skilful multimedia manipulation of texts, audio and visual elements. It often uses techniques such as punning, pastiche, burlesque, lip-synching and remixing of digital footage. *E'gao* products are highly intertextual; that is, they are designed for insiders, people who are already familiar with Chinese language, prototypical works or formats of *e'gao*, and Chinese political culture. This explains the popularity of *e'gao* on the Chinese internet, and yet very few can be translated into English for global consumption.

A 20-minute online spoof of a 2005 blockbuster film directed by China's renowned filmmaker Chen Kaige, *The Promise* (Wuji), set the scene for the craze for the *e'gao* cultural phenomenon by the average Chinese netizens, researchers, observers and journalists with a focus on China. This *e'gao* video, called *A Bloody Case Caused by a Steamed Bun*, has been central to almost all discussions about *e'gao* and Chinese internet culture in the twenty-first century (Gong and Yang, 2010; Li, 2011; Meng, 2011; Yu, 2007, 2015). These discussions have unpacked the techniques in *e'gao*, their political significance and cultural implications. It is argued that *e'gao* is a networked practice of online political satire (Yang and Jiang, 2015); an alternative means of social engagement with, political critique of and cultural intervention in mainstream culture (Voci, 2010; Meng, 2011); and a digital reproduction of a rich repertoire of satire, humour and parody in oral and written forms in Chinese popular culture, and a product of Chinese post-socialist techno-political conditions (Yu, 2015).

This chapter explores the *e'gao* phenomenon as a networked digital leisure practice. It argues for a rethinking of the de facto 'democratic ethos' of popular practices, and questions both the 'repressive hypothesis' (with the state as the culprit of media censorship of popular discourses, including *e'gao*) and the 'empowerment hypothesis' (with the Chinese netizens as rebels and heroes in producing a resistance culture). Rather, *e'gao* represents the networking and play elements in Chinese leisure culture. Its strength comes from its ability to play with the establishment culture and structure, and to engage in playful conversations with power.

E'gao as a networked digital leisure practice

China not only has a long history of popular dissent through humour, irony and satire, but also a turbulent history in leisure culture. Popular leisure activities, including making and sharing jokes, were highly politicised in the Mao era (1949–1976). People were criticised and punished for engaging in 'petty bourgeois amusements' if they were involved in any leisure activity (such as keeping a pet or collecting stamps) (Wang, 1995: 156). The withdrawal of the party state from everyday life and the depoliticisation of Chinese society in the Deng era led to a gradual restructuring of people's work and leisure lives. Leisure spaces grew and expanded, from parks, museums, streets and public squares to shopping malls, tea houses, cinemas, bookstores, restaurants and internet cafés, and to the more 'sexy' nightlife spaces such as massage parlours, discos, karaoke parlours, nightclubs, bars, dancing clubs, saunas and beauty salons.

The arrival of the internet to the Chinese public in 1996 provided an alternative space for young people to enjoy leisure activities such as gaming, networking or simply surfing the net. For a long time, chatting with friends via QQ (a Chinese instant messaging tool), playing computer games, listening to music and watching movies via desktop computers at home or visiting internet cafés was a popular pastime among the young technical enthusiasts and social elites. The internet café first emerged in 1996 around China's Ivy-league universities in Beijing. It was not long before internet cafés in China migrated from being salons for the intellectual and social elites to everyday spaces for students, migrant workers and other information-poor working classes. Internet cafés, as the major venue of leisure for Chinese youths, have declined since 2008, as broadband and smartphones are readily available at home in urban areas, but internet cafés remain the main venue for underdeveloped areas and the floating population (Qiu, 2009). In the countryside and small towns the internet café penetration rate was still as high as 54.9 per cent among youth as of 2009 (CNNIC, 2010).

Chinese leisure spaces are highly stratified and reinforce forms of socio-economic inequality. People in large cities enjoy a vibrant leisure scene with a strong consumerism flavour, while those in the countryside, less developed urban areas or at the lower end of the socio-economic ladder have less choice. Urban middle-class youths are more likely to engage in a rich variety of online leisure activities, including producing, sharing and consuming *e'gao* products, than their counterparts at the lower end of the socio-economic ladder. There is no evidence to suggest that the 'little people' (such as peasants, rural-to-city migrant workers, laid-off factory workers and ethnic minorities) engage in *e'gao* cultural production, whether for profit or social networking, for self-expression or simply fun-seeking. Their use of online leisure space (accessible often via internet cafés and mobile phones) is often guided by pragmatism. It is an extension of their social networks, a practical and emotional tool and space to live out both sociality and intimacy (Wallis, 2013).

The structural inequality in accessing online space is further compounded by the nature of leisure in the context of China's consumer culture. The rise of the new rich in China, rampant consumerism and commodity fetishism render any potential civil discourse and resistance less conspicuous in the public sphere. Rather, leisure activities are associated with spending money, building *guanxi* (a personalised network of influence and benefit) and establishing status (Davis, 2000). Online political satire, such as *e'gao*, is used to accumulate and advance one's cultural and social capital. The networked practices in producing, circulating and meaning construction through *e'gao* have offered opportunities for amateur online spoofers to benefit both politically and financially as they ostensibly express dissent while having fun at the same time (Yu, 2015). Similar to the state's regulation of public leisure spaces and activities, as long as *e'gao* and *e'gao* spoofers do not pose any serious threat to the Chinese social and political order, stability or moral sentiments, the party state simply keeps one eye on them while keeping the other closed. This explains the prevalence of *e'gao* on the Chinese internet.

The discussion of *e'gao* as an innocuous digital leisure practice is not intended to deny its political significance as a practice of everyday life. As Michel de Certeau (1984: xiv) has argued, the unnoticed, mundane, inconspicuous qualities of everyday (leisure) activities make them an important site for resistance to the disciplinary power 'by means of a multitude of "tactics" ... taken by the dispersed, tactical, and make-shift creativity of groups or individuals already caught in the nets of "discipline"'. In the Chinese context, leisure activities offer opportunities for socialisation and social mobility to people who provide leisure services (including migrant workers), even though they are subject to the web of subordination and inequality in contesting power relations (Zheng, 2008). Leisure activities and spaces can be 'productive in terms of new social relations and cultural expressions' and 'new spaces for alternative expressions of identity, including political aspirations' at the same time (Farrer, 2008: 2). Even internet cafés can be a vital site for Chinese citizens to engage in guerrilla warfare with the state, with owners providing illegal websites and not complying with the state regulation on user ID registration in order to attract more customers, and with users occasionally posting pieces in their blogs or Youku on social and political issues (Sun, 2012).

The tension between (individual) agency and (political) structure and between official and popular leisure ethics has been played out in both online and offline spaces. The official leisure ethics promote 'healthy' leisure activities that are used to maintain social order and harmony, and increase the cultural competence or *suzhi* (quality) of individuals and thereby the *suzhi* of the population indirectly (Rolandsen, 2011: 65). The popular desire is more about play (or 'wan' in Chinese), about having and poking fun at whatever subject that can cause resonance and reactions among fellow citizens, and about sharing such fun with friends. This is often played out in the digitised and networked leisure space (the internet) and practice (*e'gao*).

E'gao as a networked digital leisure practice exemplifies the many contradictions and incongruities of Chinese leisure culture and digital culture, as briefly discussed above. It demonstrates the creativity of Chinese people, as it often plays with the 'establishment' culture by mocking and poking fun at it. At the same time it affirms the cultural authority of the 'establishment' that it is supposedly to subvert and resist. Hu Ge's famous *e'gao* video is not meant to challenge or subvert Chen Kaige's authority as one of China's best filmmakers; nor has it succeeded in doing so inadvertently. As the following case study demonstrates, playing with the 'establishment' can be an easy way to unleash popular creativity without bearing too much political risk.

Playing with the 'establishment'

China Central Television (CCTV) is one of the most popular targets for netizens to 'play with', from its logo, headquarters building and presenters to its brand programmes. Established in 1958, CCTV is one of the 'big three' party state organ media organisations, along with *People's Daily* and Xinhua News Agency, which are the so-called 'tongue and throat' of the party state. It is under the direct control of the State Administration of Radio, Film and Television (SARFT) – one of the highest decision-making institutions to formulate China's media policies, industry standards and regulations. This endorses CCTV with both authority and monopoly over China's television market. It is now a network of 42 channels, 31 domestic and 70 international bureaux, and over 1.2 billion viewers globally. CCTV's official background, state-sanctioned discursive power and market monopoly sustain each other, making it both a powerful mouthpiece and a successful 'money spinner' (Zhao, 1999).

CCTV's dominance in the Chinese television market has been constantly challenged from regional broadcasters (Zhong, 2007), digital content providers, as well as viewers. The rapid development of online broadcasting, IPTV, mobile TV and the internet has unprecedentedly increased ordinary people's sources of information (Keane, 2015), and their dissatisfaction with CCTV's dominance. Since 2005, *e'gao* has become a popular way for ordinary viewers, particularly internet-savvy young viewers, to tactically and playfully express their dissatisfaction with CCTV. Many of CCTV's established programmes have become the prototypes of online *e'gao*. *Network News* (*Xinwen lianbo*), the most watched television programme in China, is one such case.

Network News is CCTV's flagship programme broadcast daily from 7 p.m. to 7.30 p.m. Commonly known in China as the 'weather vane of Chinese politics', it focuses on government announcements, national leaders' activities, commentaries of state media and inspiring events of the nation. Although in recent years more social news has been included, *Network News* remains very authoritarian, propagandistic and formulaic. A popular joke aptly sums up its content in 'three segments': 'The first ten minutes show how busy the national leaders are; the second ten minutes on how the motherland is developing rapidly; and the last ten minutes about how chaotic Western countries are.' Moreover, *Network News* is the only TV programme in China that is required to be simultaneously relayed by broadcasters at provincial, municipal and county levels. This makes *Network News* China's most-watched news programme. Watching *Network News* has become a national ritual and routine for ordinary Chinese at the dinner table. The programme is like an everyday media ritual and a virtual 'family head' to guide dinner table discussions, and as such construct an enhanced 'family–state' relationship (Guo, 2012: 105).

The 'popularity' and pervasiveness of *Network News* makes it an easy target in the networked digital leisure practice of *e'gao*. Its formulaic format, vacuous content and didactic style have 'inspired' many spoofers. A search on Baidu.com, China's leading search engine, using the Chinese keywords 恶搞 (*e'gao*) and 新闻联播 (*Network News*) on 20 August 2015 revealed 3.13 million results. These *e'gao* works may be divided approximately into three categories: *duanzi*, digital remix and copycatted video production.

Duanzi refers to textual jokes or anecdotes that critically reflect social problems in a humorous and satirical way, and it is one of the most popular cultural genres in Chinese society (Yang and Jiang, 2015). With a long tradition in China's satirical literature, theatres and cross-talk, *duanzi* has gone digitised in the internet age. Making, sharing and consuming *duanzi* via the internet, text message and social media platforms has become one of the most important leisure and entertainment activities in Chinese people's everyday lives. *Duanzi* to mock and make fun of *Network News* abound on Chinese digital platforms. One of the most widely circulated *duanzi* online is *I Have a Dream* (*Network News* Version).

I Have a Dream is an internationally well-known public speech delivered by American civil rights activist Martin Luther King in 1963, which has greatly inspired civil rights movements throughout the world. Chinese netizens selected the climax part of the speech and replaced the original speech with satirical words to poke fun at *Network News* as follows.

> I have a dream: to live forever in *Network News*, where all government officials perform duties honestly, all ordinary people are moral models. Though occasionally a corruptive official is caught, this would only cause brief news reporting as if nothing had happened.... I have a dream: to live forever in *Network News*, where all children can go to school, poor people could afford medical treatment, people pay only 77 *yuan* per month for renting a house, wage growth has reached 11.2%, the employment rate of university students has reached 99.13%.... I have a dream: to live forever in *Network News*. It is a place full of love, a paradise on earth and a world of dream.
>
> (Woyou yige meng, 2011)

E'gao *a networked leisure practice in China* 157

This *duanzi* mocks the selective reporting of *Network News* on positive rather than negative news and critiques the so-called objectivity and credibility of China's most powerful broadcaster in news reportage. The mash-up of the pattern of Martin Luther King's speech with the flamboyant style, flowery language and rosy picture that is typical of *Network News* and its content is meant to highlight contrast and evoke laughter.

In addition to textual *duanzi*, tech-savvy netizens also use multimedia, such as Photoshop, one of the most popular image-editing software, and other video-dubbing software to remix parts of original images or texts of *Network News* with images or texts from various sources to create a humorous effect. One of the most widely shared remixed pictures is the transplanted heads of Guo Degang (a well-known cross-talk actor and comedian) and Chen Luyu (a famous talk show host described as 'China's Oprah') as the male and female anchors of *Network News* (see Figure 12.1). Moreover, some netizens have dubbed CCTV's *Network News* with local dialects, making it more approachable and attractive to local audiences who do not speak Mandarin. The head transplantation and dialect dubbing make the *e'gao Network News* hilarious to Chinese viewers for their transgression of both linguistic boundaries and political correctness.

The *e'gao* spoofers do not stop at Photoshop-edited pictures and re-dubbed videos. Some go further to produce copycatted *Network News*. These copycatted

Figure 12.1 Transplantation of head images of Chen Luyu (left) and Guo Degang (right) into the anchors of CCTV's *Network News* (http://news.qq.com/a/20090616/000691.htm).

videos are different from the re-dubbed videos that are highly reliant on the original texts. They are more innovative and original with little remixing work. They are more like self-produced mini-films, in which anchorpersons and people featured in the news are acted out by amateurs such as university students, kindergarten kids or bloggers. These videos imitate the rhetoric and style of *Network News* to report fictitious news stories about mundane events such as toilet blockages in student dormitories. The contrast between their low-quality video production and the CCTV's high-quality production, as well as the discrepancy between official discourses and personal stories, make the copycatted versions satirical and entertaining. *Dormitory Network News* (*Sushe xinwen liabo*) is one such video that plays with *Network News*.

Dormitory Network News begins with the familiar prelude of CCTV *Network News*. One male and one female university student broadcast news in a classroom sitting behind the teacher's desk in front of the blackboard. On the blackboard, a world map and a map of China are sketched with chalk. The bottom of the screen reads 'Student Flat TV Station, *Network News* November 10, 2011' (see Figure 12.2). The two anchorpersons use the stereotyped official language of *Network News*, filled with flowery, empty and clichéd phrases and slogans, to report fictitious news happening in Nos 343 and 435 student dorms. One of the news items reports that the toilet in No. 343 dorm has become blocked. The news item is presented in the same way that serious accidents, such as mining disasters, were reported in *Network News*. Similarly, the emphasis is not on the victims but on rescue efforts and the leadership of such efforts. In the 'news', the

Figure 12.2 Dormitory Network News (http://bbs.tiexue.net/post_5606847_1.html).

security captain, chief officials of the Ministry of Water Resources and Ministry of Pipeline of the dorm come to the toilet to lead the 'rescue and relief work'. Accompanying staff hold up umbrellas and fans for the leaders at the toilet door. The news ends with a formulaic phrase used conventionally in China's crisis reporting:

> [C]hief officials from relevant departments immediately arrived at the scene, guided the rescue and relief work, commanded to eliminate dangerous situation quickly, cope with the aftermath issues properly, identify the cause of the accident and settle the consolation affairs in a proper way for the victims' relatives and families.

To a Chinese audience this copycatted *Network News* highlights many of the abnormalities of Chinese politics that have become routine, such as the incompetency of China's Leviathan bureaucracy, official corruption and arrogance, and the nature of crisis reporting in China (with a focus on the activities of government officials rather than on the victims and causes of accidents).

Netizens' *e'gao* craze to play with the 'establishment' does not stop with *Network News*. Other popular programmes of CCTV are also spoofed in similar ways, though not as much as *Network News*, such as its *Spring Festival Gala* (*Chunjie lianhuan wanhui*) and *Lecture Room* (*Baijia jiangtan*). The popular practice to play with and tease the cultural establishment can provoke a critical contemplation of the so-called 'mainstream' cultural products that people have taken for granted. Nevertheless, such playful and symbolic resistance is usually light-hearted, without posing any challenge or bringing changes to the reality. *Network News* is still the ideology and money spinner for CCTV. CCTV's dominance in Chinese TV industry and its role as an ideological apparatus remain unchallenged and unchallengeable under the current political system.

As a networked digital leisure practice, *e'gao* forms a symbiotic and parasitic relationship with power (both market power and political power), even when it purportedly resists and subverts it. Its playfulness can be dialogical and a safe way to start a conversation with power by mobilising public emotions, particularly in online protests involving official wrongdoings, which in turn forces the latter to respond to the e-public opinion represented by *e'gao* pieces.

Playful conversation with power

Humour, satire and irony have long been used in social movements as effective means to publicly express and display subversive emotions in democratic and authoritarian societies (t'Hart, 2007). In the digital era, playful resistance has gone digitised and viral in popular protests. For example, political jokes, humour and satire greatly increased on social media sites and became the propeller of protests in the Arab Spring and Occupy Movements (Hassan, 2013; Vila, 2011). In China, *e'gao* has constituted a very important component of the 'contentious conversation' (Tilly, 1998) to converse with power in online protests. It allows netizens to tactically avoid using politically sensitive keywords and circumvent internet censorship. Being widely circulated on the networked digital platforms, *e'gao* posts are most likely to cause strong resonation among participants, effectively mobilise public emotions and force the government to respond to the public concerns.

On 23 July 2011, two high-speed trains collided on a viaduct at Shuangyu near Wenzhou in Zhejiang Province. Six carriages were derailed, four of which fell off the viaduct. The crash killed 40 people and injured 192. After the accident, the government hastily oversaw rescue operations, ordered the burial of the derailed carriages, and issued directives to limit media coverage. This immediately evoked public outrage online. On Sina Weibo, the most popular microblogging platform in China, millions of users posted, commented and reposted on aspects of the accident to push the government to release the truth. Among millions of posts, *e'gao* posts played an important role in mobilising public sentiment against the government's shoddy crisis management and communication.

A bone of contention came after the government ordered the burial of the train wreckage. In the first press conference following the collision, held by the Ministry of Railways (MOR) on the evening of 24 July, Wang Yongping, the spokesperson for MOR, declared that the burial was for the convenience of the emergency rescue operation rather than to destroy the evidence. He added: 'whether you believe it or not, I certainly do.' When asked why rescuers had pulled a toddler out of the wreckage alive hours after the rescue effort had been officially called off, Wang said: 'it was a miracle.' Wang's attitude and the perfunctory answers he gave at the press conference immediately provoked an online relay of 'national sentence-making' (*Quanmin zaoju*), a networked practice of remaking satirical sentences by using popular internet buzzwords, phrases and sayings (Yang and Jiang, 2015: 5). Netizens generated a series of national sentence-making relays to mock Wang and MOR, such as following examples (Long, 2011):

> *Sentence 1*: 'Burying the derailed carriages was for harvesting more new high-speed trains in autumn. Whether you believe it or not, I certainly do.'
>
> *Sentence 2*: 'Baby formula made in China does not contain sex hormone. Whether you believe it or not, I certainly do.'
>
> *Sentence 3*: 'Beijing didn't have traffic jam today. It is a miracle, but it did happen. Whether you believe it or not, I certainly do.'

Dubbed 'high-speed train style' (*gaotie ti*), these sentences are a sarcastic commentary on Chinese corrupt bureaucracy, notorious road safety and traffic congestion, and food safety. The expression 'whether you believe it or not, I certainly do' is adopted to end such sentences. Netizens often compete with one another to come up with the next witty sentence. The networked practice encouraged mass consumption, reproduction and circulation as a way to start a dialogue among netizens and with the government.

E'gao *a networked leisure practice in China* 161

Netizens' *e'gao* practices in the context of the train crash do not stop at witty play with words. They have extended to include visual effect. In an *e'gao* poster called 'Never colliding high-speed train', the spoofer places several government officials in the first and last carriages, where they will be spared from the full impact of any train crash (see Figure 12.3). This simple poster makes clear a public secret: the lives of government officials are more valued than the common people. In another poster, pictures of Sheng Guangzu (the Party Chief and Minister of Railways), Wang Yongping, and Long Jing (the head of the Shanghai Railway Bureau) are Photoshopped into the background of the train wreckage. The three government officials are sarcastically named as leading actors in a make-believe disaster film called *Fatal Bullet Train* to celebrate the ninetieth anniversary of the founding of the Chinese Communist Party (CCP) (see Figure 12.4).

In China, where the internet is heavily censored and open critique of the government and the CCP may cause trouble, tactical critiques in the form of humour, satire and irony are relatively safe ways for ordinary people to engage in online disobedience. As Guobin Yang (2009) argues, satire is one of the most important emotional powers to mobilise online collective action in China. The stronger the satirical emotion, the stronger online public opinion would be, and the more likely the protest message would reach the wider public and finally set an agenda for the government. *E'gao* has been used as a communicative strategy by Chinese netizens to engage with power. The *e'gao* pieces discussed above invoke anger, frustration and outcry among Chinese netizens as they produce, share and consume them. The sympathy towards the victims and anger at the official cover-up and irresponsibility caused a strong emotional tide among the public. This tide became too strong to be confined in the online space. The authorities were forced to respond to public emotion. The MOR finally admitted that faulty signal technology had led to the collision, and relevant officials were demoted (Siu, 2011). Netizens' *e'gao* finally got a response from the 'power'. A playful conversation, rather than simply a monologue, is realised through *e'gao*.

Conclusion

This chapter has argued that *e'gao* takes on mainstream cultural forms and established media formats and reinterprets and reconstitutes them as a way to engage and start a conversation with power. It either plays with the establishment culture

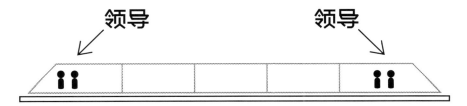

Figure 12.3 Design of the 'never colliding high-speed train' (http://danhuaer.com/t/15442).

Figure 12.4 Movie poster of *Fatal Bullet Train* (http://cn.uncyclopedia.wikia.com/wiki/伪基新闻:惊魂动车组在大陆全线 上映, 铁道部回应有关质疑).

and structure to satisfy consumer desires and popular needs, or engages in playful conversations with power in order to provoke a response from the latter. In both cases, it deconstructs and mimics elements from the 'authentic', 'established' and 'legitimate' cultural and political norms and structures. In both cases, it has not been able to challenge or reconstruct the establishment cultures. Nor has it altered the power relationship between the grassroots, which *e'gao* supposedly represents, and the political, economic and intellectual elites who own, regulate and control the basic architecture, facilities and services of Chinese leisure spaces, both online and offline.

Scholarly focus on the content and format of selected and often 'spectacular' *e'gao* cases should not overemphasise the narrowly defined and opportunistic understanding of empowerment and resistance in everyday leisure activities. As Wanning Sun (2008: 33–45) warns us, such 'spectacular visuality' dictates media reproduction (both online and offline) to focus on 'the eventful, the heroic and the entertaining' and 'articulate middle-class concerns, priorities, sentiments and sensibility', rather than the mundane, the ordinary and the routine of the everyday, and of the insignificant, peripheral and silent 'little people'. We concur with this observation. The impact of *e'gao* upon the ordinary and little people, who constitute the majority of the Chinese population, will determine the political significance of such a networked digital leisure practice. This is, understandably, difficult to measure.

With such a limitation in mind, we support Andrew Chubb's argument that the resistance embodied by China's *shanzhai* culture and the popular 'Grabism' practices 'appears either superficial, or paralleled by contradictory impulses of affirmation of the same authority it purportedly subverts' (Chubb, 2015: 276). Chinese online spoofers choose to mock, clone, make fun of and pick a fight with the cultural and political establishment (such as CCTV), but fall short of challenging or subverting the discursive violence and dominance of such an establishment. *E'gao* provides the venue for Chinese people to talk back to the structure of domination and an imagined sense of empowerment when the establishment structure or institution chooses to respond to such grassroots ethos. As Haiqing Yu (2015: 63) argues, the laughter invoked by *e'gao* pieces should be viewed as:

> a celebration of grassroots creativity in transgressing social and political boundaries and in capitalizing on such transgressions for personal gains, both financially and symbolically. The expected counterdiscourse, however, is most likely to be silenced and drowned in the sanitized online carnival, which promotes a spiral of silence and cyber-dislocation of open and serious discussions of political significance.

E'gao does not constitute a countercultural movement, which is concerned with reaching out to mass audiences, engaging in highly visible public acts to create alternative politics and transform public spaces, or generating and reconstructing a new cultural consciousness (Cox, 2011). Nor does it constitute a resistant culture where humour, satire and irony are used in social movements as a potentially subversive tool (t'Hart, 2007). *E'gao* has not been able to transcend cultural barriers to reach out to a wider audience than the Han Chinese, or class barriers to transmit alternative messages to the 'little people'. It may best be viewed as a mild form of culture jamming that aims to engage audiences emotionally, rather than politically or intellectually, so that they can see established cultural codes, norms and practices in a new light. However, even this aim cannot be guaranteed, as the 'ambiguity and multiplicity of meaning' implied in cultural resistance – in this case *e'gao* – may be misinterpreted, rejected, 'ignored, or missed altogether' (Fominaya, 2014: 99). As *e'gao* becomes routinised, commodified and normalised as part of the 'mainstream' leisure activity on the Chinese internet, it is no longer alternative or cutting-edge.

References

Chubb, A. (2015) China's Shanzhai culture: 'Grabism' and the politics of hybridity. *Journal of Contemporary China*, 24(92): 260–279.
CNNIC (2010) 2009年中国青少年上网行为调查报告 (*2009 Survey Report on Chinese Youth Online Behaviours*). China Internet Network Information Centre. Available at: https://www.cnnic.net.cn/hlwfzyj/hlwfzzx/qwfb/201004/t20100426_31164.htm (accessed 11 September 2015).
Cox, L. (2011) *Building Counter Culture: The Radical Praxis of Social Movement Milieu*. Helsiniki. Available at: Into-ebooks (accessed 10 September 2015).
Davis, D. (ed.) (2000) *The Consumer Revolution in Urban China*. Berkeley: University of California Press.
De Certeau, M. (1984) *The Practice of Everyday Life*. Berkeley: University of California Press.
Farrer, J. (2008) Play and power in Chinese nightlife spaces. *China: An International Journal*, 6(1): 1–17.
Fominaya, C.F. (2014) *Social Movements and Globalization: How Protests, Occupations and Uprisings are Changing the World*. New York: Palgrave Macmillan.
Gong, H. and Yang, X. (2010) Digitized parody: The politics of egao in contemporary China. *China Information*, 24(1): 3–26.
Guo, J. (2012) 'Family' vs. 'state' in media ritual: Fieldwork in an ethnic minority village in Yunnan province. In W. Sun and J. Chio (eds) *Mapping Media in China: Region, Province, Locality*. London and New York: Routledge (pp. 94–106).
Hassan, B.A. (2013) The pragmatics of humor: January 25th Revolution and Occupy Wall Street. *Mediterranean Journal of Social Sciences*, 4(2): 551–562.
Keane, M. (2015) *The Chinese Television Industry*. New York: Palgrave Macmillan.
Li, H. (2011) Parody and resistance on the Chinese internet'. In D.K. Herold and P. Marolt (eds) *Online Society in China: Creating, Celebrating, and Instrumentalising the Online Carnival*. London and New York: Routledge (pp. 71–88).
Long, W. (2011) 高铁体 成网络流行语 (*High-speed Train Style has Become Buzzword Online*), 26 July. William Long: Blog. Available at: www.williamlong.info/blog/archives/857.html (accessed 2 September 2015).
Meng, B. (2011) From steamed bun to grass mud horse: E Gao as alternative political discourse on the Chinese internet. *Global Media and Communication*, 7(1): 33–51.

Qiu, J.L. (2009) *Working-class Network Society: Communication Technology and the Information Have-less in Urban China*. Cambridge, MA: The MIT Press.

Rolandsen, U.M. (2011) *Leisure and Power in Urban China: Everyday Life in a Chinese City*. Abingdon: Taylor & Francis.

Siu, T. (2011) China rail firm boss, blamed for crash, dies of heart attack. Available at: www.reuters.com/article/2011/08/23/us-china-railways-idUSTRE77M2H820110823 (accessed 2 September 2015).

Sun, H. (2012) *Internet Policy in China: A Field Study of Internet Cafes*. Lanham, MD: Lexington Books.

Sun, W. (2008) The curse of the everyday: Politics of representation and new social semiotics in post-socialist China. In K. Sen and T. Lee (eds) *Political Regimes and the Media in Asia*. London and New York: Routledge (pp. 31–48).

t'Hart, M. (2007) Humour and social protest. *International Review of Social History*, 52(S15): 1–20.

Tilly, C. (1998) Contentious conversation. *Social Research*, 65: 491–510.

Vila, S. (2011) Social media and satire fuel Arab Spring in Tunisia, Egypt. Available at: http://mediashift.org/2011/07/social-media-and-satire-fuel-arab-spring-in-tunisia-egypt195/ (accessed 2 September 2015).

Voci, P. (2010) *China on Video: Smaller-screen Realities*. London and New York: Routledge.

Wallis, C. (2013) *Technobility in China: Young Migrant Women and Mobile Phones*. New York: New York University Press.

Wang, S. (1995) The politics of private time: Changing leisure patterns in urban China. In D.S. Davis, R. Kraus, B. Naughton and E.J. Perry (eds) *Urban Spaces in Contemporary China: The Potential for Autonomy and Community in Post-Mao China*. Cambridge and New York: Cambridge University Press (pp. 149–172).

Woyou yige meng (2011) 我有一个梦想》——要永远生活在新闻联播里 (*I Have a Dream* – To live in the *Network News* forever). Available at: http://bbs.tiexue.net/post_5220300_1.html (accessed 30 August 2015).

Yang, G. (2009) 悲情与戏谑：网络事件中的情感动员 (Of sympathy and play: Emotional moblisation in online collective action). 传播与社会学刊 (*Communication and Society Quarterly*), 9: 39–66.

Yang, G. and Jiang, M. (2015) The networked practice of online political satire in China: Between ritual and resistance. *International Communication Gazette*, 77(3): 215–231.

Yu, H. (2007) Blogging everyday life in Chinese internet culture. *Asian Studies Review*, 31(4): 423–433.

Yu, H. (2015) After the 'Steamed Bun': E'gao and its postsocialist politics. *Chinese Literature Today*, 5(1): 55–64.

Zhao, B. (1999) Mouthpiece or money-spinner? The double life of Chinese television in the late 1990s. *International Journal of Cultural Studies*, 2(3): 291–305.

Zheng, T. (2008) Complexity of life and resistance: Informal networks of rural migrant karaoke bar hostesses in urban Chinese sex industry. *China: An International Journal*, 6(1): 69–95.

Zhong, Y. (2007) Competition is getting real in Chinese TV: A moment of confrontation between CCTV and HSTV. *Media International Australia*, 124: 68–81.

13 Teju Cole's *small fates*
Producing leisure space and leisure time on Twitter

Stuart J. Purcell

Josef Pieper, the liberal arts and leisure

As Western society moves ever deeper into the digital age (or digital ages) and networked digital tools become an ever-more pervasive part of everyday life – of contemporary existence – we are forced to re-evaluate our conceptions of space and time. The digital age has prompted an intensification and acceleration in human communications to such an exponential extent that our notions of space and time need not only be re-evaluated, but dynamically and recursively restructured through forms of engaged practice that expose and challenge the spatial and temporal biases of digital tools. The ramifications of the digital age are keenly felt across all areas of contemporary scholarship but the need to engage with concepts of space and time is particularly pressing for leisure studies. But that is not to say that the issue itself is entirely unheralded within the spheres of leisure and culture.

Originally writing in 1948, philosopher Josef Pieper was concerned that postwar Germany, overly focused on economic recovery, was in danger of redefining society solely upon principles of planned diligence and total labour: 'a world of nothing but work' (1952: 26). For Pieper, the result was that 'leisure', as a concept, was progressively defined as 'not-work', where work was of central importance in human affairs. Pieper suggested that this constituted an inversion of classical antiquarian values. For the Greeks, argued Pieper, 'leisure' was the central tenet of human society and 'work' was conversely defined '[t]o be unleisurely' (1952: 27). 'Work' was essentially the 'servile work' that was necessary to ensure survival, whereas 'leisure' was any activity that required no justification beyond itself. It is from here that the more modern concept of 'the liberal arts' originates, as those subjects or skills concerned with knowledge and freedom not requiring legitimation by their usefulness. In this sense, the concepts of the liberal arts and leisure in their truest forms are innately linked by virtue of their transcending the world of work.

In our contemporary technocultural context, the unabated development of networked digital tools has produced environments which are characterised by control, surveillance, commodification and speed – environments more conducive to work (and not-work) than leisure. In other words, digital tools are built with a functional and structural bias towards work. Online environs, through social media and networking platforms in particular, have transcended their original playful identity and they are now 'a place for getting things done' (Morozov, 2012). Tools designed initially to make our working lives less demanding in exchange for freeing up more of our daily lives for leisure pursuits have only succeeded in drawing us further into the world of total labour and normalised their functional and structural bias towards work. As Pieper feared, we are in danger of engineering leisure out of digital human affairs. Leisure requires 'stepping beyond the workaday world' and 'appears as something wholly fortuitous and strange, without rhyme or reason' (Pieper, 1952: 57, 48). It is 'a receptive attitude of mind, a contemplative attitude'; 'it means not being "busy", but letting things happen' (Pieper, 1952: 52). Leisure, by its very nature it would seem, is increasingly incompatible with the work-based logic and systematic nature of networked digital tools.

But Pieper also stated that the sphere in which leisure appears and comes to fruition is both spatial and temporal, and contemporary leisure studies scholars continue to define leisure within these terms. Rojek (1989) has notably used the terms 'leisure space' and 'leisure time' in stressing that space and time are not fixed and definite features of society. They are instead continuously formed and reformed in people's actions. At the same time, McGillivray (2014) notes that technological innovations render accepted understandings of 'time' and 'space' as fixed concepts problematic, placing particular emphasis on the need to consider technology's role in creating concepts of space and time. Space and time are neither axiomatic nor constitutive of themselves, and therefore leisure, as a product of specific spatial and temporal relations, is not inevitably incongruous to digital environs. To reconcile a concept of leisure within a digital environment, both the human (sociological) and technological aspects of that environment – and their constitutive roles in its spatial and temporal dimensions – must be accounted for. This is the task facing many digital practitioners at the vanguard of the liberal arts: finding ways of using but also actively engaging with networked digital tools that expose and/or challenge their functional and structural biases in order to carve out a place for leisure and leisurely practice within the tools' digital environs.

Taking Twitter as his medium, author Teju Cole has published several experimental works of literature on the platform, perhaps most prominently his *small fates* project (2011–2013). By adopting Cole's *small fates* project as literary exemplar of a liberal arts practice that both uses and engages with a networked digital tool, Twitter, this chapter demonstrates how the *small fates* project exposes and challenges the platform's functional and structural biases on spatial and temporal fronts, effectively carving out a place for leisure, as defined by Pieper, within its digital environs.

Small fates

The *small fates* project began in 2011 when Cole was in Lagos writing his novel *Every Day is for the Thief*, and it finished two years later, after nearly

1000 *small fates*, in 2013. The genesis point for the project came once Cole had amassed a collection of Nigerian news stories from the crime section of local newspapers which he felt contained 'a different quality of everyday life ... life in the raw' (Cole, 2011). As they did not fit with the tone of the text he was working on, being too abstract or too bizarre, Cole decided to find another medium for these stories of Nigerian everyday life. The medium he chose was Twitter. As a digitally networked social media platform, Twitter provided a very different kind of outlet to the print medium novel he was working on and the *small fates* then needed a form compatible with Twitter. The form he chose was the *fait divers*.

Cole adopted and adapted his project's name from the *fait divers*, a French form of literary journalism that has no direct translation in English. The closest translation may be 'incidents' but the form itself is that of 'news briefs', 'sundry events' or 'strange news'. More precisely than simply co-opting the *fait divers* form in a general sense, Cole retrieves the concisely crafted miniature novels popularised by Félix Fénéon, a Parisian writer, journalist, art critic, editor and anarchist born in 1861. Fénéon published his *fait divers* anonymously in *Le Matin*, a French daily newspaper of the period, as *Nouvelles en Trois Lignes* (News in Three Lines) and in his hands the *fait divers* became a modernist form. Although their basis was in news events, Barthes (1979: 194) stated that 'the *fait divers* is literature'. They are very brief pieces, but complete in and of themselves. Barthes (1979: 187) suggested that, if anything, 'It is immanence which defines the *fait divers*'. Their causality, their past and outcome, was 'without duration and without context'; they were 'the classification of the unclassifiable' (Barthes, 1979: 187, 185). They were typically witty and often, but not always, featured an ironic twist of fate; they spoke of 'scandal, sensation, disruptions of the norm ... which occur in the byways of everyday life' (Walker, 1995: 1–2). For example, from Fénéon's *Novels in Three Lines*:

> A dishwasher from Nancy, Vital Frérotte, who had just come back from Lourdes cured forever of tuberculosis, died Sunday by mistake.
> There was a gas explosion at the home of Larrieux, in Bordeaux. He was injured. His mother-in-law's hair caught on fire. The ceiling caved in.

Cole retrieves the *fait divers* as a modernist literary form à la Fénéon from obsolescence and obscurity, translating it from the French cultural context into a Nigerian one, and transforming it for the digital medium of Twitter. To denote the process of metamorphosis, Cole called them *small fates* as opposed to *fait divers*, partly because he appreciated the near-rhyme of fates and fait, though they are fundamentally unrelated. For example, from Cole's (2013) collection of 45 *small fates* for *The New Inquiry*:

> Children are a gift from God. In the returns department: a baby girl, left by the side of Effiom Ekpo Street in Calabar.

Police will never catch Ojo, alias Palaga, one of Akure's most notorious criminals. With a noose, he escaped to the afterlife.

Wives are flammable, a police inspector, Waisu, of Okokomaiko, has found.

Leisure space

Twitter is a web-based social networking and media platform that is often referred to as a 'micro-blogging' site which, at the time of writing, has 288 million monthly active users (see https://about.twitter.com/company). It was created in 2006 and was designed to work within the functional constraints of the SMS (short messaging service), which provides the rationale for the character length of a Twitter post, or 'tweet'. One SMS message is 160 characters long, and anything exceeding this threshold is split into a second separate post (tweet). Twitter – a tweet – works within the limits of one SMS message where, within the available 160 characters, '20 was reserved for the name space, and the other 140 characters for the message' (Roger, 2014: x).

A tweet, in spatial terms, is, first, defined by and expressed as a number of characters within a set range. As such, one of the first things Twitter stresses is brevity. Tweet character limits are capped at 140 characters and any communiqué to be tweeted must remain within this specified count. The name of the platform itself similarly emphasises concision, as well as hinting at the supposed immateriality of the communication it enables. 'Twitter means *bird calls*, as well as "a short burst of inconsequential information"' (Roger, 2014: xi–ii). In both its functional design (software) and its nomenclature, Twitter amplifies brevity. In this way, Twitter was an ideal medium for the *small fates*.

The *small fates* were defined by their brevity. The only extant collection of Fénéon's work in the *fait divers* form, from which the two earlier examples are culled, bears the title *Novels in Three Lines* (recalling *Nouvelles en Trois Lignes*), and many of Cole's *small fates* were even shorter; often, they were as brief as a single line. For example, again from Cole's (2013) collection:

Arrested for theft in Mecca, the Nigerian immigrant Ibrahim is now learning to use his left hand.

The *small fates* used Twitter's functional and structural bias towards brevity in its imposing a limit of 140 characters on each tweet in order to appear typical. Although incredibly short in literary terms, in relation to a novel or even a short story, the *small fates* appeared entirely average in length – or spatial terms – against the backdrop of Twitter.

Simultaneously, the character restrictions and stand-alone nature of each individual tweet – its separation from surrounding tweets – suited the essential immanence of the *small fates*. Each *small fate* was complete in and of itself, telling a whole story, if, indeed, not the whole story. Once more, from Cole's (2013) collection:

> Boarding her London-bound flight in Lagos, grandma Fatimat Abike absent-mindedly exceeded the cocaine carry-on limit by 1.74 kg.

> Ude, of Ikata, recently lost his wife. Tired of arguing with her, he used a machete.

All the relevant details are included in the *small fates*, yet they provided little elucidation as to the motivation or the consequence of the events described – as Barthes stated, their causality was without context. Why did Ibrahim steal? What did he steal? Why was a grandmother carrying several kilograms of cocaine onto a plane? Was she arrested? Did she go to jail? Why was Ude arguing with his wife? Did he go to prison? There was an enigmatic quality to the *small fates*; there was a feeling that something is excluded or withheld from the reader. They were also defined by the spaces, or gaps, they left in their narratives via the platform's bias towards brevity. But it is through these spaces and the resultant strange narrative causalities, happenstance and often ironic turn the tales took that the *small fates* started carving out a space for leisure on the platform.

The *fait divers* derived much of their meaning by the virtue of not being the central content of the newspaper and, at once, in opposition to the central content. As Walker (1995: 2) stated, it is 'precisely because they are located on the margins of the social consensus they may point to, or illustrate, realities that the conventional wisdom leaves out of account'. They were immanent within their own spatial restrictions, but they did not exist in a vacuum. By their nature they challenged existing systems of meaning, as symbolised by the supposedly more central content of the newspaper. Although complete in and of themselves, they were defined as marginalia or sundries, collected together on account of their not being deemed important enough to be stand-alone stories. This gave them a sort of context-in-numbers, with their strange otherness diluted by their abundance and homogeneity. Their intrinsic brevity, the space they were permitted to take up, was a condition of the secondary status of their content in relation to the more expansive and avowedly more important news of the day, and their marginality was expressed in a spatial and visual sense on the printed page. If headline stories appeared in the highways of the newspaper, then the *fait divers* occupied its byways.

The fact that the *small fates* were not differentiated in a spatial sense – by their length, size and position on the page; the space they occupy – was crucial to their place, and how it was defined, within the global milieu of Twitter. The rationale for the project meant that the *small fates* had to appear among other tweets, amidst users' 'streams' (timeline of tweets) and seem, at first glance, to be typical tweets. In many ways they were. Given the sheer volume and relative variety of material published on Twitter it can be difficult to define non-typical material or differentiate a particular tweet from the larger body of tweets published on the platform at any given time, even if that is the author's express intention. But even though they appeared conventional at first glance, they gained much of their meaning and effect in their essential strangeness. The *small fates* re-created the *fait divers*' spatial marginality and defined themselves in opposition to the more typical types of content on Twitter through their lack of context. As Cole explains:

> Part of the appeal of Small Fates is that I could put something into people's day that I knew was completely different from what they were seeing. It wasn't the only serious thing in their timeline, but it would be the only thing that would arrive with this extreme lack of context – because you have a context for the jokes, you have a context for the news reports that had links ... the Small Fates sort of arrive with a kind of intricate and decontextualized detail about lives that you knew nothing about. Each Small Fate was completely new and completely out of context.
>
> (Zhang, 2013)

While the *fait divers* had the context of being based on news stories and being published within a newspaper, the *small fates* had no such contextual link to Twitter. Cole also chose not to directly explain the project to his 'followers' (the other users in whose streams his tweets would appear) during the period in which he was publishing the *small fates*; neither did he provide any form of indexing within the tweets, eschewing common keywords or 'hashtags' that would have linked the tweets together. Although he did eventually post a description of the *small fates* on his own website shortly after the project had begun in 2011, he did not link to this via Twitter, and it was not until much later in the year that news and cultural outlets such as *NPR*, *The New Yorker* and *The New Inquiry* reported and outlined the project. As a result, *small fates* simply started to appear in Cole's follower's streams: strange, often tragic short stories from the periphery of Nigerian everyday life appearing at random, without elucidation or rationale, among the links (news, articles, etc.), updates, images, gifs, and all the other miscellaneous tweets that make up Twitter's environs.

As Barthes (1979) stated, the *fait divers* occurred in 'the byways of everyday life' and were 'disruptions of the norm' in reference to the stories they told. The *small fates* described similarly unusual events, but also disrupted Twitter's functional norms through their extreme lack of context in relation to the other material on the platform. The *small fates* appeared 'wholly fortuitous and strange, without rhyme or reason' in and among Cole's followers' streams, emblematic of Pieper's description of leisure's emergence. They used the platform's instrumental rationality and homogeneity as a means of subverting it through the contextlessness of their content.

Many observers have argued that the urge to update and communicate is secondary to maintaining a connected presence on Twitter, that the communication or content itself is merely the means of maintaining connection. As a result, the content of communications is rendered phatic. Roger (2014) suggests that the purpose of Twitter is to maintain and sustain a connected presence, meaning the platform is almost utterly devoid of substantive content. Hence he refers to Twitter as 'shallow media'. Similarly, Miller (2008) believes that, as social networks have developed in the digital age, there has been a shift from the purpose of these networks being to facilitate users' exchange of substantive content towards the maintenance of a network itself becoming the primary focus. As Spracklen (2015: 86) states from a leisure studies perspective, '[i]ndividuals who check their Twitter accounts do not stop to engage in meaningful conversations'.

At the time when Cole began using Twitter for his *small fates*, its reputation as a medium was characterised by insignificance and superficiality – 'a short burst of inconsequential information'. It had no standing or utility as a more profound, reflective, literary medium, and it had few serious contributors outside of a handful of poets and comedians given its image as 'a sort of ephemeral and unworthy venue' (Pearce, 2011). As with the *small fates*' strange stories from the byways of Nigerian everyday life, there was no context for the type of literary material the *small fates* represented. Simply by using Twitter as a literary medium, Cole was 'stepping beyond the workaday world' of its ordinary utility, as Pieper (1952) suggested was necessary for the emergence of leisure. By bringing his strange, tragic, violent, poignant and blackly humorous *small fates* to Twitter through retrieving and repurposing the *fait divers* for a digital medium, Cole was providing the type of substantive content the platform had previously lacked. He was paving substantive byways in and among Twitter's phatic highways, carving out a space for liberal arts practice – in this case literary practice – on the platform. In the process, the *small fates* concurrently challenged conceptions of literature in a contemporary context. They showed that it is not restricted to the domains of printed texts and eBooks, and that literature can be something placed in people's daily lives without fee-based subscription or direct commodity value to the author. Cole's view with regard to Twitter was, 'that's where the people are, so bring the literature to them' (Pearce, 2011).

However, in choosing to publish the *small fates* via the medium of Twitter, Cole was also ceding to a concept of authorial agency that applied solely to the content of the works. He could choose when to publish and where to publish from, but as soon as Cole tweeted a new *fate*, it was in the figurative hands of the Twitter platform and its operational logic. In practice, the Twitter network became a collaborator in the works in that its algorithms decided when and how each *small fate* appeared in each individual follower's stream – Cole controlled the content and Twitter controlled the context in which they appeared. As Langlois *et al.* (2009) suggest, Web 2.0 established the conditions within which content can be produced/shared and the sphere of agency of users defined. While there was a degree of user input on the part of Cole's followers, in terms of their personal norms and behaviours on and in relation to Twitter (for example, in how often they accessed the platform, how long for, and the number of other users they had chosen to follow), the network controlled how long a *small fate* stayed in users' streams and controlled what other tweets the *small fate* was displayed next to. As much as Cole was yielding to the instrumentality of the Twitter platform, he was doing so in a manner that exposed its functional and structural biases in order to produce the 'extreme lack of context' he described.

Each and every *small fate* tweeted was uniquely threaded through the specificities of the platform's operational logic so that they appeared scattered throughout his followers' streams in a 'wholly fortuitous' fashion.

Appearing spaced out amidst the other material that filled Cole's followers' streams, in constellation rather than collection and in a position operatively decided by the network rather than the author, served to enhance the *small fates*' lack of context in relation to other material and reflected the same strange causalities and happenstance of the stories themselves. The *small fates*' content, the bizarre stories from the periphery of Nigerian everyday life they described, was mirrored by the space they occupied within Twitter, where they appeared as strange, singular tweets that arose seemingly 'without rhyme or reason' in and among users' streams. In other words, how they materialised, how long they remained in users' streams and in what specific context (which other tweets they appeared next to) was in itself an act of *fate*, albeit one based on the operational logic of the Twitter network. For the author, this sphere of agency involved an element of 'letting things happen', another characteristic of leisure articulated by Pieper (1952). But, as their *raison d'être* made clear, ceding a degree of agency also allowed the *small fates* to provide an 'intricate and decontextualized detail about lives that you knew nothing about'.

The *small fates* were expressly concerned with telling stories from the periphery of Nigerian everyday life. Of principal importance was that, though the events they described were indeed bizarre, they were no more or less bizarre than the events that transpired anywhere else. The *small fates* showed that the everyday occurrences that took place in the rest of the world – especially in the Western world – also occurred in Nigeria. When Cole spoke of the *small fates* being a way to 'put something into people's day that [he] knew was completely different from what they were seeing', this not only referred to their being out of context as literary works or via their strange subject matter and odd causalities: it indicated the hegemonic Western bias on platforms such as Twitter. According to Forbes, the ten countries with the most Twitter users are the US, the UK, Canada, Australia, Brazil, Germany, Netherlands, France, India and South Africa (Lipman, 2014). The list is largely populated by North American and European nations, with only Brazil, India and South Africa (the sole African nation) falling outside of those categories. By bringing stories of Nigerian everyday life to the platform, the *small fates* challenged Twitter's hegemonic Western bias, although admittedly on a relatively small scale.

Leisure time

At the top of every Twitter user's home page is the text box in which the content to be tweeted is written. Immanent to this text box is Twitter's default prompt for the user's tweet: 'What's happening?' (see https://blog.twitter.com/2009/whats-happening).

The question is pointedly in present tense and creates a time-critical sense of 'nowness', of perpetual presence. Twitter 'favours the present, the popular, and the ephemeral' (Roger, 2014, p. xv) where tweets, regardless of their content, are always composed in response to a present-tense prompt. But the platform also amplifies this sense of perpetual nowness in functional ways.

Tweets are published on Twitter sequentially in reverse chronological order based on 'the representation of time generated from the timestamp in the tweet template', and also include the narrative cues of the tweeter's username and profile picture (Page, 2012: 100). The visible sequence of tweets a user sees is then filtered through each individual user's network selections, depending on the other users they follow. Within this sequence, the newer a tweet, the closer to the top of a user's stream it will appear. As newer tweets are published, older tweets are pushed further and further down the user's stream. 'Twitter relies on the logic of "not first things first but the newest things first" and, unlike perhaps most narratives, focuses on what has just happened rather than what happened in the beginning' (Thomas, 2014: 103). It cultivates an exigent sense of time, enabling instant updates and real-time publishing, encouraging users to respond instantaneously to what is happening. These cues and queues have a palpable effect on users' patterns of linguistic expression on the platform, providing evidence of the ways in which this perpetual sense of nowness influences their communications.

In her analysis of communication practices on Twitter, Page (2012) compared temporal reference use on Twitter to that in general language, using two reference corpora as her sample set. She found that references to time occurred three times more frequently on Twitter than in general usage. Of the temporal references used on Twitter, she found that the adverbs 'tonight, today, and tomorrow' were the most commonly used and that 'yesterday' was ten times less frequently used than 'today' on Twitter. Her analysis of the reciprocal deictic pairs 'now' and 'then' and 'here' and 'there' bore out the same sort of conclusions in that, in each case, 'the adverb which indicates close proximity to the time and the place of the speaker (here and now) occurs more frequently ... than those that indicate distance (then and here)' (Page, 2012: 102). In her study, Page also noted the typicality of nonfinite verb forms on Twitter. The clausal ambiguity which nonfinite verb forms create, when combined with temporal adverbs such as 'tonight', 'today' and 'tomorrow', establishes a feeling of a perpetual present. The results of Page's (2012) analysis underlined the emphasis on the present moment – the sense of nowness – fostered by the Twitter platform, in which '[a]ny sense of retrospection is diminished, as each episode is received within the context of an ever-present now'. However, this time-critical sense of nowness was notably absent from the *small fates*.

As a general rule, the *small fates* did not contain temporal adverbs to anchor them in any particular time frame. Of a sample of 45 *small fates* compiled by Cole (2013), not one contained any of the three most prevalent temporal adverbs noted by Page – 'tonight', 'today' and 'tomorrow' – nor did they contain any temporal adverbs at all. On one occasion, a day of the week (Monday) is referenced, but only in order to draw out the ironic twist in the tale:

Prince Monday Whiskey was, on Monday, whisked away by persons unknown.

The *small fates* were distinct from the majority of the content published on Twitter on the basis of their temporal ambiguity. In other words, they were out of step with its exigent time dynamics. The *small fates* were not about what was happening now, as Twitter pointedly prompts: they were an echo; they were an interpretation of an event that had already transpired; they were stories composed from the Nigerian news clippings collected by Cole. This is underscored by the ambiguity of tense evident in the *small fates*, as they often drifted between past, present and future tense, further enhancing the enigmatic quality of the tweets. Unlike more typical tweets that emphasised the platform's pervasive sense of nowness, the *small fates* seemed to exist in a free-floating and abstract temporality amidst the dynamic ebb and flow of Twitter streams.

At the same time, Cole published the *small fates* without adhering to any particular timetable as to when they were published or how frequently, so that they would appear 'without rhyme or reason' at infrequent intervals, at irregular times, making no attempt to stay in step with the platform's time-critical dynamics. While the *small fates* were still functionally subject to the platform's time logic – its time-stamping and sequential, chronological arranging of tweets – they also used the instrumentality of their linguistic structure and Cole's irregular use of the platform as a means of simultaneously, ambiguously, 'stepping beyond the workaday' nature of Twitter's exigent time relations. The *small fates* used Twitter's time-critical focus as a means of defining themselves as other in relation to it. As with the *fait divers*, they gained meaning in relation to the content that they were not, as much as what they were. The *small fates* used their gnomic quality as a means of reducing other content to oppositional 'white noise', homogeneous and phatic static in relation to their 'black noise', interruptive, obscure and strange stories from the periphery of Nigerian everyday life. This again drew attention to the point they made about the hegemonic Western bias of the platform.

Through its perpetual nowness and the routine ephemerality of tweets, Twitter pushes aside contemplation. Currently, according to IBM Social Business, the estimated average half-life of a tweet is just eight minutes (see https://twitter.com/ibmsocialbiz/status/540226185804779520). Twitter's operational logic and the speed at which tweets digitally dematerialise leave little room for pause or contemplation. Unless a tweet is specifically recorded by a user, it swiftly disappears off the screen. Newer tweets perpetually push older tweets further and further down users' streams until they are no longer visible and they eventually drop out of active circulation. In its functional logic and subtle semantic prompts, Twitter emphasises response times and the swiftness thereof; its stress is upon responding rather than reflecting. Through their strangeness and their contextlessness, the *small fates* prompted users – particularly those as yet unaware of the greater scope of the project – to delay refreshing their stream to view newer tweets, even if only for a brief moment.

They urged users to reread and reflect on their unusual subject matter and odd causalities, or even carry out further investigations to try to discover their *raison d'être*.

At the time that the *small fates* were appearing on the platform, between 2011 and 2013, Twitter had yet to announce its advanced search function and make available an indexed archive of hundreds of billions of users' tweets. At this point, as Roger (2014: xv) states, it seemed 'ephemerality was built in' to Twitter. Within the platform, at this point, there were only two main ways of recording a tweet: a user could mark it as a 'favourite' (which has since been changed to 'like') or 'retweet' it. Through their black humour and unusual causalities the *small fates* encouraged users to favourite and/or retweet them to view again at a later time or to share with their own followers. The first tweet from the two below *small fates* was retweeted 50 times and favourited 30 times, and the second was retweeted 87 times and favourited 21 times:

> down. The Lagos office of Xerox burned down. The Lagos office of Xerox burned down. The Lagos office of Xerox burned down. The Lagos

> Some ladies whisper sweet nothings to their boyfriends. Into the ears of hers, Ejima, 35, in Asaba, poured hot Indomie noodles.

Storing or sharing a tweet removes it from the exigent time relations of a user's stream and in this way promotes a more 'contemplative attitude' towards the tweet, which Pieper (1952) suggested was key to leisure coming to fruition. The favouriting of a *small fates* tweet took users from the dynamic ebb and flow of their streams to the more calm and static space of the favourites tab on their profile page, while retweeting a *small fate* had the potential to start a conversation, using Twitter as a medium, between one (or multiple) users. In either scenario, the user moves away from being focused on 'What's happening?' as an imperative prompt and towards treating the question as more of 'a receptive attitude of mind, a contemplative attitude', a form of calm awareness in 'letting things happen' without the urge to respond or react.

Conclusion

In the relatively short space of time since Cole published his *small fates* on Twitter, the platform has already undergone a significant process of metamorphosis. In introducing the advanced search function and opening up its extensive tweet archive, adding a pinning function to allow users to keep specific tweets at the top of their timelines, and by displaying tweet conversations in chronological, sequential order denoted by a blue line that visually links the replies, the platform's dimensions of time and space have already been altered in relation to the instance of Twitter discussed above. This only serves to highlight the dynamic and recursive nature of digital tools' development. But as Cole and his *small fates* project show, these developments are not purely deterministic unless we allow them to be:

they may be restructured through forms of engaged practice that expose and challenge the spatial and temporal biases of digital tools. If the temporal and spatial dimensions of digital tools can be restructured, then a place for leisure can be carved out within their environs. To actively find ways of working through and creating a place for their work to be received in digital environs that retains and reaffirms the true meaning of 'the liberal arts' is increasingly the ongoing challenge for those at the vanguard of liberal arts practice. But as long as engaged practitioners such as Teju Cole continue to strive to demonstrate means of meeting this challenge while simultaneously providing new ways of thinking about the liberal arts in and through networked digital environments, Josef Pieper's fear that we have forgotten the true sense of 'leisure' to be left only with a world of planned diligence and total labour will prove to be unfounded.

References

Barthes, R. (1979) The structure of the fait-divers. In *Critical Essays*. Chicago, IL: Northwestern University Press (pp. 185–196).
Cole, T. (2011) Small fates. Available at: www.tejucole.com/small-fates/ (accessed 15 August 2015).
Cole, T. (2013) 'I don't normally do this kind of thing': 45 small fates. *The New Inquiry*. Available at: http://thenewinquiry.com/blogs/dtake/i-dont-normally-do-this-kind-of-thing-45-small-fates/ (accessed 12 April 2015).
Langlois, G., McKelvey, F., Elmer, G. and Werbin, K. (2009) Mapping commerical Web 2.0 worlds: Toward a new critical ontogenesis. *Fibreculture*, 14. Available at: http://fourteen.fibreculturejournal.org/fcj-095-mapping-commercial-web-2-0-worlds-towards-a-new-critical-ontogenesis/ (accessed 5 January 2016).
Lipman, V. (2014) Top Twitter trends: What countries are most active? Who's most popular? *Forbes*. Available at: www.forbes.com/sites/victorlipman/2014/05/24/top-twitter-trends-what-countries-are-most-active-whos-most-popular/ (accessed 24 August 2015).
McGillivray, D. (2014) Digital cultures, acceleration and mega sporting events narratives. *Leisure Studies*, 33(1): 96–109.
Miller, V. (2008) New media, networking and phatic culture. *Convergence*, 14(4): 387–400.
Morozov, E. (2012) The death of the cyberflâneur. *New York Times*. Available at: www.nytimes.com/2012/02/05/opinion/sunday/the-death-of-the-cyberflaneur.html?pagewanted=all&_r=0 (accessed 20 August 2015).
Page, R.E. (2012) *Stories and Social Media: Identities and Interaction*. Oxford: Routledge.
Pearce, M. (2011) Death by Twitter. *The New Inquiry*. Available at: http://thenewinquiry.com/essays/death-by-twitter/ (accessed 7 April 2015).
Pieper, J. (1952) *Leisure: The Basis of Culture*. London: Faber and Faber.
Roger, R. (2014) Debanalising Twitter: The transformation of an object of study. In K. Weller *et al.* (eds) *Twitter and Society*. New York: Peter Lang (pp. ix–xxvi).
Rojek, C. (1989) Lesiure time and leisure space. In C. Rojek (ed.) *Leisure for Leisure*. London: Macmillan (pp. 191–205).
Spracklen, K. (2015) *Digital Leisure, The Internet and Popular Culture*. London: Palgrave Macmillan.

Thomas, B. (2014) 140 characters in search of a story. In A. Bell, A. Ensslin and H.K. Rustad (eds) *Analyzing Digital Fiction*. Oxford: Routledge (pp. 94–108).

Walker, D.H. (1995) *Outrage and Insight: Modern French Writers and the 'Fait Divers'*. Oxford: Berg.

Zhang, S. (2013) Teju Cole on the 'empathy gap' and tweeting drone strikes. *Mother Jones*. Available at: www.motherjones.com/media/2013/03/teju-cole-interview-twitter-drones-small-fates (accessed 1 March 2015).

14 Street hauntings

Digital storytelling in twenty-first-century leisure cultures

Spencer Jordan

Introduction

Stories are at the heart of how we understand the world. They allow us to pass on knowledge in a way that is at once personal and subjective while at the same time rooted in the wider world. It has even been argued that stories lie at the very heart of consciousness itself, what Jameson (1981: 13) called the 'central function or instance of the human mind'. From this ontological position, concepts such as 'place' are no longer fixed and stable. Instead, they are 'created through performance' (Coleman and Crang, 2004: 1), where performance describes both the physical interaction of the body with the external world and cognitive sense-making. This notion of the active construction of experience provides a key theoretical underpinning for this chapter. Critical here is the degree to which stories not only augment existing perceptions of the world but also facilitate new ways of understanding.

This need for adaptation and change, for the radical and transgressive, has become ever more significant as cities across the globe come under new challenges and pressures. Population growth, ecological impact and social unrest are just some of the issues placing enormous strain on communities and governments. As the United Nations Population Fund (UNFPA, 2007) recognises, urbanisation remains one of the world's most pressing issues. But if there are challenges, then there are also opportunities. The technology company, Ericsson, estimates that the number of mobile phones in Africa will rise to 930 million by 2019, almost one per African (Economist, 2015). In the United Kingdom, 80 per cent of households are already connected to the internet (Economist, 2014). In the first quarter of 2014, 61 per cent of UK adults owned a smartphone (Ofcom, 2014).

Understanding the potential that such technologies afford society is an imperative recognised by an increasing number of global organisations. Yet, as the collection of chapters in this volume demonstrates, a tension exists here. On one side is the view that technologies simply extend systems of control and hegemonic surveillance. On the other, digital technology is seen as supporting what de Waal (2014) calls the 'libertarian urban ideal' (p. 11). This chapter offers insight into these debates. A particular focus is on the degree to which digitally enhanced leisure activities can change the way in which the urban environment is itself experienced. The outputs of two research projects are discussed which have specifically examined the role that digital storytelling can play in this process, both in terms of the creation of stories, but also as a means by which the physical journey through the city itself can be re-envisioned. It will be argued that such narrative construction may be understood as a transgressive form of 'mapping', a re-haunting of our cityspace in which the evocation of 'the past' remains a significant feature.

Digital technology and the city

Contemporary anxieties about the social and cultural impact of urbanisation are just the most recent in a long line of concerns in which notions of 'belonging' and 'community' are seen to be undermined. Simmel (1997), for example, saw the modern nineteenth-century metropolis as characterised both by strangers and by the experience of 'shock'. And as Jacobs (1961: 40) noted, 'cities are, by definition, full of strangers. To any one person, strangers are far more common in big cities than acquaintances.' Whereas, historically, cities were seen as having a clear centre around which the urban form radiated (Sassen, 1991), modern cities came to be characterised more by their lack of identifiable centres: 'We live ... in an exploding universe of mechanical and electronic invention.... This technological explosion has produced a similar explosion of the city itself: the city has burst open' (Mumford, 1973: 45). Fishman (1994: 398) is even more dogmatic, suggesting that 'The new city ... lacks what gave shape and meaning to every urban form of the past: a dominant single core and definable boundaries'. The result is a new kind of space, neither city nor countryside, what Ferrarotti calls 'an urban–rural continuum' (1994: 463), a city without a place, 'ageographical' to use Sorkin's description (1992: xi), or Soja's 'postmetropolis' (2000: 95).

This radical development in both the form of cities and the lives of its citizens has become a global phenomenon. China already has 160 cities with a population of over a million. Of these, five have metropolitan areas with more than ten million people. Yet, as the UNFPA (2007) recognise, population growth will be greatest in smaller towns and cities, predominantly in Asia and Africa. A global imperative now exists to understand how citizens can live successfully and sustainably in these new urban centres. Although still in its infancy, there is a growing body of research focused on the role digital technology may be able to play in this process. Although some of this draws upon the experiences of Europe and America, it is important to note the work being done elsewhere, such as Wong and Ling's (2011) analysis of digital interactions between 'poor urban youth' in Bangladesh. What characterises a lot of this research, however, is its exploration of how digital technology can support what might be termed 'playful' interaction with a particular urban environment. Indeed, as Crawford (2013: 568) notes, new technology has impacted 'nowhere more visibly than in terms of leisure patterns and practices'.

Yet the impact of digital technology is not without controversy. For some, digital media is just the latest in a long series of iniquitous socio-economic reconfigurations of city space. Virilio, for example, sees a loss of coherence as central to this, a growing urban illegibility, a process reinforced by electronic media in the creation of 'accidental, discontinuous and heterogeneous space' (Virilio, 1991: 35). Yet for others, the picture is not so bleak. Both McQuire (2008) and de Waal (2014) celebrate the benefits that digital technology can bring. For them, 'augmented reality', 'mixed reality' and 'augmented space' are concepts to be embraced, enhancing citizen engagement and choice. De Waal in particular champions the use of the smartphone as 'an intelligent compass' (2014: 9), allowing the citizen to digitally interact with his or her environment. This chapter provides one small step in furthering our understanding of this relationship between digital participation and playfulness, or what Williams and Mascioni (2014: xi) call 'digital out-of-home entertainment'.

Of course, one should not simplify the impact that digital technology will have upon our lives. The increasing speed of our 'connectedness', what Scheuerman (2009) calls 'social acceleration', needs to be explored. The home has become an interactive node, permanently online, blurring the boundaries between place and experience, self and stranger. Technological speed and ubiquitous connectivity has therefore affected our relationship to space in fundamental ways. One important aspect of this is how digital technology undermines notions of locality, proximity and distance. Through a smartphone, for example, we can just as easily be connected to someone or something on the other side of the world as we can to those things within our immediate physical vicinity. McQuire adopts the term *relational space* to help explain this phenomenon, 'in which the horizon of social relationships has become radically open' (2008: 22), breaking down previous restraints of place and time. The critical debate is perhaps here. If digital technology prioritises an *other-orientated* and heterotopic understanding of space, how can it also support our own emotional attachment to the physical space around us? And what might that attachment actually look like? Ben-Ze'ev's (2015) work with young people in Israel-Palestine, in particular the relationship between mental maps and spatial perception, reminds us that this is no simple academic exercise. Behind this lie significant global issues to which this chapter, in its own small way, provides some tentative insights.

Digital storytelling and the city

In their discussion of digital leisure culture, Williams and Mascioni note the rise of what they call digital out-of-home entertainment (DOE):

> Perhaps one of the most significant trends affecting the DOE market is the growing convergence between real and virtual experiences, afforded by such interactive forms as mobile AR [augmented reality], location-based games and social media. New technologies, such as smartphones, and new consumer habits are hastening the increasing convergence of the interactive consumer and DOE markets in public places, and much greater convergence is likely to spawn huge opportunities in the next decade.
>
> (Williams and Mascioni, 2014: 160)

182 S. Jordan

A significant part of this new leisure activity is digital storytelling, with user-generated content and personalised interactivity becoming increasingly important (Williams and Mascioni, 2014). The ability to create and share on the fly, as one moves through the city, 'adds life to tourism by highlighting the interplay between movement and materiality as people navigate themselves from one place to the next' (Palmer and Lester, 2013: 240). Yet these technological interventions are not just entertainment. Instead, such 'urban media', as de Waal (2011) calls them, are also central to the creation of 'place' itself. As the use of digital technology proliferates, the city is becoming a hybrid, its space constituted through both the digital and the physical worlds, forming a new urban form.

This new urban form involves both a reconfiguring of the physical environment (space) as well as the subjective constructions that arise from it (place). It is here, in the interplay between space and place, that narrative maintains a key role, one that pre-dates the rise of digital texts. Perhaps this should not surprise us. Miller (1995) has argued that every story may be considered to be a map of some kind, in which the spatial architecture of places, dwellings, paths and roads is encoded. For Azcárate (2014), the physical city is also a story, one constructed from countless numbers of individual human acts. Zhang (1996) takes this further, arguing that the city is in essence a ritualised collection of customs and traditions. Lynch (1960: 12) used the term 'wayfinding' to describe the process of navigating through the 'vast sprawl of our cities', mentally reconfiguring the urban form through the ongoing creation of stories.

Such stories are conjured through the spatial practices of its citizens, the physical and subjective performance that reflects our lives. As these narratives are constructed, second by second, then so too is the cityspace around us. Our interaction with the environment is therefore critical in terms of how we understand and experience it. Yet, as this chapter demonstrates, it also offers the potential for change and adaptation. Prieto, for example, reminds us that narratives can also be radical and transgressive, helping to 'change the ways their readers view the world ... making possible new ways of understanding what is actually there' (2013: 9). As we have seen, cities across the globe are facing unprecedented social challenges. This chapter argues that narrative performance will play an important role in helping these communities find sustainable solutions to these pressures.

One key area where narrative performance or 'storifying' can make a significant intervention is in the mediation of 'past' and 'present'. How the city is experienced is not just a spatial phenomenon but one that also has an important temporal dimension. De Certeau noted the importance of what he called 'verbal relics', superstitions, myths and legends – in effect, old stories have slowly accumulated in a place. De Certeau saw that, in this way, all places are 'haunted' by the past; in fact, 'haunted places are the only ones people can live in' (de Certeau, 1984: 108). It is this very haunting of space by stories that allows a place to become 'home' (1984: 106); without them the habitable city becomes annulled.

These ideas have attracted academic interest. In particular, there is concern about the gap between individual and community memory, and what might be termed official or authorised history. Rosenberg, in her study of Berlin, notes that places remain continually haunted by past meanings and artefacts (2012: 131) and, as Huyssens (2008) has shown, cultural and collective memory can become highly politicised as a consequence. For Edensor (2005), the exploration of 'haunted' sites continues to remain attractive because such places stand outside of any authorised attempt at establishing official 'history'. As he notes, 'the objects, spaces, and traces found in ruins highlight the mystery and radical otherness of the past, a past which can haunt the fixed memories of place proffered by the powerful' (Edensor, 2005: 847).

This chapter argues that it is the ability to map this subjective interplay between past and present that remains a key aspect of digital storytelling. Concepts such as 'relational space' provide clues as to how such digital interventions might offer a real-time interplay between the physical exploration of the 'here', overlaid with the digital exploration of the 'absent' and, through that process, generate new stories and understandings of twenty-first-century cityspace.

Digital storytelling: two examples

Two digital projects, both funded by the Creative Exchange Wales Network (CEWN), provide the empirical component of this chapter. These projects build on earlier work that has explored the creative leisure opportunities afforded by digital storytelling. *Ghosts in the Garden* (http://old.react-hub.org.uk/heritagesandbox/projects/2012/ghosts-in-the-garden/) (2012), *City Strata* (http://old.react-hub.org.uk/heritagesandbox/projects/2012/city-strata/) (2012) and *I Tweet Dead People* (http://old.react-hub.org.uk/heritagesandbox/projects/2012/the-ivory-bangle-lady/journal/i-tweet-dead-people/) (2012), all funded through REACT (Research and Enterprise in Arts and Creative Technology, an AHRC-funded Knowledge Exchange Hub), are important in their exploration of the interplay between digital technology and storytelling. Projects such as *Linking the Chain: A Network for Digital Heritage in Wales* (http://gtr.rcuk.ac.uk/projects?ref=AH/H033807/1) (2010) have shown ways in which storytelling may be used within a digital heritage context. And *These Pages Fall Like Ash* (http://old.react-hub.org.uk/books-and-print-sandbox/projects/2013/these-pages-fall-like-ash/) (2013) pushed the boundaries of storytelling by inviting readers to visit physical locations, locating digital fragments and uploading their own responses. In their exploration of location-based interactive narratives, Paay and Kjeldskov (2011) note the immersive nature of augmented reality when played out across a city. Von Jungenfeld (2014) explores the project *Walking Through Time* which uses the superimposition of historical maps on a smartphone app to guide users around Edinburgh. She notes how digitally layered mapping returned the 'map' to historical, mythical and encyclopaedic representations of space, as encapsulated by medieval maps such as the Mappae Mundi (von Jungenfeld, 2014).

Even authors themselves are increasingly intrigued by the potential offered by digital storytelling. Koehler (2013) examines how Twitter stories such as Rick Moody's 'Some contemporary characters' (2010) and Jennifer Egan's 'Black box' (2012) explore what he calls 'new ways of understanding craft as a synthesis of

184 S. Jordan

readers' affect and participation in an unfolding narrative' (Koehler, 2013: 387). In this sense then, the two projects examined here may be understood to be building on a range of earlier work concerned with the interplay between physical and digital exploration. The first, *Walkways and Waterways* (2013), was a collaborative project involving Cardiff Metropolitan University, the University of South Wales and the digital media startup, Fresh Content Creation. The purpose of the project was to explore how creative exploration, mediated through mobile technology, could help users re-explore their own city, in this case the Welsh capital, Cardiff (one of 22 cities included in the UK government's 'SuperConnected Cities' programme). The event consisted of a digitally mediated journey, retracing the last two miles of the Glamorganshire Canal, from Cardiff Castle to the Bay. The canal itself fell into ruin soon after the Second World War and has long since been removed. Retracing it through the centre of the city involved traversing a variety of terrains, including a large modern shopping centre, before finishing up at the location of the canal's old sea lock, beneath the A4232 flyover. The event was advertised through social media. Twenty participants attended, ranging from young children to the retired. While the physical journey was led by project members, exploration was digitally augmented by Twitter through which further guidance and information was given in real time. The smartphone allowed each participant to upload photographs and commentary to *#GlamCan*, providing a shareable, real-time forum through which every individual itinerary could be recorded. Embedded within the walk were 12 'treasures', forming a 'treasure trail'. In this way, *Waterways and Walkways* employed real-time gaming and 'play' as a way of enhancing participation and engagement. Tweets sent by the project team prompted participants to both find and then record the next 'treasure'. Sometimes, as in the case of the marooned paddle post in the subway beneath the A470, participants were invited to discuss its function (see Figure 14.1).

The use of the smartphone within the project recalls de Waal's notion of 'an intelligent compass, guiding the city dweller through the bustle and chaos of everyday life' (de Waal, 2014: 9). Each participant recorded their own journey which was then shared in real time across Twitter. The writing was clearly not what may be considered to be a traditional piece of prose, a single block of crafted text. Instead, it consisted of a series of tweets (short textual responses limited to 140 characters, including spaces) through which each participant captured their mood and thoughts but also responses to the pre-planned questions and prompts as they navigated from treasure to treasure. In other situations, the limitations of a tweet might be considered to be unnecessarily restrictive. Yet, out on the street, the brevity and concision imposed by the medium became a strength. Two further aspects of Twitter enhanced the creative responses. First, each tweet offered the opportunity to add up to four photographs taken on the smartphone. This allowed the participants to explore the interplay between text and image as they progressed along the path of the canal, a simple yet powerful augmentation of their creative output. Second, each tweet became part of a single, collective narrative on *#GlamCan*, a real-time amalgamation of over 20 stories that each participant could access alongside their own individual record.

Figure 14.1 Paddle post in the subway under the A470 (source: author).

The smartphone was able to support the event in a number of ways that a more traditional format could not. As well as an intelligent compass, de Waal notes how a smartphone also operates as an 'experience marker', recording and sharing experiences, and a 'territory device', influencing the subjective experience of an urban area (2014: 19). Both of these features were evident in *Waterways and Walkways*. The technology allowed real-time mapping across Cardiff using the phone's global positioning system (GPS). It also provided a means of geographically triggering audio, video and images, augmenting the physical experience of the contemporary city with historical photographs, records and testimony. As 'territory devices', the smartphones were able to digitally link stories to the historical legacies of specific sites. Finally, the phones allowed each participant to record and post their own creative responses through Twitter, and then to read each other's, as the journey progressed.

Neuhaus (2014) notes how his own mapping of Twitter activity across a number of smart cities, including New York City and London, produced parallel virtual landscapes, created through the narrative activity of the cities' populations. In *Waterways and Walkways*, stories emerged on Twitter but they were also generated verbally as the participants moved along the route. At one point, beside the extant post of a crane on what would have been the Sea Lock Pound

(Figure 14.2), one of the participants began to sing a sea shanty, evoking the life of the stevedores and bargemen who had worked on the canal. The author's role consisted of leading the group along the path of the canal. Qualitative data consisted of the tweets themselves as well as verbal feedback gathered during the course of the walk. Quantitative data were collected through the metrics available on Twitter and from a questionnaire distributed to all participants at the end of the walk. Participants were also asked to review their experiences and submit them through an online survey after the event. The author's position as both researcher and walk leader was therefore ameliorated by the triangulation of these qualitative and quantitative data. Although the conclusions can only be tentative at this stage, there is enough evidence to suggest that by the end of the journey the participants had engaged with each other both physically and digitally, and through that interaction had begun to reconfigure their relationship to the spaces of the city and its citizens. The qualitative data in particular record how the exploration helped participants see the city in new and interesting ways. Two examples will suffice. First, participants described how passage through the shopping centre allowed them to experience it in a new way, released from the role of customer or consumer. Feedback recorded that being asked what we were doing by the centre's security guard was a particular highlight. Second, one participant did the walk again a few days later, with their children, something of which the project team was unaware until they saw the Twitter feed.

Figure 14.2 Extant crane post in Canal Park (source: author).

The second project, *People's Journeys*, was undertaken in Cardiff in the autumn of 2014 and involved a collaboration between the author and a small enterprise (Centre for Creativity Ltd). The project sought to explore the intersection between storytelling and cityspace, de Certeau's (1984) 'space of enunciation', through the creation of digitally mediated 'journeys. These dérives were deliberately transgressive, community-generated journeys reflecting local experiences and places. To do this, the project set out to record individual narratives across a discrete locale, tagging them electronically to specific locations. The users of the *People's Journeys* app would be able to retrace these 'journeys' using a mobile phone to engage with audio, image and video, in effect creating their own 'journey' or 'storyspace' as they moved across the city. Given the limited nature of the project, it was decided to start with a series of discrete narratives relating to the First World War. Drawing upon various community members through the local history society, the project team identified and then recorded nine biographical stories, each of a soldier killed in the Great War from a single district in Cardiff. These recordings were co-scripted and recorded by community members. Images and video were again sourced by the local community, overseen by the project team.

The app itself was built using the *AppFurnace* mobile application development platform. These narratives were brought together by the app to create the first of what was ultimately conceived of as a limitless number of 'journeys' criss-crossing a community. It was decided that the start of the 'journey' should be the war memorial in the local park (see Figure 14.3). The app incorporated a live Twitter feed through which participants could leave textual responses and photographs. The project team used an *experience design framework*, which stresses the importance of iteration in terms of the design of prototypes. At key stages the app was trialled by community representatives and their feedback integrated into the final version. The app was published on both Google Play and Apple's App Store. Some of the locations used in the app are buildings associated with the soldiers' lives, though certain locations have been demolished. Photographs and community memory are able to bring such places back into existence as the user journeys across the city.

In this sense the project was an overt exploration of McQuire's (2008) concept of relational space. Yet it was also an exploration of how digital technology can help address issues of alienation and community estrangement. In its own small way, the app facilitated the physical and emotional reattachment of citizens to the space around them through the exploration of stories. Yet, by moving from story to story, each participant created their own unique narrative. The smartphone in this case really was an intelligent compass, helping to navigate each user both physically along the streets, but also temporally, through links to audio-visual material, historical photographs and text. In that sense, the user navigated the hybrid space of here and 'other', the other being that which has been lost, the digital hauntings of voice, place and image.

188 S. Jordan

Figure 14.3 The start of the journey, the Grangetown War Memorial (source: author).

Conclusion

This chapter has discussed two projects which have specifically explored the use of digital storytelling as part of twenty-first-century leisure cultures. Key here has been the use of pervasive connectivity, something that is not without controversy. As Crang and Graham warn, embedded within the everyday life of what they call 'sentient cities' is a 'politics of visibility' in which the freedom of individuals is both increasingly anticipated and regulated by 'sentient systems' (2007: 789). Edensor notes that official sites of memory will always 'rely on pervasive spatial regulation for their power' (2005: 831). If technological devices such as the smartphone are to be used effectively, and if walking itself is to remain what Rosenberg (2012: 132) calls a transformative encounter, then the technology itself must ensure that digital storytelling and the leisure practices they support do not themselves become part of a growing technological network of regulation and surveillance.

Yet, it is also clear that smartphones, and the technological infrastructure of the modern city, are not going to disappear any time soon. Ben-Ze'ev's (2015) analysis of spatial perception in Palestine, and Wong and Ling's (2011) study of mobile interactions among the urban poor in Bangladesh, are indicative of the global interest in the potential offered by digital technology. Decisions about what is remembered and what is forgotten by any society are not neutral actions. As Urry notes (1998: 50), 'forgetting is as socially structured as is the process of remembering'.

This chapter has shown how digital technology may be used to support bottom-up, community-based 'landscapes of memory'. Both *Waterways and Walkways* and *People's Journey's* involved disruptive and oppositional events, taking users on a dérive well beyond the parameters of any official or authorised tour. Both walking and storifying remained important elements for both projects in what amounted to a personalised remapping of a cityspace. As Selby notes, 'these "landscapes of memory" are not constructed out of national historical facts, but out of the local, contextual, everyday life of visitors' (2004: 57). Over the course of this chapter some of the key features of digital storytelling have begun to emerge. Critical is the degree to which the technology can support an understanding of place as embodied performance (Coleman and Crang, 2004). Crouch calls tourism nothing more than the 'embodied practice of space' (2004: 208) and the two projects discussed here suggest that a recourse to the digital can have a significant impact upon how an individual engages with the environment around them. As Sheller and Urry note, 'the playfulness of place is in part about the urge to travel elsewhere' (2004: 1); yet that 'elsewhere' need not be a geographically 'new location'. Digitally enhanced playfulness embraces the ability to see old places anew and in different ways, especially for those already living within those communities.

The mobility of the smartphone through a wi-fi-enabled cityspace is critical here, as is the ability to engage with multimedia, including sound and image. Social media platforms, such as Twitter, facilitate the real-time sharing of content while the GPS function allows real-time location positioning, but also the geo-spatial tagging of content. This facilitates the physical walking of a journey (a traditional spatial mapping) but also the geo-spatial mapping of emotion, thought and memory. De Waal's (2011) two uses for the smartphone, namely 'experience markers' and 'territory devices', perhaps requires a third, 'temporal devices', in which the participants are able to tag their stories to objects and urban features that have long since been removed.

As we have seen, one of the key features of McQuire's (2008) 'relational space' is the concept of being both 'here' and 'other'. Such a dichotomy exists as part of any digital intervention where the user has a presence in the physical world, but also a focus on a 'digital' that is always 'absent'. Yet this chapter has shown that it also embraces the ability of digital media to interweave the past and present in a way that augments reality. As Tenedório *et al.* state, 'An AR [augmented reality] system expands the real world scene (requiring the user to maintain the sense of presence in that world, as opposed to a total immersive virtual world)' (2014: 221). Yet such virtual spaces are innovative not only because of their enhanced leisure opportunities. As Lester and Scarles note in their analysis of leisure and tourism, virtuality is also important because of its ability to offer individuals a space through which 'to present themselves and their travel experiences to others' (2013: 263).

This chapter has also shown that bottom-up, community-based approaches to digital media can play a powerful role. The creative responses captured by Twitter on the navigation of the lost Glamorganshire Canal in *Walkways and Waterways*, and the production and use of the soldiers' stories for *People's Journeys*, highlight the importance of 'the past' in any transgressive spatial practice. As Till notes on the politics of memory in Berlin, 'places are not only continuously interpreted; they are haunted by past structures of meaning and material presences from other times and lives' (2005: 9). Sheringham (2010) states that 'a city is a memory machine' (p. 10), and, for de Certeau too, the city is built on what is no longer there. Writers such as W.G. Sebald and Iain Sinclair make us aware that the past is never truly expunged from the high street but lurks ghost-like in its shadows. In this sense we are always among the ruins of what has gone before, both in physical space but also in human memory. This chapter suggests that it is digital media's ability to reconnect these two phenomena, to re-attach memory to the lost physical places of our cityscapes, that remains one of its strongest features.

References

Azcárate, A. (ed.) (2014) *Cityscapes: World Cities and Their Cultural Industries*. Champaign, IL: Common Ground Publishing (Kindle File).

Ben-Ze'ev, E. (2015) Mental maps and spatial perceptions: The fragmentation of Israel-Palestine. In L. Roberts (ed.) *Mapping Cultures: Place, Practice, Performance*. London: Palgrave Macmillan (pp. 237–259).

Certeau, M. de (1984) *The Practice of Everyday Life*. Berkeley, CA: University of California Press.

Coleman, S. and Crang, M. (2004) Grounded tourists, travelling theory. In S. Coleman and M. Crang (eds) *Tourism: Between Place and Performance*. Oxford: Berghahn Books (pp. 1–17).

Crang, M. and Graham, S. (2007) Sentient cities: Ambient intelligence and the politics of urban space. *Information, Communication and Society*, 10(6): 789–817.

Crawford, G. (2013) Virtual leisure. In T. Blackshaw (ed.) *Routledge Handbook of Leisure Studies*. London: Routledge (pp. 560–570).

Crouch, D. (2004) Surrounded by place: Embodied encounters. In S. Coleman and M. Crang (eds) *Tourism: Between Place and Performance*. Oxford: Berghahn Books (pp. 207–218).

Economist, The (2014) Cybercrime: Thieves in the night. *The Economist*, 20 December, p. 35.

Economist, The (2015) The pioneering continent. *The Economist*, 25 April, p. 45.

Edensor, T. (2005) The ghosts of industrial ruins: Ordering and disordering memory in excessive space. *Environment and Planning*, 23: 829–849.

Ferrarotti, F. (1994) Civil society as a polyarchic form: The city. In P. Kasinitz (ed.) *Metropolis: Centre and Symbol of Our Times*. London: Macmillan (pp. 450–468).

Fishman, R. (1994) Megalopolis unbound. In P. Kasinitz (ed.) *Metropolis: Center and Symbol of our Times*. London: Macmillan (pp. 395–412).
Foth, M., Forlano, L., Satchell, C. and Gibbs, M., (eds) (2008) *Handbook of Research on Urban Informatics: The Practice and Promise of the Real-time City*. Hershey, PA: Information Science Reference, IGI Global.
Gordon, E. (2008) Towards a theory of networked locality. *First Monday*, 13(10). Available from: http://firstmonday.org/article/view/2157/2035 (accessed 8 August 2015).
Harvey, D. (1990) *The Condition of Postmodernity: An Enquiry into the Origins of Cultural Change*. Oxford: Blackwell.
Huyssens, A. (ed.) (2008) *Other Cities, Other Worlds: Urban Imaginaries in a Globalizing Age*. Durham, NC: Duke University Press.
Jacobs, J. (2000) *The Death and Life of Great American Cities*. London: Pimlico. First published 1961.
Jameson, F. (1981) *The Political Unconscious: Narrative as a Socially Symbolic Act*. Ithaca, NY: Cornell University Press.
Jungenfeld, R. von (2014) Exploring the changing texture of the city. In A. Azcárate (ed.) *Cityscapes: World Cities and Their Cultural Industries*. Champaign, IL: Common Ground Publishing (Kindle File) (pp. 394–407).
Koehler, A. (2013) Digitizing craft: Creative writing studies and new media: A proposal. *College English*, 75(4): 379–397.
Lester, J. and Scarles, C. (2013) Mediating tourism: Future directions? In J. Lester and C. Scarles (eds) *Current Developments in the Geographies of Leisure and Tourism: Mediating the Tourist Experience: From Brochures to Virtual Encounters*. Brookfield, VT: Ashgate Publishing (pp. 255–269).
Lynch, K. (1960) *The Image of the City*. Cambridge, MA: The MIT Press.
McQuire, S. (2008) *The Media City: Media, Architecture and Urban Space*. London: Sage.
Miller, J.H. (1995) *Topographies*. Stanford, CA: Stanford University Press.
Mumford, L. (1973) *The City in History*. Harmondsworth: Penguin Books.
Neuhaus, F. (2014) The use of social media for urban planning: Virtual urban landscapes created using Twitter data. In N.N. Pinto, J.A. Tenedório and A.P. Antunes (eds) *Technologies for Urban and Spatial Planning: Virtual Cities and Territories*. Hershey, PA: Information Science Reference (pp. 113–134).
Ofcom (2014) *The Communications Market Report*. London: Ofcom.
Paay, J. and Kjeldskov, J. (2011) Bjørnetjeneste: Using the city as a backdrop for location-based interactive narratives. In M. Foth, L. Forlano, C. Satchell, M. Gibbs (eds) From Society Butterfly to Engaged Citizen: Urban Informatics, Social Media, Ubiquitous Computing and Mobile Technology to Support Citizen Engagement. Boston, MA: The MIT Press (pp. 253–273).
Palmer, C. and Lester, J. (2013) Maps, mapping and materiality: Navigating London. In J. Lester and C. Scarles (eds) *Current Developments in the Geographies of Leisure and Tourism: Mediating the Tourist Experience: From Brochures to Virtual Encounters*. Brookfield, VT: Ashgate Publishing (pp. 237–254).
Prieto, E. (2013) *Literature, Geography and the Postmodern Poetics of Place*. London: Palgrave Macmillan.
Rosenberg, E. (2012) Walking in the city: Memory and place. *Journal of Architecture*, 17(1): 131–149.
Sassen, S. (1991) *The Global City: New York, London, Tokyo*. Princeton, NJ: Princeton University Press.

Scheuerman, W.E. (2009) Citizen and speed. In H. Rosa and W.E. Scheuerman(eds) *High-speed Society: Social Acceleration, Power and Modernity*. Philadelphia: Pennsylvania State University (pp. 287–306).

Selby, M. (2004) *Understanding Urban Tourism, Image, Culture and Experience*. London: I.B. Tauris.

Sheller, M. and Urry, J. (2004) Places to play, places in play. In M. Sheller and J. Urry (eds) *Tourism Mobilities. Places to Play, Places in Play*. London: Routledge (pp. 1–10).

Sheringham, M. (2010) Archiving. In M. Beaumont and G. Dart (eds) *Restless Cities*. London: Verso (pp. 1–17).

Simmel, G. (1997) *Simmel on Culture*. London: Sage.

Soja, E. (2000) *Postmetropolis: Critical Studies of Cities and Regions*. Malden, MA: Blackwell.

Sorkin, M. (ed.) (1992) *Variations on a Theme Park: The New American City and the End of Public Place*. New York: Hill and Wang.

Tally Jr, R.T. (2013) *Spatiality*. London: Routledge.

Tenedório, J.A., Henriques, C.D., Rebelo, C., Marques, L., Estanqueiro, R. and Goncalves, J.A. (2014) New developments in geographical information technology for urban and spatial planning. In N.N. Pinto, J.A. Tenedório and A.P. Antunes (eds) *Technologies for Urban and Spatial Planning: Virtual Cities and Territories*. Hershey, PA: Information Science Reference (pp. 196–227).

Till, K. (2005) *The New Berlin: Memory, Politics and Place*. Minneapolis: University of Minnesota Press.

UNFPA (2007) *State of World Population 2007: Unleashing the Potential of Urban Growth*. New York: UNFA.

Urry, J. (1998) How societies remember the past. In S. MacDonald and G. Fyfe (eds) *Theorising Museums*. Oxford: Blackwell (pp. 45–68).

Virilio, P. (1991) *The Last Dimension*. New York: Semiotexte.

Waal, M. de (2011) The ideas and ideals in urban media. In M. Foth, L. Forlano, C. Satchell and M. Gibbs (eds) *From Society Butterfly to Engaged Citizen: Urban Informatics, Social Media, Ubiquitous Computing and Mobile Technology to Support Citizen Engagement*. Boston, MA: The MIT Press (pp. 5–20).

Waal, M. de (2014) *The City as Interface: How New Media are Changing the City*. Rotterdam: nai010 Publishers.

Wearing, S. and Law, A. (2013) The leisured nature of tourism: A sociological critique. In T. Blackshaw (ed.) *Routledge Handbook of Leisure Studies*. London: Routledge (pp. 280–292).

Williams, K, and Mascioni, M. (2014) *Out-of-home Immersive Entertainment Frontier: Expanding Interactive Boundaries in Leisure Facilities*. Farnham: Ashgate Publishing.

Wong, A. and Ling, R. (2011) Mobile interactions as social machines: Poor urban youth at play in Bangladesh. In M. Foth, L. Forlano, C. Satchell and M. Gibbs (eds) *From Society Butterfly to Engaged Citizen: Urban Informatics, Social Media, Ubiquitous Computing and Mobile Technology to Support Citizen Engagement*. Boston, MA: The MIT Press (pp. 275–290).

Zhang, Y. (1996) *The City in Modern Chinese Literature and Film*. Stanford, CA: Stanford University Press.

15 Literary work as a leisure activity
Amateur literary forums on the Czech internet

Karel Piorecký

Introduction

The aim of this chapter is to analyse the changing face of literary culture as new opportunities for publishing and literary communication are opened up by the internet and particularly by Web 2.0 and the associated principles of 'participative culture'. Hence, it is the author's intention to verify the hypothesis that the advent of open publication platforms (blogs, discussion forums with literary content, websites for writing communities, social networks and the like) has started to change the social status and social function of literature and its creators – literature is beginning to be presented and perceived as the product of leisure activity with primarily a relaxational and auto-therapeutic function. This objective will be achieved by analysing the structure and communicative practice of amateur literary forums which make up a substantial proportion of the content on the Czech literary internet, and are found in a number of other national literatures.

Democratisation of literary discourse

Literature has traditionally been perceived as a prestige discourse for intellectual elites, as well as an institution with socially important cultural and political functions – but postmodernism has relativised its status. Norman Fairclough described this process involving the transformation of prestige discourses and the loss of its exclusivity as the 'democratisation of discourse'. In his book *Discourse and Social Change*, Fairclough (1992) speaks of the discourse democratisation process as involving the removal of asymmetry in the rules, obligations and prestige of individual groups of language users, including the expansion of access to prestige types of discourse (e.g. political, professional and media, as well as artistic and literary). At the same time, however, he points out that although the democratisation of discourse may be natural and authentic, it can also be artificial and simulated. Contemporary culture holds informal discourse in high regard, so a dominant trend is to adapt written forms to spoken forms. Fairclough claims that, as a result, conversational discourse has penetrated from its primary, private sphere into the public: conversation is colonising the media and various public discourses are acquiring a conversational character. In this sense the boundaries between public and private spheres are being restructured (Fairclough, 1992).

Digital media did not start off this long-term process, but they did accelerate it. It may already be said that the democratisation process started when book printing weakened the Church's monopoly on the written word and offered written culture to the broader public. I see the idea of participative culture elaborated by Henry Jenkins in his book *Convergence Culture* and, in particular, his concept of the culture vernacularisation process as an extension and elaboration of the linguistic and philosophical framework presented by the discourse democratisation theory, and as its adaptation for the sphere of digital culture. Jenkins uses the term 'vernacular culture' to represent a culture created by amateurs, judging that new digital tools and distribution networks have bolstered the average person's capacity to participate in this culture: 'Having felt that power, fans and other subcultural groups are not going to return to docility and invisibility' (Jenkins, 2006: 162).

From the narrower leisure studies methodological toolkit, the 'serious leisure perspective' (SLP) seems to be a productive theoretical framework to think about literary cultures. Stebbins (2007) differentiates between serious leisure, casual leisure and project-based leisure. This triad enables us to assess the literary activity of those using open internet publication platforms in a differentiated way – in a different relationship to literature undertaken professionally and at a different distance from it. However, Stebbins and Cohen (2013) focus exclusively on the meaning of leisure activities for the individual and his or her individual identity – focusing less on the impact of mass and publicly operated leisure activity on the identity of the artistic circles and institutions that traditionally mediate it – the primary issue that this study attempts to deal with. Stebbins' concept of serious leisure will therefore play more of a supplementary and auxiliary role in the final analysis. The concepts of discourse demoncratisation and vernacular culture play a much more substantial role, as they support the primary aim of this study, to undertake a discourse and cultural analysis, the individual findings of which will be correlated under the literary system model put forward by Schmidt (2008).

It is within the framework of these theoretical ideas that the following observations and analyses are made. The objective of these analyses will be to define the role of amateur internet literary forums within the process of the vernacularisation of literature – the weakening of its status as a prestige discourse with important social functions – while the concept of literature as a tentative leisure activity is strengthened.

Amateur literature: towards a terminological framework

The very concept of 'amateur literature' is problematic in that it immediately implies its own antonym – 'professional literature' – whose meaning conflicts with actual literary practice. On (not only) the Czech literary scene, literary work has only ever been a profession in the true sense of the word for a narrow circle of authors. By no means all writers whose work is considered to be of literary merit fall within this circle.

Ways of distinguishing professionals from amateurs commonly used in other areas of human activity and always closely associated with the presence or absence of financial remuneration for a particular activity cannot be straighforwardly applied to literary culture. This economic criterion is also used, for example, by Stebbins (2007), so his concept is only partly usable within this study. The rule that a professional or a high-standard author can command financial remuneration and thus distinguish him- or herself from the amateur is not straightforwardly applicable in literature. Even many of the best authors, particularly in literatures with small book markets, are unable to rely on income from royalties, with their reward often being just the publication of the book itself or several copies for the author. This terminological dilemma will not be resolved by a sociological definition of the difference between professionals and amateurs. For an author to become a literary professional it is not enough for him or her to become involved in the writing community's social structures. Professionalism in literature (and art) is a much more dynamic entity than it is in other fields of human activity.

Nevertheless, it is possible to adhere terminologically to the term 'amateur literature', but the measure of amateurism or professionalism cannot be derived from writers' life experience, professions or social roles, but rather from their literary competence. Literary scholars define literary competence (and professionalism in literature) as a precondition for understanding (Culler, 1975) as well as for the creation (Svedjedal, 2000) of literary texts, for which it is essential to understand the rules of how literary discourse functions. Literary work is always part of a particular tradition, following certain literary (e.g. genre) conventions, and situated in the current literary and extraliterary context. It also has both intentional and unintentional intertextual connections and certain value frameworks are in operation as part of the literary culture, as are certain preconditions (e.g. mastery of literary language and its linguistic devices, editorial finalisation of the texts and so on).

I understand amateur literature as the creative work of those authors who have not adopted, or who have only partly adopted, these rules of literary discourse, either because their tender age does not allow them to, or because adoption of these rules is beyond their individual capacities. In the first case we might speak of beginning authors, and in the second case literary dilettantes. The activity of beginning authors shows the typical characteristics of serious leisure: intentionality, ambition and an attempt to launch a literary career. These authors crave feedback, and they see the publication opportunities awaiting them didactically as an opportunity for personal artistic development. On the other hand, the literary activity of dilettantes (or rather, in Stebbins' terminology 'the Hobbyists') is a typical example of casual leisure because it is random, it has the character of uncommitted experiments and of occasional, random texts that are stylised with only a sketchy notion of the nature of literary language (Piorecký, 2014a). The dilettante does not strive for any evaluative feedback, finding the very opportunity to publish and take part in prestige discourse to be quite absorbing.

The term 'blogomania' may be applied to the literary activities of dilettantes, as used by Dariusz Śnieżko in his study *Grafomania w sieci* (Śnieżko, 2009). In his view we cannot speak of graphomania in the case of online publication platforms, because the regularity and relatively high frequency of publishing does not so much stem from an individual's pathological aberration as from a structural component of these publication platforms, which are deliberately planned to make their users regularly spend their leisure time engaged in community communications and interactions. Hence, the literary activities of dilettantes are not motivated by literary ambitions, but by the very mechanism of digital publication, which may actually be of an addictive nature (Spitzer, 2014).

Amateur literature, in my sense, is an umbrella term for the creative work of both types of authors referred to above, whose common characteristic is a lack of literary competence and a conception of literary work as a leisure activity. A suitable example that enables us to narrow down this concept of literary work as a leisure activity seems to be what are known as literary websites, which on the Czech internet and elsewhere have become centres for amateur literary activity. I will now proceed to analyse the structure of these websites and characterise the media behaviour of their users.

Czech 'literary websites': media characterisation

With only the minimum quantitative restrictions, freely available web services facilitating the publication of literary texts have been available on the Czech internet since the late 1990s. The first website to offer this was *Písmák.cz* in 1997, at the same time as a similar German-language site *Leselupe.de* (1998) and English-language *Deepundergroundpoetry.com* launched in 1999. In 1999 the *Totem.cz* website entered this literary space and in the following few years a number of other websites also appeared (e.g. *LiTerra*, *Liter.cz* and *Epika*), offering a similar service, for which the expression 'literary website' came to be used. Since 2000 over 20 websites of this kind have been operating online in the Czech Republic, many of which operate to this day. The term 'literary websites' is indeed well established, but also somewhat misleading: there are more literary websites, where content of a literary nature is gathered, than websites offering amateur work – hence use of this term stakes a claim to a general meaning that does not actually match the subject. Literary websites are, in fact, better described as, de facto, a form of the discussion forums that abound online. I would therefore prefer to call these web services *literary forums* and define them as freely accessible spaces for publishing literary texts and discussing or evaluating their qualities.

Literary forum users and their media behaviour

Web-based literary forums have eased the way for amateur authors to publicly present themselves and hide their authorial identity, while entirely eliminating the geographical location of the author and the regional aspect of interactions within literary communities, which previously played (and to a certain extent continues to play) its role in literary clubs and competitions. In particular, they have changed the temporal conditions for these activities: the option of publishing, communicating and interacting is always available to amateur authors, so it just depends on what time of day and how much leisure time they spend on activities on literary forums, including periods formally designated as working time (procrastination during working hours).

The first step to be taken by those interested in publishing on a literary forum is to register and select a user name and nickname (nick). The option of presenting oneself in a brief profile is, for the most part, not used by contributors, who often fill it with hoax, ironic or humorous content. It is a relatively common practice to set up several nicks for the same contributor. These 'alternicks' are then used primarily to support the initial nick, whose identity has been built up by the user over a substantial period, for example, to publish a text of dubious standards which may be to the detriment of his relative celebrity. If the rules for publishing on a particular forum (to which the user expresses consent when he registers) are breached, the administrator may block the user account in question and delete published contributions, which is practically the only risk to which literary forum contributors are exposed. Of course, nobody can stop them creating a new user account.

Like other forms of online publication, literary forums facilitate the subsequent editing of texts that have already been published. Contributors take advantage of this by responding to objections sent to them in the comment boxes. However, this textual event (Pellizzi, 2006) has become difficult to decipher recently as the original version of the text is not available. The facility to make additional edits is one of the strongest factors minimising the risk of failure to which forum contributors are exposed. In contrast to publication in printed media, any lapse is always a priori temporary, because the text can be amended at any time or removed from public circulation without trace. Hence, literary forums are a domain for provisional, uncommitted publishing, in contrast to printed media, which fix the text in a single version, with the moment of publication in their case being an irreversible divide between the genesis and the reception to which the text is destined.

Likewise, when a contribution is being edited, the author decides in which category to include it. These are not just categories based on literary types and genres, but also on the specific intention which makes a particular author publish a text. For example, the structure of the *Literra* website does not automatically assume that the aim of an act of publication will be to enter into literary communication. In addition to the category of 'creative writing', another two alternative categories are also available: 'For fun' and 'Daily consumption/needs'. Hence graphomania (or blogomania) is anticipated, and no obstacles are placed in its way, but only 'sensible' graphomaniacs are given the opportunity to practise their deviant concept of literature. The actual structuring of literary forums into genre categories shows that in contrast to older media forms, this case does not just involve amateur literary content, but the literary forums are also amateur in their very structure: in the way they relate to the published content from the position of a medium and in the presumptions which they articulate with regard to this content. For example, the *Písmák* website is divided into two basic sections: 'Serious prose'/'Serious poetry'. This contrasts with the 'Stupidities' category. The *Literra* forum includes such categories as *Fixed Verse, Free Verse, Short Stories, Fairy Tales and Shout in the Dark* or *Taking Off*. The *Totem* forum has genres that go against mere scholastic convention: *Classic Verse, Poetic Word, Potpourri*. Hence, the architects of these websites and their administrators do not a priori expect any literary competency among their contributors and indeed do not show any themselves. In the case of literary forums it is not just the production of their content that has the character of amateur leisure activities, but the very creation and operation of forums as publication platforms – in this second case we can speak more of project-based leisure.

After a contribution has undergone this self-service editing it can be published almost immediately. The time the text is completed and the time it is published are almost identical in the case of literary forums, and it is this speed as well as the 'low-threshold' nature of these publication forums that make them popular. Not least, their popularity is also fostered by the absence of literary criticism in the original sense, even though considerable attention is paid to alternative forms of evaluation.

Absence of value perspective

In literary forums, published texts are immediately exposed to potential evaluation. Evaluation is only actively available to registered literary forum users, who are also contributors to the forum in question and participants in the activities within the community. The ideal of quality feedback is thus often not attained, and evaluation is more of a device for establishing social contacts between contributors; hence reciprocity is involved. The atmosphere is dominated by a shared common interest and a conviction that there is something to appreciate about every text, if only the author's effort. However, this is not always the case on foreign literary forums. For example, the *Leselupe* forum offers free 'lectoring' of texts by established writers, while the *InterBoard Poetry Community* website evaluates contributions from a set of over 20 literary forums in the form of competitions refereed by winners of prestigious literary awards. On fan fiction websites the role of critics (and to some extent editors) is assumed by what are known as 'beta readers', who are recruited from inside the amateur community but whose evalation is not public, and given to the author alone before the text is published. However, the rules for beta readers do not clearly indicate that a negative evaluation is required to be formulated in this context, merely as a suggestion, and authors should be praised for something in all cases.

It is also important to emphasise that the value of a contribution on a literary forum does not derive only from the quality of the text itself, but also from the overall behaviour of its author on the website. Also subject to evaluation are the author's statements on the contribution in question, as well as those of other participants in the conversation. Communication is determined more by the collegial atmosphere and conversational character of discourse in literary forums. It is common to see reciprocal praise of contributions among authors, and less frequent to see reciprocal criticism. The conversational nature of 'criticism' on literary forums is evident in the ability to block negative comments and evaluations, which the author in question finds unpleasant or off-putting – as in any other conversation this is merely a question of personal choice regarding with whom the author enters into communication contact. Criticism is not an independent voice from outside, but just another contribution to the broad-branching conversation formed by the entire speech activity taking place within the literary forum.

Literature as conversation

In addition to the evaluation method and the forms of criticism, the conversational character of literary communication on internet forums is made evident in the intertextual relations (citation, allusion, dedication, etc.) between the contributions of individual users of a particular forum. For example, on the *Litweb* forum the practice is relatively widespread whereby a poem by one forum member explicitly carries on from and reacts to the poetic text of another. This is done repeatedly, for example, by two contributors with the nicks Marek and JC senior, either by publishing contributions which are dedicated in the introductory comment (known as the prologue) to a friendly nick and indicates an association with his text, or in the form of a comment beneath a contribution, which is stylised into verse involving some motif or stylistic feature of the prototext. Or, finally, the contribution is intertextually linked to the prototext in the form of a versified review.

This intertextual nexus indicates the conversational nature of the literary communication taking place within literary forums. Here, a literary text does not act as a work which the author makes available to readers, but as a contribution to a constantly ongoing informal and artistic objective not following any group conversations. The literary text becomes a reply within a dialogue. Here, intertextuality does not only have the character of inspiration or allusion, but also of dialogue. Texts are consumed in conversations, in which they exhaust their meaning. A literary forum is a social formation but then, paradoxically, the texts that circulate there have a very weak social function. They are a vehicle for community conversation, not an artistic work as a social fact with a dominating aesthetic function. Hence, it should also be understood that a large number of contributors on literary forums make it explicitly clear (e.g. in the form of paratexts, comments and so on) that they have given up on literary ambitions and present their participation in the life of the literary forum as mere uncommitted fun.

In a number of cases it is clear that the authors are distancing themselves from the texts they have published by the very poetics of their titles and a self-deprecating judgemental tone. For example, the titles of the 'collections' on *Písmák* often have deprecatory expressions which indicate in advance the experimental, unfinished, occasional and random character of the texts included in the collection: *Silliness, Winter sillinesses, Spring sillinesses, Summer sillinesses and so on, The poor collection of an ignorant machine operator, Beginner's hocus pocus and the like.*

Community nature of literary forums

Not all registered nicks may be considered to be members of the literary forum community, but only those actively taking part in communication and collaboration. In the case of Czech literary forums active contributors make up approximately one-tenth of the overall total of registered users, but even so, particularly in the case of the oldest forums, these are communities of respectable size. For example, in January 2009, there were 35,675 users registered on *Písmák*, of whom website owner Roman Plojhar estimates the number of active contributors totals 8000. In 2011 some 2800 users joined the forum every day. In 2009 the *Totem* forum had around 30,000 registered users and offered 265,000 contributions (this information is publicly available at pismak.cz and totem.cz).

This size shows that Czech literary forums are an extraordinary and atypical phenomenon in comparison with those elsewhere. For example, the German literary forum *Leselupe.de* with 4744 registered users presents itself as a large, or even one of the largest, German literary forums. The number of users is only a fraction of the number of users at the Czech forums *Písmák* or *Totem*, while *Leselupe* accepts its users from a much broader language area. Czech literary forums are not even matched by the anglophone *deepundergroundpoetry.com* with 16,071 registered users. What is significantly higher is the number of contributions: in 2009 some 265,000 works were available on *Totem*, while that same year *Leselupe* offered around 70,000. Also noticeable is the number of visitors to the German website. It was visited monthly (in 2009) by around 150,000 users with an average of around 5000 users every day, which is a significantly higher figure than the number of registered users (of whom there were around 4000 that year). In 2011 *Písmák* achieved a maximum visitor rate of 2800 per day. One of the differences between Czech websites and *Leselupe* is probably the presence of 'lurkers' among the website visitors – unregistered readers who only come to the site to browse. In the case of Czech literary forums this group barely appears, and quite definitely not to the same extent (1000 'pure' readers a day). Clearly, this is one of the specific features of Czech literary forums. However, in her international research into online communities, Baym came to the conclusion that 'lurkers' are the most common and frequent type of participants in these groups, whereas the 'posters' (i.e. authors of contributions) are in a clear minority (Baym, 2010: 87).

Contributors' activities on literary forums have the character of leisure-time pursuits. This is confirmed by Košinská (2009), who points out that a difference may be observed in visiting rates during working days and weekends, when the number of visitors (slightly) increases. Differences in visiting rates during the working week and the year as a whole can be identified, but they are not in any way sizeable. Even at Christmas the number of visits to literary forums does not substantially fall. Hence, these are communities that share all their time equally: working time (procrastination), free time and time that is traditionally set aside for family gatherings (holidays) (Košinská, 2009).

In addition to publication activity, contributors and administrators normally organise various events that allow community members to spend free time together not only in the virtual environment of an internet forum, but also physically at various meetings, literary soirées and social outings. Thus, the primary virtual form of existence of these communities also has its extension into physical spaces. However, even on these occasions, community members maintain their role as representatives of the virtual identities they have built up on the internet, addressing each other not with their actual names but with their 'nicks', just like online. For example, it shows the photographic documentation for the Totem literary forum (Totem během více než 10 let – 2010).

The literary communication system in literary forums tends to be closed. An audience is desirable, but it has to be predisposed towards (amateur) literature. The closed, cohesive nature of the communities is demonstrated by works based on many years of personal experience of communication within these communities. It is also telling that reactions towards occasional attempts by established authors to enter into community conversations are negative (e.g. the attempt made by poet Lubor Kasal to obtain feedback on his poem *Dvanáct* before it was published as a book).

A logical consequence of the closed nature of forums is the fairly strong coherence of the communities and the low membership turnover among the different literary forums. However, these communities are not homogeneous in terms of opinions or interests. Among their participants there are clear differences in the attitudes they adopt towards this way of spending leisure time together – those present include both people who try to make use of the literary forum environment for personal improvement (serious leisure), and those who do not hesitate to publish texts in this way that have emerged entirely by chance without any literary ambitions (casual leisure). The serious segment of literary communities is characterised by their 'unique ethos', which Stebbins counts among the basic characteristics of serious leisure: 'An ethos is the spirit of the community of serious leisure participants, as manifested in shared attitudes, practices, values, beliefs, goals and so on' (Stebbins, 2007: 12).

Communities in literary forums in the Czech Republic are not homogeneous in terms of age or generation. The age range of literary forum contributors has been changing as the internet has developed and its accessibility has improved. During the first phase (at the end of the 1990s), contributors were primarily those who had access to the internet at work (in the 18–35 age group) (Košinská, 2009: 21). Since 2000, the internet has become more accessible and the circle of users has begun to expand to include a strong group of young authors of secondary school age, as well as (in the case of some websites like *Epika* and *Litweb*) older users who while away the time on literary forums when they retire. The generational differences between literary forum users are evident and may be interpreted in terms of the dichotomy between 'digital natives' and 'digital immigrants' (Palfrey and Gasser, 2008). Literary forums naturally play the greatest role for authors whose age places them in the digital natives category, and are accepted by them as a natural first opportunity to enter into literary communication. Digital immigrants are to a large extent in a numerical minority. They are either authors who are using the internet to make up for the lack of literary clubs (which for the most part closed down in Czechia after 1989), or pensioners who welcome these websites as an opportunity to pass their leisure time in an active way.

The position of amateur literature in contemporary culture

In spite of the above, literary forums cannot be seen as an isolated sphere separate from literary culture as a whole. Quite the contrary, since Generation Y authors' literary forums have become not only a space for spending leisure time, but also (for the best ones) a primary publication space in which to launch their literary work. Literary forums have become a 'level zero', as it were, in the literary system (Schmidt, 2008) through which it is possible to get into literature. Whereas in the age of printed media, publication platforms for literary amateurs (e.g. specialised journal features) adopted rules of literary discourse and were used de facto to broaden literary competence, in the case of online literary forums quite the opposite is the case. Literary forums as an inherent, functional and stabilised part of the literary system cast the shadow of amateurism over the entire system. Literature is then presented as a leisure-time activity for creative writers without any greater ambition to penetrate beyond their literary context and exercise their influence. The publication space afforded by literary forums is broader than in the case of older media forums for presenting amateur literature, as it is organised systematically and the entire sphere of amateur literature enters public communication with a much higher self-confidence than before. Literary forums relativise the boundary between amateur and professional (literarily competent) work. This is a consequence of technological and media conditions, as well as the overall cultural shift away from professionalism towards amateurism (Keen, 2007).

Literary forums are by no means the only phenomenon in contemporary literature that operate as vehicles for the vernacularisation of literary culture. Working on a similar principle to that of literary forums is the *Poetizer* mobile application, which differs from older literary forums not only in its mobile internet orientation, but also in its commercial nature, as users of this service have the option of sending a financial gift to the authors of poems that have appealed to them. The company that is developing and operating *Poetizer* takes 10 per cent commission from each gift (while another 30 per cent covers *Poetizer* distribution on Google Play). This actually involves the technical and organisational professionalisation of amateur literary discourse. The vernacularisation function of *Poetizer* is emphasised by the application inventors themselves in their promotional texts, which say, inter alia, 'Poetizer is a mobile application for all poetry lovers whose aim is to raise interest in poetry, make it available to the broadest possible public and demonstrate that it is not just a literary form for the elect' (Poetizer, 2015). A similar approach also characterises numerous Facebook pages for amateur literati, which stress a radically democratised concept of literature as public self-expression available to anyone without restriction. For example, the administrator at *Verše pro všechny* has addressed Facebook users as follows: 'This page is for all those who, like me, wish to express their feelings. Do it. You won't harm anything with poetry. Say what you feel' (Böhm, 2014). The vernacularisation process also has its supporters outside of digital media. These literary phenomena adopt a concept of literature as a leisure-time pursuit that is dynamically developing on the internet and also establish it in the sphere of printing (publishing books by means of print-on-demand services) and literary events (slam poetry, open mic literary events and guerrilla poetry) (Fišerová, 2014). A common characteristic of these various literary activities is that their organisers successfully create a positive media image, which is facilitated to a considerable extent by the inability or unwillingness of mainstream media to distinguish between amateur and professional literary output (e.g. the Czech Television report on the prank Facebook page *Městská poezie Brno* as an example of contemporary poetry (Události v culture, 2014)). Or the approach of the same mass media to the Poetizer mobile application, which Czech Television presented as hope for the 'Renaissance of poetry' (@online, 2015).

The systemic consequences of these processes are also evident in the imaginary core of the literary system, which is supposedly made up of authors with a high degree of literary competence and professionalism – this is traditionally associated with professional literary organisations. Currently, the Writers' Guild, the largest Czech organisation of its kind, is led by people who define themselves as literary amateurs and who cannot demonstrate reliable literary activity (Piorecký, 2014b).

Literature as a leisure activity

The question then remains whether, even after this 'invasion of dilettantes', literature will remain a 'prestige type' of discourse, as Fairclough describes it, as literary amateurs not only endeavour to expand access to literary discourse, but also to colonise it. They create integrated literary communication microsystems and present them as an alternative or as a parallel literary culture comparable in value to the core of literary discourse residing in the printed media sphere. The question also remains whether the new, unprecedentedly strong role played by amateurs in literary culture is a positive manifestation of its democratisation, eliminating previous social, ideological, geographical and other obstacles, or an invasion of literary dilettantes, taking advantage of the free space they have colonised, gaining in self-confidence and increasingly making demands as this space expands. Keen is right to some extent when he says that the process of democratisation that was supposed to come together with the internet is just a *great seductive illusion* (Keen, 2007: 16). In (civic) journalism, for example, the discourse democratisation process has the advantage of speed. In open source software development, another obvious benefit is that of cost savings. Wikipedia is used to efficiently distribute knowledge. However, it would be difficult to find similar benefits in the case of the democratisation of literary discourse, where the democratisation is more of an illusory nature. Authors who begin their literary life in online literary forums and who have literary competence and talent ought in all probability to enter into literary discourse without the aid of such literary forums. In any case they get into printed literary media not because of any journals' or publishers' quest or interest, but again thanks to their own activities.

Literary forums on the Czech internet would be a positive democratising factor in literary discourse if they also broadened literary competence within literary culture. But this does not happen, at least in the case of Czech literary forums. In contrast to British and American specialist websites, which declare their operating principle to be that of 'writing communities' with an openly didactic function – as a rule by means of online creative writing lessons (*UKAuthors*, 2002; *Leselupe.de*, 1998; *Slavonica.sk*, ludo, 2014), competitions with the participation of a panel of judges from the ranks of respected literary figures (*Interboard Poetry Community*, 1999), a combination of contributions by amateur writers and classic literary texts presented as a model (Classic Poetry, 2004) or other forms of targeted enhancement of literary competence among website users.

The difference between Czech and Anglo-Saxon literary forums is clearly associated with the different tradition behind the teaching of creative writing in the two language spheres. The stronger didactic focus of English-language literary forums points to their cultural connection with the well-established tuition of creative writing in the educational systems of these countries. Hence, Czech literary forums are much more than just democratising forces in the true sense of the word, as vehicles for entertainment and experiential culture (Simanowski, 2008), which also injects the 'enjoyment' imperative into literature and eliminates the traditional distinctions between roles. After all, who would not like to enjoy the role of writer at least for a while?

Conclusion

This analysis of literary forums and their contextual connections supports the initial hypothesis that literature in contact with digital culture and in connection with the growing position of literary amateurs is changing from a prestige discourse to a free-time activity. This primarily involves the systemic nature of the change which amateur literature, disseminated by digital media, brings about. Amateur free-time literary activities (performed at the level of serious leisure) have become a part of the literary system, which is in contrast to the pre-digital era, when they were relegated to an underground existence or to publication in media with marginal coverage (magazine features for neophyte authors, student magazines and so on).

Another fundamental difference is the legitimisation of texts created by chance through literary activities at the level of casual leisure. This is facilitated by the fact that in the digital media environment the conversational aspect of literary communication has been markedly bolstered, along with the concept of literature as a community entertainment at the expense of the social and aesthetic function of literature. This analysis of amateur literature on the Czech internet has also indicated the paradigmatic nature of this new form of literary amateurism. The leisure-time character of literary production has ceased to be a unique attribute of selected literary websites and has started (in line with post-digital culture) to penetrate beyond the internet and to influence the paradigms of highbrow literature itself.

Acknowledgement

This chapter was written as part of Czech Science Foundation grant project P406/12/P603.

References

@online (2015) @online. Available at: www.ceskatelevize.cz:8080/ivysilani/10659215431-online/315281381880328 (accessed 14 November 2015).
Baym, N.K. (2010) *Personal Connections in the Digital Age*. Cambridge: Polity Press.
Böhm, T. (2014) Verše pro všechny. Available at: https://www.facebook.com/Verseprovsechny/?fref=ts (accessed 14 November 2015).
Classic Poetry (2004) Classic poetry. Available at: http://poems.writers-network.com/ (accessed 14 November 2015).
Cramer, F. (2014) What is 'post-digital'? *APRJA*, 3(1). Available at: www.aprja.net/?p=1318 (accessed 14 November 2015).
Culler, J. (1975) *Structuralist Poetics*. London: Routledge.
Deep Underground Poetry (1999) Deep underground poetry. Available at: http://deepundergroundpoetry.com/ (accessed 14 November 2015).
Donath, J.S. (1999) Identity and deception in the virtual community. In M.A. Smith and P. Kollock (eds) *Communities in Cyberspace*. London: Routledge (pp. 29–59).
Epika (2002) *Epika*. Available at: http://epika.cz (accessed 14 November 2015).
Fairclough, N. (1992) *Discourse and Social Change*. Cambridge: Polity Press.
Fišerová, B. (2014) Guerilla poetring. Available at: http://guerillapoetring.webnode.cz/ (accessed 14 November 2015).
Interboard Poetry Community (1999) Interboard poetry community. Available at: http://ibpc.webdelsol.com/ (accessed 14 November 2015).
Jenkins, H. (2006) *Convergence Culture. Where Old and New Media Collide*. New York: New York University Press.
Keen, A. (2007) *The Cult of the Amateur*. New York: Doubleday.
Košinská, E. (2009) *Čtenáři v internetových komunitách (zaměřených na literaturu)*. MA dissertation, Charles University in Prague, Faculty of Arts.
Krapovich, A.I. (2006) The audience as editor. The role of beta readers in online fan fiction communities. In K. Hellekson and K. Busse (eds) *Fan Fiction and Fan Communities in the Age of the Internet*. Jefferson: McFarland (pp. 171–188).
Leselupe.de (1998) Leselupe.de. Available at: www.leselupe.de/ (accessed 14 November 2015).

Liter (2004) Liter. Available at: www.liter.cz/ (accessed 14 November 2015).
Literra (2003) Literra. Available at: www.literra.cz/ (accessed 14 November 2015).
Litweb (2012) Litweb. Available at: www.litweb.cz (accessed 14 November 2015).
ludo (2014) Cvičenie: Poviedka. Available at: www.slavonica.sk/cvicenia/1402394466/cvicenie-poviedka/ (accessed 14 November 2015).
Palfrey, J. and Gasser, U. (2008) *Born Digital. Understanding the First Generation of Digital Natives.* New York: Basic Books.
Pellizzi, F. (2006) Dialogism, intermediality and digital textuality. Available at: www.iasl.uni-muenchen.de/discuss/lisforen/pellizzi_dialogism.pdf (accessed 14 November 2015).
Piorecký, K. (2014a) Amatérská literární fóra na českém internetu. Mezi demokratizací a diletantstvím, *Mediální studia*, 8(2): 127–148.
Piorecký, K. (2014b) Invaze diletantů. Obec spisovatelů – odvrácená tvář demokratizace literatury? *A2*, 10(13): 18–19.
Písmák (1997) *Písmák*. Available at: www.pismak.cz/ (accessed 14 November 2015).
Poetizer (2015) *Poetizer*. Available at: www.poetizer.cz (accessed 14 November 2015).
Schmidt, S.J. (2008) *Přesahování literatury.* Prague: Institute of Czech Studies CAS.
Simanowski, R. (2008) *Digitale Medien in der Erlebnisgesellschaft.* Reinbek bei Hamburg: Rowohlt.
Śnieżko, D. (2009) Grafomania w sieci. In A. Gumkowska (ed.) *Tekst w sieci 2.* Warsaw: Wydawnictwa Akademickie i Profesjonalne (pp. 13–20).
Spitzer, M. (2014) *Digitální demence. Jak připravujeme sami sebe a naše děti o rozum.* Brno: Host.
Společenství amatérských spisovatelů (2005) *Společenství amatérských spisovatelů.* Available at: www.saspi.cz/ (accessed 14 November 2015).
Stebbins, R.A. (2007) *Serious Leisure: A Perspective For Our Time.* New Brunswick, NJ: Transaction.
Stebbins, R.A. and Cohen, E.G. (2013) *Serious Leisure and Individuality.* Montreal: MQUP.
Svedjedal, J. (2000) *The Literary Web.* Stockholm: Kungl. Biblioteket.
Totem (1999) *Totem*. Available at: www.totem.cz/ (accessed 14 November 2015).
Totem během více než 10 let (2010) *Totem*. Available at: www.totem.cz/endb.php?nm=20&pg=3 (accessed 14 November 2015).
Writers University (2002) *Writers university*. Available at: http://archive.is/Pe7OJ (accessed 14 November 2015).
Události v kultuře (2014) *Události v kultuře*. Available at: www.ceskatelevize.cz/ivysilani/1097206490-udalosti-v-kulture/214411000120826/obsah/346088-policejni-poezie (accessed 14 November 2015).
UKAuthors (2002) *UKAuthors*. Available at: http://ukauthors.com/ (accessed 14 November 2015).

16 Sexual desire in the digital leisure sphere
Women's consumption of sexually explicit material

Diana C. Parry and Tracy Penny Light

Introduction

Sexual desire in the digital leisure sphere is complicated for women. Technology has opened up a new leisure culture for female consumers of sexually explicit material (SEM) – such as pornography and erotica. New technologies, such as e-readers, chat rooms, blogs and websites open up space for a broad intersection of women to access, consume, produce and discuss SEM both online and in face-to-face communities (Parry and Penny Light, 2014). The increased diversity of women accessing SEM may be viewed as liberatory because the sexual practices and experiences they seek 'are important parts of many people's self-recognition as sexual subjects' (Albury, 2009: 650). Yet, SEM can also constrain women's liberation by depicting patriarchal sex acts (Attwood, 2007). Even the newer 'by women, for women' (BWFW) genre of SEM tends to reproduce traditional paradigms of sexuality that reinforce harmful, heteronormative stereotypes of femininity and masculinity. Despite these representations, many women see their engagement with SEM as positive, enabling them to acknowledge, embrace and explore their 'dark [digital] desires' (Kipnis, 2007; James, 2011). The complexity surrounding women's use of digital technology to consume SEM in their leisure time begs a feminist analysis. Thus, the purpose of our chapter is to critically examine women's use of digital technology to consume SEM as a case study in the changing nature of leisure culture.

Our chapter is based on in-depth, conversational interviews with 29 women that lasted 90 minutes on average. The interviews explored SEM and digital engagement across participants' sexual histories and sexual practices, as well as their feelings/attitudes about sexual culture and sexual well-being. We recruited participants through *Good for Her*, which is a sexual workshop centre that seeks to empower women by celebrating their sexuality. Employing experienced and knowledgeable sex educators since 1997, *Good for Her* attracts a large and diverse group of women. This diversity was reflected in our group of participants who ranged in age from 21 to 54. They represented a wide variety of sexual identities including heterosexual, lesbian, pansexual, kinky, queer, fluid and bisexual. Many of the women were in committed relationships (married or common law), but others were single, divorced and/or dating. Most were employed full time in a variety of careers, including the fashion industry, accountancy, education (both teachers and students), art, retail and service industries. Five of the participants were mothers. Most of the participants identified as Caucasians, but others self-identified as mixed race, West Indian, Sri Lankan or European. The education levels of participants ranged from some college courses through to completion of a Master's degree. The household incomes of participants ranged from $20,000 to over a $100,000.

Through a feminist lens, our findings reveal the complexities of women's consumption of SEM due to the shifting cultural and digital contexts in which sexually explicit materials are made available to them in their leisure time. Our analysis considers both the positive and negative impacts of digital technologies upon women's sexual health and well-being. In so doing, we explore how women's use of digital technology to consume SEM is closing the 'digital gap' by recovering a sphere traditionally associated with the masculine for women (Puente, 2008: 435). Similarly, we examine how digital leisure cultures, including online SEM, impacts upon the pleasure gap that many feminists argue exists between men's and women's sexuality (Orenstein, 2000). Finally, we analyse digital leisure culture (through SEM) as a context for the simultaneous reproduction and resistance of gendered ideologies.

Our chapter is guided by a cyberfeminist theoretical orientation. Cyberfeminism 'refers to a range of theories, debates, and practices about the relationship between gender and digital culture' (Daniels, 2009: 102). Resisting a monolithic, totalising vision, cyberfeminist research often includes critiques about equality in cyberspace, challenges to gender stereotypes, and examinations of the relationships between women and technology (Flanagan and Booth, 2002). While much literature on gender and technology has usefully documented ways in which technology can contribute to women's oppression (Eble and Breault, 2002), cyberfeminism often emphasises the possibilities of technology to *enhance* women's lives. Cyberfeminist perspectives recognise that women's experiences with technology can facilitate worldwide networking and the creation of women's own spaces of dialogue and action on the internet (Orgad, 2005). We begin by contextualising the impact of technology upon SEM production and consumption in contemporary culture.

SEM consumption in the digital era

In her book *Pornland*, Dines (2010) clearly outlines how the 'the Internet caused a revolution in porn' (p. xiii). Indeed, the advent of the internet has made SEM – including pornography and erotica – more accessible, affordable and anonymous, what Cooper (1998) refers to as the Triple-A engine. The SEM that is available today is strikingly different from the print materials that pre-date the invention of the World Wide Web (Dines, 2010). The internet has facilitated a seismic shift in the scope, type and variety of material that is available for consumption (Attwood, 2010). The technological influence is so great that SEM is embedded in our everyday lives, resulting in a pornification of society (Paasonen *et al.*, 2007), including leisure. Towards this end, Spracklen posits that 'masturbating to pornography is the biggest form of leisure associated with the Net' (2015: 173).

Historically, men have been the primary producers and consumers of SEM and thus associated with this type of leisure behaviour (Attwood, 2010; Spracklen, 2015). Today, women are one of the fastest-growing groups of SEM consumers and producers (Doring, 2009). Using technology, women are subverting the gendered politics of shame by consuming SEM whenever and wherever they like (Parry and Penny Light, 2014). Adding women's voices to the consumption and production of SEM offers 'new thinking about the richness and complexity of porn as a genre and as an industry' (Taormino et al., 2013: 9). This chapter contributes to that body of scholarship by exploring the changing nature of leisure culture brought about, intensified and accelerated by women's use of digital technology to consume SEM. We turn next to the exploration of contemporary feminist debates surrounding SEM.

Anti-pornography feminist perspectives in the digital era

Contemporary debates about the impacts of SEM consumption tend to contrast sex-positive feminists and those who are anti-pornography. The latter group argues that SEM, online and offline, caters to a male, heterosexual consumer and thus constructs and maintains female oppression by depicting women as skilled sexual servants of patriarchal needs (Sonnet, 1999). This feminist position believes porn is 'debased, dehumanized, formulaic and generic' with negative impacts for women's sexuality (Dines, 2010: x). From this feminist perspective, porn is 'inherently oppressive to women – … women are debased when they have sex on camera' (Taormino et al., 2013: 15). Doring (2009) explains that SEM aimed at male audiences contributes to negative attitudes and abusive behaviours because the images of women are sexist and reinforce idealised versions of women's bodies and their sexual prowess that can negatively influence perceptions of their abilities. Other feminists raise concerns with forms of SEM that showcase sexual freedom because they 'set the stage for sexual liberalism and "amoral" or "irresponsible" sexual behaviour' (Doring, 2009: 1093). This type of sexual imagery can make women feel pressured, manipulated and coerced into 'porn sex', which is anonymous, disconnected and devoid of intimacy (Dines, 2010). Taken together, anti-pornography feminist critiques emphasise that SEM can be dangerous, as it objectifies, dehumanises and depersonalises its subjects, mostly women (Attwood, 2007). With the emergence of new technologies that enable more people to access, consume and produce SEM, these feminist concerns are more prevalent than ever (Penley et al., 2013).

The concerns raised by anti-pornography feminists are not unfounded insofar as almost all the women in our study accessed SEM through new digital technologies, including laptops, tablets and smartphones, which speaks to increased availability and access. Even those who were consuming erotic literature often did so digitally through e-readers. Moreover, the feminist critiques about the sexist images and subsequent behaviours associated with SEM consumption were reflected in our findings. For example, some of the women in our study spoke directly about the limited visual representations of women in SEM, noting that porn stars are thin, mostly white and young, except for those who fulfil niche interests such as size (i.e. BBW – big, beautiful woman), ethnicity (i.e. Asians) or older (think MILF or Mother I would like to Fuck). Many participants were aware that porn stars may not represent 'real bodies', having undergone cosmetic surgeries such as breast augmentation and labiaplasty to enhance their sex appeal (Penny Light and Parry, forthcoming).

And yet, the visual images in pornography did serve to make some of the women feel badly about their bodies, sexual capabilities and/or support harmful behaviour. For example, one woman in our study put pictures of naked female porn stars up on the walls of her apartment to remind herself not to overeat and to stick to her diet. Some participants referred to problems which SEM consumption caused in their intimate relationships, including partners who became jealous of their porn consumption. Towards this end, Julia (all names are pseudonyms) said, 'I think he was kind of jealous of it though. Just weirdly jealous of it' and others whose partners developed harmful porn addictions: 'He honestly turned out to be addicted to it. So it was weird. A weird situation.' Perhaps one of the most striking issues raised by the women using digital technology to consume SEM in our study was the lack of representation of the type of sex they themselves were having in real life. For example, Carolyn stated, 'I touch myself while having sex and I always orgasm that way at least once. But I never saw that in the porn I watched online.' These points highlight some of the problematic aspects of SEM consumption on women's sexual well-being, thereby supporting the concerns raised by anti-pornography feminists.

The sex positive feminist perspective in the digital era

In contrast to the anti-pornography feminist position, sex-positive feminists argue that focusing on the dangers of SEM has subsumed the feminist project of examining how women's sexual desires and pleasure may in fact benefit from their consumption (Vance, 1992). Given that 'online pornography [i]s used by ... women with considerably greater frequency' (Doring, 2009: 1092), the possible benefits of its consumption also warrant attention. These benefits are particularly relevant in light of a rapidly expanding market of a 'by women, for women' (BWFW) genre of SEM (Ray, 2007). In contrast to male-oriented SEM, the BWFW genre 'focuses more on plot and characterisation, foregrounds emotional connection between actors and actresses, and eschews conventions such as the ubiquitous external ejaculation' (Beggan and Allison, 2009: 448). Such materials purport to tap into the female point of view, foregrounding women's sexual tastes and desires (Sonnet, 1999). According to Schauer (2005), this genre of SEM reworks sexist pornography conventions. Penley *et al.* explain, 'women-authored erotica and pornography speaks to fantasies that women actually have' (2013: 14).

The most recent and visible example of the BWFW genre of SEM is the *Fifty Shades of Grey* trilogy by author E.L. James. The books are best known for the explicitly erotic narrative and have topped bestseller lists worldwide, earning E.L. James a number of accolades. '*Fifty Shades* popularized – and, to a greater extent, destigmatized – erotica' so that now more and more women are surrendering to the seductive stories (Bello, 2013: 23). Much of the success attributed to the *Fifty Shades* series is linked to the discreet nature of e-reading devices that enable women to consume SEM without shame whenever and wherever they like (Parry and Penny Light, 2014). Lyons (2012) explains,

> the unprecedented popularity of the novels stems in part from their original publication as e-books. Previously, erotic novels were for private consumption, to be kept on the bed stand, probably rarely even displayed on one's bookshelf. One of the reported pleasures found in reading the trilogy emerged from its furtive consumption on new mobile technologies, in particular the Kindle, which allows the reader to hide the books and, indeed, themselves under a cloak of erotic invisibility.
>
> (Lyons, 2012: 885)

The overwhelming popularity of the *Fifty Shades* series demonstrates that there is great demand among women for explicit sexual representations (Penley *et al.*, 2013). Indeed, the women in our study support this argument. Many had even read the *Fifty Shades* series. While most were not fans of the books – noting they were poor examples of literature that contain inaccurate representations of bondage/discipline, dominance/submission and sadism/masochism (BDSM), and sex scenes that were unrealistic and at times boring – they did appreciate the series as an important entry into SEM for many women. Other benefits of the new technological avenues for women to access and consume SEM included increased sexual pleasure (both with partners and alone), self-acceptance regarding sexual interests and practices, improved communication between sexual partners, but also friends, and a widening of traditional gender roles and sexual scripts. Many women in our study specifically highlighted that technology enabled them to access new (to them) sexual practices that broadened their sexual repertoire. For example, Fiona referred to a site she frequented called FetLife that provides information on specific sexual fetishes. She stated,

> it was kind of nice to have it because I was able to explore BDSM without actually being involved in the activities and I could kind of figure out what I'd be interested in and what I wouldn't be. So then when I started a new relationship I knew what was OK in that relationship. I kind of already knew what I wanted.

The importance of technology in facilitating women's access to SEM should not be underestimated: in a provocative way it 'offers popular pleasures with a view to enhancing women's understanding of the possible role of erotica in developing personal sexual practices' (Sonnet, 1999: 183).

Digital technology and the transformation of SEM consumption

Digital engagement is key to contemporary SEM consumption and production (Taormino *et al.*, 2013; Dines, 2010). Indeed, all of the women in our study reported using some form of digital technology to consume SEM. As just one example, in discussing the various types of SEM she consumes, Amanda spoke about the use of her phone: 'I have some pictures on my phone that I'll look at.' Most of our participants spoke about how digital technologies afforded access to SEM that opened a whole new world for them. For example, Ella stated, 'having a laptop and the ability to access and just look through the internet was kind of eye opening for me.' Annika talked about the affordability of SEM online when she stated, 'the internet's a really good cheap outlet for me for looking at porn'. Many spoke about the anonymity afforded through online technology: for example, Lisa said, 'anonymousness, anonymity is something that's really meaningful to me'. These findings support Cooper's (1998) notion of technology serving as a Triple-A engine (accessible, affordable, anonymous) in SEM.

Digital engagement was also critical to consuming new (to the women) and varied forms of SEM. Many women spoke of initially seeking out one type of SEM online and discovering other forms that they found sexually satisfying. For example, Lauren used her laptop to search mediated SEM images ('I went to search for still images of women and sometimes men') and videos, but through her search she discovered live sex acts. In her words,

> I developed this knowledge that things could be live. I got into cams and ChatRoulette [an online website that randomly pairs people around the world for web-based conversations]. When I went to university that was the same year that I heard about ChatRoulette and I had kind of this knowledge that things could be live and not videos so I was kind of drawn to that. I guess I wanted some interaction to feel like I was part of it.

Digital engagement, therefore, facilitates exposure to new genres of SEM for women.

While consumption of SEM often happens in isolation or with a sexual partner, some of the women in our study were using technology to move beyond the individual pleasure of consuming SEM. Through digital technologies such as social networking sites and chat rooms, some of the women formed online communities within which they expressed their sexual desire, shared their sexual knowledge, and even learned about how to perform new sexual acts (Parry and Penny Light, 2014). For example, Betsy stated,

> I do have a lot of – I do have some chums online and we do email porn to each other and so I have a lot of graphics and visuals and some little gifs with looping action happening, that kind of thing.

Beth talked about sharing SEM with friends: 'I have girlfriends that I share the stuff that I get.' Anna talked about the online communities she joined: 'I'm in some Facebook groups around women's sexuality and some references are shared there, not like check out this hot clip, but go check this out, it's a good director or there's a sale on at this place.'

Our interviews point to the ways in which women are using new digital technologies to create a collective identity grounded in a shared, sexual fantasy world (Sonnet, 1999). These practices reflect a 'participatory culture', which occurs when technology brings together groups of like-minded people who would not connect otherwise face-to-face (Attwood, 2007). Webblogs serve as a good example. According to Muise (2011), online sexual webblogs provide women with spaces to discuss their sexuality in communities where they can articulate sexual desires while potentially avoiding shameful feelings about sex acts. In her words, 'online blogs and zines are one place where women can develop vocabularies of sexual desire, reduce shame around sex, and build communities to share experiences and information' (Muise, 2011: 412). Thus, Muise demonstrates the liberatory potential of online technology for women's sexuality.

Other researchers have noted that the ability to access sex sites on the internet empowers women to explore their own sexuality. Technology such as fan fiction websites, e-books, virtual publishers, social networking sites and online communities of interest are opening up new avenues for women's consumption and construction of their sexuality and sexual practices (Milhausen, 2012). Attwood explained, 'It is now possible to create, distribute and access a much more diverse set of sexual representations' (2007: 441). Moreover, newer forms of representation and access want to draw in audiences that have traditionally been ignored by porn, including women (Attwood, 2007).

Technology, SEM and women's sexual well-being: liberation *and* constraint

Emergent technologies open up space for a broad intersection of women to access and consume SEM online. The women who participated in our study demonstrated much diversity in terms of age, sexual identity, relationship status, employment, education and socio-economic status. By most accounts, our participants represented a fairly diverse group of women accessing and consuming SEM. The diversity in participants and increased access may be viewed as liberatory given that the sexual practices and experiences such as those found in SEM help people embrace their sexual selves and sexual desires (Albury, 2009). Yet, as noted earlier, the depictions of women in SEM often include patriarchal sex acts and storylines that reproduce harmful, heteronormative ideals which are constraining (Attwood, 2007). For example, so-called 'gonzo' porn, 'which is all over the Internet ... depicts hard-core, body-punishing sex in which women are demeaned and debased' (Dines, 2010: xi). Many of the women in our research reported consuming SEM that was geared towards a male audience. In talking about the type of SEM she consumes, Lucy explained,

> I think most of the stuff I do look at is technically geared at men. I get the feeling it is anyway. I seem to watch a lot of threesome stuff and like girl-on-girl stuff. That's what I end up watching. It's usually not geared at women, I find anyway.

Certain genres of SEM that objectify women for men's sexual pleasure still exist. Attwood explained that 'hardcore' commercialised pornography:

> is still organized around a set of sexual 'numbers' derived from 1970s ... [that include] the oral, vaginal and anal penetration of women by men, girl on girl scenes and threesomes. Porn of this kind tends to focus on the explicit display of women's bodies, with male display limited to ejaculation, usually onto the body or into the mouth of a woman – the so-called money shot.
>
> (2007: 449)

Even the newer BWFW genre of SEM tends to reproduce traditional paradigms of sexuality that reinforce harmful, heteronormative stereotypes of femininity and masculinity. This issue is perhaps best evidenced in the ubiquitous *Fifty Shades of Grey* series in which the main male character, Christian Grey, introduces the female character Ana to sexual activity, but also BDSM. In so doing, he controls her sexual activity (i.e. punishing her by preventing her from orgasming) and engages in non-consensual behaviour that sexually excites him, but mortifies her. After reading the series, Peyton stated, 'He does things without her consent. She says you're not allowed to hit me and he hits her.' Clearly, technology can enable and empower women to consume whatever they like (and perhaps experiment with their sexuality), but what they consume may have constraining/disempowering influences.

Despite patriarchal representations, almost all the women in our study saw their engagement with SEM as positive, enabling them to acknowledge, accept and explore their 'dark desires' (Kipnis, 2007; James, 2011). As Becky explained about her SEM consumption, 'It made me feel normal to search this stuff out and find it. And it wasn't just me looking at it. At times, it's nice just to feel normal.' The sexual practices and experiences represented and sparked off by SEM, therefore, play an important role in helping people recognise themselves as sexual beings, even though some may consider those representations to be stereotypical or harmful (Albury, 2009). Consuming SEM, therefore, has the potential to be a liberating leisure practice. Indeed, consuming SEM makes people think about 'what we regard as pleasure and danger, joy and pain, conformity and rebellion, and how we relate to social norms and conventions in these areas of behavior' (McNair, 2009: 559).The ability of women to negotiate social norms and values while also acting as agents in the development of their own personal sexual practices is an important aspect of consuming SEM for leisure. Towards this end, Penley *et al.* note that women's consumption of SEM requires them to 'negotiate power constantly, including in their imaginations and desires' (2013: 14). This is particularly important today as women (and men) are bombarded with the availability of SEM in popular culture, which Kolehmainen (2010) describes as 'pornographication'. She notes that this phenomenon 'can be understood to cover the development in media technology and the expansion of porn; transformations in media regulation and legislation; and the visibility of porno chic in connection to a general sexualisation of culture (Kolehmainen, 2010: 180). Critically, pornographication has ushered in a new era of SEM, which 'pays attention to the portrayal and address of women as active, desiring and powerful sexual subjects rather than erotic objects of the male gaze in contemporary media' (Kolehmainen, 2010: 180).

A key element of this new era is a genre of SEM referred to as feminist porn. According to Penley et al., feminist porn:

> uses sexually explicit imagery to contest and complicate dominant representations of gender, sexuality, race, ethnicity, class, ability, age, body, and other identity markers. It explores concepts of desire, agency, power, beauty, and pleasure at their most confounding and difficult, including pleasure within and across inequality, in the face of injustice, and against the limits of gender hierarchy and both heternormativity and homonormativity.
>
> (Penley et al., 2013: 10)

Seeking to disrupt traditional notions of sex and expand concepts of sexual and erotic activity, feminist porn troubles expressions of identity, power exchange and cultural commodity. Feminist porn is not based on a single, monolithic female viewer, but rather assumes multiple viewers with different sexual preferences. Producers of feminist porn strive to create fair, ethical and consensual work environments for their employees. Ultimately, through its consideration of sexual representation and production, feminist porn is a site for resistance, intervention and change (Penley et al., 2013). By mobilising a collective vision for change, feminist porn is a form of erotic activism that 'works within and against the marketplace to imagine new ways to envision gender and sexuality in our culture' (Penley et al., 2013: 15). Clearly, feminist porn is forwarding a new politics of pleasure (Penley et al., 2013).

Taken together, the liberating *and* constraining aspects reflected in women's use of digital technology to consume SEM demonstrate that careful consideration is needed when exploring the implications for women's sexual well-being and subsequent quality of life.

The digital democratisation of desire

SEM, through technology, is playing an ever-increasing role in women's (and men's) sexual well-being. Dines notes,

> before the advent of the Internet, it used to be that some men sporadically 'used' porn when growing up; it was the more soft-core type of porn, and they often had to steal it from older males, most likely their fathers.
>
> (Dines, 2010: p. xi)

Today, technology has not only changed who is accessing SEM – including women and children – but also how it is being consumed. To this point, our research reveals that women are using technology to move beyond the individual pleasure of consuming SEM. Through digital technologies such as social networking sites like FetLife mentioned earlier, and chat rooms, the women in our study were joining and forming online communities within which they express their sexual desires, share their sexual knowledge and even learn about how to perform new sexual acts (Parry and Penny Light, 2014). Accessing and discussing SEM online, as opposed to face-to-face, can lower inhibitions and lead to more open, honest discussion. According to Doring (2009: 1095), in online communications, 'sexual inclinations and preferences otherwise concealed in the real world due to fear of rejection can be acted out ... participants experience this as liberating and it often encourages self-acceptance'. In this way, the participatory culture created through SEM enables women to move beyond the gendered shame of sexual desire and practice. According to Doring (2009), sexual wellbeing (and avoidance of sexual problems) requires access to sex-related information that contributes to new and different behavioural skills and the motivation to try them – all of which women gain through participatory cultures. Through SEM, women are forming new relationships, connections and communities that are produced, enabled and encouraged among women digitally consuming SEM (Brickell, 2012). Exploring these cultures is crucial in helping us understand 'new kinds of cultural production and consumption' (Attwood, 2007: 442).

Participatory culture, in this regard, fuels a 'collaborative eroticism' (Van der Graf, 2004) in which sexuality becomes an important component of both individual and group/collective definition and is intentionally used as a form of resistance to the way in which sexual activity is presented in mainstream pornography (Attwood, 2007). A collaborative eroticism is important, as it recognises that everyone can have sexual desires. Tisdale explained it best when she said, 'pornography tells me ... that none of my thoughts are bad, that anything goes.... The message of pornography, by its very existence, is that our sexual selves are real' (1992: 44). In other words, normal sexuality may include a variety of practices and interests, assuming that they are legal. In this way, participatory cultures contribute to what McNair (2009: 191) refers to as the 'democratization of desire'. According to Kolehmainen (2010), the democratisation of desire troubles the dominant representations of male heterosexuality by adding to the public discourse different representations of sexual desire, including those of marginalised groups such as women and those who identify with other sexualities. In this way, women's use of technology to develop SEM participatory cultures could be seen as closing 'the so-called digital gap by recover[ing] a [leisure] sphere traditionally associated with the masculine for women' (Puente, 2008: 435).

A digital dilemma: technology of sexiness in leisure

Closing the digital gap suggests a strong element of empowerment through women's SEM consumption that is an important aspect of this new leisure culture. Notions of empowerment are complex, however, because they are mediated by a cultural context wherein 'we are confronted with images of "empowered sexuality" that really objectify women' (Gill, 2012: 743). In other words, empowerment is inextricably linked to sexism. Gill (2012) explains,

> 'sexual empowerment' – or at least its proxies: 'adventurousness' or 'confidence' – has itself become a compulsory part of normative, heterosexy, young female subjectivity – part of a 'technology of sexiness' that has replaced virginity or virtue as a dominant currency of feminine desirability (whilst not altogether displacing earlier valuations and double standards).
>
> (Gill, 2012: 743)

Dines (2010) points to the same issue when she notes that women are at the centre of an increasingly hypersexualised society, which puts pressure on women to look and act like porn stars. She explains,

> whether it be thongs peeping out of low-slung jeans, revealing their 'tramp stamp', their waxed pubic area, or their desire to give the best blow job ever to the latest hookup, young women and girls, it seems, are increasingly celebrating their 'empowering' sexual freedom by trying to look and act the part of a porn star.
>
> (Dines, 2010: xii)

It is not just girls and young women who face these sexual pressures As Marshall. (2012) points out, older adult or 'third age' identities are also subject to such constructions of sexuality.

Given the discourses that promote and reinforce these ideas, it is difficult to ascertain whether there is a 'feminist quality' associated with sexual acts and representations, despite assertions by women themselves to the contrary (Gill, 2012). In our study, it was notable that the women overwhelmingly viewed their participation in SEM consumption as positive and empowering because this leisure activity afforded them opportunities to explore their sexuality in a variety of ways. However, troubling notions of empowerment might speak to another issue at play with women's sexuality. That is, despite increased access, consumption and production of SEM among women, there is still a sense that men are more entitled to sexual pleasure (Attwood, 2007) reinforcing a gendered pleasure (Orenstein, 2000). As Orenstein notes, a

> pleasure gap says something profound about women's deepest feelings of legitimacy, the license to ... 'ask for what you want,' and expect to get it. Will a woman who suppresses her needs during sex be able to assert them in other realms of her life?
>
> (Orenstein, 2000: 26)

This is an important question that needs further exploration. As some of the women in our study noted, at times their consumption of SEM was problematic for their male partners and for themselves in terms of their inability to live up to prescriptions for women that exist in SEM images, or their desire to push beyond what have been traditionally viewed as acceptable leisure practices. Thus, while this new digital leisure culture has the potential to open up space for women to explore their sexual desires in ways that were not previously possible, there is clearly a need to continue to question how and why women experience SEM and whether their consumption really does close the digital gap. It may be that this gap will be addressed by the social movement reflected in feminist porn that seeks to advance a collective vision for change around women's sexuality (Penley et al., 2013).

The politics of pleasure make leisure a political practice

Women's use of digital technology to consume SEM highlights digital leisure as an important context in which gender may be resisted and/or reproduced. When conceptualised as resistance, leisure is seen as a site for women, either individually or in groups, to challenge ideologies that perpetuate unequal power distributions or the ways in which power is implemented within patriarchal society (Shaw, 2001). Under this premise, leisure becomes one arena where women's power is gained, maintained, reinforced, diminished, lost, or all of the above. Thus, women's leisure becomes a political practice (Shaw, 2001).

When applying this conceptualisation to women's consumption of SEM, there is evidence that such leisure is resistant. Women's sexual agency as represented in their open consumption, and discussion of SEM enables them to develop a sexual vocabulary, learn about various sexual practices and reduce shame around their sexual desire (Parry and Penny Light, 2014). Through their leisure, women are exploring their sexual selves, accepting themselves as sexual agents and thus going beyond sexual expectations of women in today's society. In short, women are claiming a new identity of a sexualised self that has positive implications for the individuals involved, but also for women as a social group.

Even so, leisure in the form of SEM consumption can simultaneously reproduce harmful, patriarchal notions of gender by adhering to traditional patriarchal roles and sexual scripts for both women and men. In other words, SEM may represent a constraining leisure pursuit for women given its role in reinforcing and reproducing oppressive gender structures and relations in the storylines (Muise, 2011; Shaw, 2001). In this regard, women's sexuality is increasingly shaped by men's SEM consumption. Dines explains, 'whether their sexual partners pressure them into anal sex, want to ejaculate on their faces, or use porn as a sex aid ... women are on the frontlines of the porn culture' (2010: xii).

Part of the solution to the constraining aspects of SEM is building women's sexual literacy. Living in a digital era means that conflicting information emerges from non-stop media reflecting multiple choices, viewpoints and opinions, making access to trustworthy information and advice about sexuality (not only SEM), should one seek it, difficult (Brickell, 2012; Dean, 2001).

A socially responsible engagement with online sexual content that encourages personal growth and that causes no harm to oneself or others is hardly something to be taken for granted, but demands the acquisition of specific competencies that not all Internet users possess.

(Doring, 2009: 1091)

More attention needs to be paid to raising women's sexual and media literacy. It is crucial that women be able to find SEM and sexual advice and information online, but also that they are able to critically evaluate its usefulness (Wood, 2008). Wood (2008) argues that women need best practices to guide their search for online sexual content, including SEM.

Clearly, leisure, as represented in SEM consumption, is a political practice insofar as it is an area where women's power is gained, maintained, reinforced, diminished, lost, or all of the above; and, whether resistant or reproductive, women's sexuality deserves attention within the leisure literature.

Conclusion

All told, women's use of digital technology to consume SEM speaks to the changing nature of leisure culture and even a new leisure culture wherein women can explore and control their sexual desires. Our research demonstrates how digitality is complicating leisure cultures, particularly with respect to sexuality. The extension of technology into nearly every area of society is purported to provide great opportunities for women (Kennedy, 2000), including the potential for empowering women and facilitating feminist activism (Blair et al., 2009; Harcourt, 1999; Sutton and Pollock, 2000). Through online communities and other contemporary forums facilitated by the internet, women can connect with one another, feel supported, and sometimes challenge broader cultural discourses (Pudrovska and Ferree, 2004; Youngs, 2001). These cyberfeminist avenues are being taken up by women consuming SEM as they embrace new technologies and new possibilities. Even so, these benefits need to be considered with the constraining influences in mind as well. The complexity of women's SEM consumption speaks to the importance of this line of leisure research. As women's bodies take on an ever-increasing focal point of sexualisation, women's leisure as political practice becomes progressively important to understand. And, given that the Net is a global technology, an important area of further research will be to understand women's SEM practices around the world, including how they differ, if at all, from the North American perspectives discussed here.

References

Albury, K. (2009) Reading porn reparatively. *Sexualities*, 12(5): 647–653.
Attwood, F. (2007) No money shot? Commerce, pornography and the new sex taste cultures. *Sexualities*, 10(4): 441–456.

Beggan, J.K. and Allison, S.T. (2009) Viva Viva? Women's meanings associated with male nudity in a 1970s 'for women' magazine. *Journal of Sex Research*, 46(5): 446–459.

Bello, G. (2013) (May 13) Aural sex: The rise. *Publisher's Weekly*, 13 May. Available at: www.publishersweekly.com/pw/by-topic/industry-news/audio-books/article/57209-aural-sex-the-rise-in-audiobook-erotica-focus-on-audio-2013.html (accessed 19 June 2013).

Blair, K., Gajjala, R. and Tulley, C. (eds) (2009) *Webbing Cyberfeminist Practice: Communities Pedagogies and Social Action*. Cresskill, NJ: Hampton Press.

Brickell, C. (2012) *Manly Affections: The Photographs of Robert Gant, 1885–1915*. Dunedin, NZ: Genre Books.

Cooper, A. (1998) Sexuality and the internet: Surfing into the new millennium. *Cyber Psychology and Behavior*, 1(2): 187–193.

Daniels, J. (2009) Rethinking cyberfeminism(s): Race, gender, and embodiment. *WSQ: Women's Studies Quarterly*, 37(1–2): 101–124.

Dean, J. (2001) Feminism in technoculture. *The Review of Education/Pedagogy/Cultural Studies*, 23(1): 23–47.

Dines, G. (2010) *Pornland: How Porn has Hijacked our Sexuality*. New York: Beacon Press.

Doring, N.M. (2009) The internet's impact on sexuality: A critical review of 15 years of research. *Computers in Human Behaviour*, 25: 1089–1101.

Eble, M. and Breault, R. (2002) The primetime agora: Knowledge, power and 'mainstream' resource venues for women online. *Computer and Composition*, 19(3): 315–329.

Flanagan, M. and Booth, A. (eds) (2002) *Reload: Rethinking Women and Cyberculture*. Cambridge, MA: The MIT Press.

Gill, R (2012) Media, empowerment, and the 'sexualization of culture' debates. *Sex Roles*, 66: 743.

Harcourt, W. (1999). *Women@ Internet: Creating New Cultures in Cyberspace*. New York: Palgrave Macmillan.

James, E.L. (2011) *Fifty Shades Darker*. New York: Random House.

Kennedy, T.L.M. (2000) An exploratory study of feminist experiences in cyberspace. *Cyberpsychology and Behavior*, 3(5): 707–719.

Kipnis, L. (2007) Lust and disgust: A short history of prudery, feminist or otherwise. *Harper's Magazine*, September, pp. 87–91.

Kolehmainen, M. (2010) Normalizing and gendering affects: How the relation to porn is constructed in young women's magazines. *Feminist Media Studies*, 10(2): 179–194.

Lyons, C. (2012). Fifty shades of frustration: Is the whole world not getting enough? Stylist Magazine, 1 August. Available at: www.stylist.co.uk/books/does-the-fifty-shades-phenomena-mean-weve-negltected-our-sex-lives#image-rotator-1 (accessed 3 April 2014).

Marshall, B. (2012) Medicalization and the refashioning of age-related limits on sexuality. *The Journal of Sex Research*, 49(4): 337–343.

McNair, B. (2009) Teaching porn. *Sexualities*, 12(5): 558–567.

Milhausen, R. (2012) *50 Shades of Sex: Women's Sexuality in the Context of Fifty Shades of Grey*. Ontario: Kitchener.

Muise, A. (2011) Women's sex blogs: Challenging dominant discourses of heterosexual desire. *Feminism and Psychology*, 21(3): 411–419.

Orenstein, P. (2000) *Flux: Women on Sex, Work, Kids, Love and Life in a Half Changed World*. New York: Doubleday.

Orgad, S. (2005) The transformative potential of online communication: The case of breast cancer patients' internet spaces. *Feminist Media Studies*, 5(2): 14–161.

Paasonen, S., Nikunen, K. and Saarenmaa, L. (2007) *Pornification: Sex and Sexuality in Media Culture*. Oxford: Berg.

Parry, D.C. and Penny Light, T. (2014) Fifty shades of complexity: Exploring technologically mediated leisure and women's sexuality. *Journal of Leisure Research*, 46(1): 38–57.

Penley, C., Shimizu, C., Miller-Young, M. and Taromino, T. (eds) (2013) Introduction. In *The Feminist Porn Book: The Politics of Producing Pleasure*. New York: The Feminist Press at CUNY.

Penny Light, T. and Parry, D.C. (forthcoming) Normalizing *Dark Desires?*: The medicalization of sex and women's consumption of pornography. In H. Brunskell-Evans (ed.) *Performing Sexual Liberation: The Sexualized Body and the Medical Authority of Pornography*. Cambridge: Scholars Press.

Pudrovska, T. and Ferree, M.M. (2004) Global activism in virtual space: The European women's lobby in the network of transnational women's NGO's in the web. *Social Politics*, 11(1): 117–143.

Puente, S. (2008) From cyberfeminism to technofeminism: From an essentialist perspective to social cyberfeminism in certain feminist practices in Spain. *Women's Studies International Forum*, 31: 434–440.

Ray, A. (2007) Sex on the open market: Sex workers harness the power of the internet. In K. Jacobs, M. Janssen and M. Pasquinelli (eds) *C'lickme: A Netporn Studies Reader*. Amsterdam, NL: Institute of Network Cultures.

Schauer, T. (2005) Women's porno: The heterosexual female gaze in porn sites 'for women'. *Sexuality and Culture*, 9(2): 42–64.

Shaw, S.M. (2001) Conceptualizing resistance: Women's leisure as political practice. *Journal of Leisure Research*, 33(2): 186–201.

Sonnet, E. (1999) 'Erotic fiction by women for women': The pleasures of post-feminist heterosexuality. *Sexualities*, 2(2): 167–187.

Spracklen, K. (2015) *Digital Leisure, the Internet and Popular Culture: Communities and Identities in a Digital Age*. Basingstoke: Palgrave Macmillan.

Sutton, J. and Pollock, S. (2000) Online activism for women's rights. *CyberPsychology and Behavior*, 3(5): 699–706.

Taormino, T., Penley, C., Shimizu, C. and Miller-Young, M. (eds) (2013) *The Feminist Porn Book: The Politics of Producing Pleasure*. New York: The Feminist Press at CUNY.

Throsby, K. and Hodges, S. (2009) Introduction: Situating technology. *WSQ: Women's Studies Quarterly*, 37(1): 11–18.

Tisdale, S. (1992) Talk dirty to me: A woman's taste for pornography. *Harper's Magazine*, February, pp. 37–46.

Van der Graf, S. (2004) Blogging business: Suicide girls.com. M/C Journal 7(4) URL. Available at: www.journal.media-culture.org.au/index.php/mcjournal (accessed 15 May 2013).

Vance, C.S. (1992) More danger, more pleasure: A decade after the Barnard Sexuality Conference. In C.S Vance (ed.) *Pleasure and Danger: Exploring Female Sexuality* (2nd edn). London: Pandora.

Wood, E.A. (2008) Consciousness-raising 2.0: Sex blogging and the creation of a feminist sex commons. *Feminism and Psychology*, 18(4): 480–487.

Youngs, G. (2001) Theoretical reflections on networking in practice: The case of the women on the net. In E. Green and A. Adam (eds) *Virtual Gender: Technology, Consumption and Identity*. London: Routledge.

17 Concluding remarks

Sandro Carnicelli, David McGillivray and Gayle McPherson

This book has taken us on a cultural journey exploring 16 chapters across the digital leisure cultures arena. These are discussed and analysed in many different ways and have looked in depth at the multiplicity of impacts they are having on our society. But what does all of this mean for the future of digital leisure cultures and the sort of agenda that as scholars we may want to pursue over the next few years? If we take it as read that we are increasingly tied into digital leisure pastimes that are double edged, then there is a pressing need for more research that tries to understand and explain these phenomena further. There are a few important elements that we feel require deeper scrutiny. First, we need to know more about the time that people spend online, the nature of the activities they participate in while there, the impact of the affordances of digital culture on existing leisure activities – whether replaced, reshaped or intensified – and the adaptability of individuals across the age range and social stratum to participate and benefit in these leisure cultures. We also need to know more about both the creative and political responses which individuals and groups make to the presence of a widespread digital leisure sphere – avoiding the temptation to accept the digital as inevitable, but also not falling into the trap of dismissing the leisure practices it brings into focus as superficial or less valid than those evident in offline spaces.

In our view we also need, as scholars of leisure and cultural practices, to explore the suitability of a range of methodologies, methods and techniques of analysis used to investigate digital leisure cultures. For example, as we go about our leisure or working lives mediated by digital platforms, we produce copious data that challenge us as researchers. *What* does it mean that a penalty shoot-out in a World Cup has produced in excess of 350,000 tweets per minute, and how might that impact upon the way in which these mass 'participation' (online, at least) events are understood? *Who* uses these data and to what ends? *Why* ought we to pay more attention to the privacy settings and terms and conditions when using social networking sites? What tools help us to make sense of these phenomena, and what are their limitations in interpreting such vast quantities of data? Recently, we have heard about new fields of digital sociology and digital humanities, and alongside these we will see new methodological approaches that involve immersion in digital spaces. As one recent example, Pink *et al.* (2015) have argued for a distinctive digital ethnography, defined by an engagement with multiplicity, non-digital-centricness, openness, reflexivity and unorthodox ways. Similarly, Lupton (2014) has suggested that a digital sociologist engages in new forms of professional practice using digital tools to network and build conversations; researches how people are using digital media, technologies and tools; uses digital tools for analysis; and engages in critical analysis of the use and consequences of digital media. We are calling for those involved in studying the digital leisure practices contained in this text and beyond to adapt their practices to ensure that the insights they gather are reflective of the complex practices, cultures and behaviours they encounter online.

As a number of contributors to this text attest, we also need to understand more about the experience of the disempowered and disenfranchised in a digitally enabled society, including further investigation into the barriers impeding participation, whether economic, cultural or social. We must look beyond simplistic dichotomies of digital immigrants and digital natives to explore the unevenness of access to, participation in and outcomes from digital technologies and platforms. Not everyone participates, and those who do participate in different ways, with ongoing struggles for recognition, power and status a feature of digital platforms, from Facebook to FIFA16.

Related to inclusion, exclusion and digital beneficiaries, we also need to understand the moral and ethical implications of leisure lives mediated in online environments and the place of the law and other regulatory agents in governing behaviour in these spaces. Those interested in the psychology of leisure might consider the stresses, anxieties and emotional responses generated by the always-on and always-on-them culture described by Turkle. Those with a focus on legal discourses might explore further the limits of national regulatory frameworks to contain and restrict the sharing of media artefacts, gambling activity and artistic property in a globalised arena, and the attendant risks and economic implications. As social media platforms become pervasive, leisure scholars need to participate in, and shape, policy debates around the rights of children to benefit from the affordances of the digital world, while being protected from its deleterious excesses.

Finally, though no less important, we need to consider the creative (and political) potential of the digital sphere as a sphere of resistance, protest and dissent – extending classical critical theory and cultural studies analyses of the leisure phenomenon but addressing the unique environment that the digital environment presents for online activism. Digitally enabled protests are not without their limitations, but while transnational corporations and states come together to monitor, survey and harvest data online, digital subcultures form and operate online to contest and challenge these powerful interests. Whether satirical (see Chapter 12 on *E'gao*) or concerned with bringing about material social change, the nature, form and activities of these subcultural activities require the attention of leisure scholars.

It is our hope that this text represents the starting point, alongside the work of those who have contributed to the book, and those whose work we have cited here, for a meaningful, critically informed and theoretically robust debate about digital leisure cultures.

References

Lupton, D. (2014) *Digital Sociology*. London and New York: Routledge.
Pink, S., Horst, H., Postill, J., Hjorth, L., Lewis, T. and Tacchi, J. (2015) Ethnography in a digital world. In *Digital Ethnography: Principles and Practice*. London: Sage.

Index

3D printing 9, 26–30, 32, 35–8
3D self-replica 31

abuse 10, 85, 120–34
accelerated culture 13–17, 19–25
affect 16, 34, 44, 47, 79, 107, 112, 128, 138, 184
ageing 36, 56, 98–100, 102–5
ageism 10, 94, 98
agency 37, 54–5, 62, 77–8, 98–100, 144, 147, 154–5, 172–3, 215, 218
ANT 9, 54–5, 62–3
authentic leisure 135–7, 139, 141–2, 147–8
authenticity 9–10, 40, 67–9, 71–9, 135, 141–2

Badiou 8, 14–15, 18–19, 21–5
Baudrillard 8, 14, 17, 19–22, 24–5, 109, 116
blogs 2, 78, 80, 82, 84–90, 92, 95, 116, 121, 134, 154, 177, 193, 207, 213, 220
body, the 9, 11, 27, 32, 34–5, 38, 43, 54, 105, 144

CCTV 96, 155, 157–9, 163, 165
Cole, Teju 11, 166–7, 177–8
commodification 116, 136–7, 166
cyberfeminism 208, 220–1

decline narrative 98
digital: age 2, 4, 25, 52, 149, 166, 172, 205, 221; citizenship 11–12; culture 41, 54, 64, 155, 194, 204, 208, 222; cultures xii–1, 7–8, 12, 39, 64, 105, 118, 177; data 9, 26–7, 29, 31–7; divide 8, 104, 106–7, 109, 111–13, 115, 117–19; inequalities 10, 107, 112–13, 115; leisure xii–2, 4–6, 8–10, 12–15, 17, 19–23, 25, 63, 82, 94–101, 103–5, 107, 112, 115, 135, 153–6, 159, 163, 177, 207–8, 218, 221–4; leisure cultures xii–2, 6, 10, 13–15, 17, 19–21, 23, 63, 94–5, 97, 99–101, 103–5, 208, 222, 224; leisure practice 153–6, 159, 163; l media 7, 10–12, 35, 50, 80, 92, 94, 97–8, 100, 102–3, 133, 194, 204–5, 223; sport 80; storytelling 11, 179, 181, 183; technology 11, 53–5, 57, 59, 61, 63, 65, 95, 180, 207–10, 212, 215, 218–19; transformations 2; turn 1, 13–14, 21

E'gao 10, 152–7, 159–61, 163–5, 223
embodiment 26–7, 32, 36, 49, 52, 145, 220
emotion 34, 72, 113, 161, 189
empowerment 97, 153, 163, 216–17, 220
environment 10, 53–4, 57, 60–1, 63–5, 73, 77, 95, 112, 120, 122, 125, 127–8, 130–1, 147, 150, 167, 181–2, 190, 201, 205, 223
erotica 207–8, 210–11, 220
experience 1, 27, 29, 39, 42, 46–7, 53–5, 58–63, 65–77, 79, 81, 88, 92, 98–100, 102–4, 108–13, 116, 120–1, 127–9, 132, 135–7, 139, 141–7, 149, 151, 179–82, 185–7, 189, 191–2, 195, 201, 216, 218, 223

fait divers 168–72, 175, 178

gendered ideologies 208
Grannies on the Net 94, 100, 102–3, 105
grassroots creativity 163

hockey 9, 80–93

ICTs 96, 102–4, 107–8, 110, 112–14, 116
individualised control 54–5

226 *Index*

labour 2, 8–9, 21, 39–42, 44–52, 89–90, 108, 114–16, 166–7, 177
leisure 15, 17, 19–23, 25–30, 36–7, 39–40, 44–5, 48–51, 53, 63–4, 66–7, 69–71, 73, 75–7, 79–101, 103–20, 133, 135–50, 152–7, 159, 161, 163–7, 169–73, 175–7, 179–83, 188, 190–8, 200–9, 214, 216–19, 221–4
leisure culture 2–3, 9, 94, 107, 109–11, 113–14, 116, 139, 148, 153, 155, 207–9, 218–19
leisure identities 137, 141
liberal art 10, 166–7, 172, 177
literary culture 193, 195, 202–3
literature 30, 35, 53–4, 62–3, 65, 94, 107, 112, 123, 131, 137, 142, 156, 165, 167–8, 172, 191–7, 199, 201–5, 208–9, 211, 219

masculinity 39, 51, 92, 207, 214
memory 9, 11, 34, 36–8, 85, 97, 145, 182–3, 188–92
MemorySpace 94, 96–7, 99, 106
modernity 10, 22, 51, 79, 95, 108–9, 116, 135–9, 141–4, 146–50, 191

neoliberalism 17, 20, 39–41, 48, 51–2
network 3–4, 7, 9–10, 17, 27, 54, 56, 62–4, 94, 106, 113–14, 116, 121–2, 132, 154–9, 164–5, 172–4, 183, 188, 221, 223

outdoor recreation 9, 53–7, 59, 61–5

parody 152, 164
Pieper, Josef 166, 177
play 1, 4, 10, 15, 17, 21, 41, 75, 96, 105–6, 110, 112–16, 135–51, 153, 155, 159, 161, 164–5, 180, 182, 184, 187, 190, 192, 194, 197, 202, 214, 217
politics 17–18, 24–5, 37, 41, 51, 91–2, 95, 105, 117, 136, 150, 155, 159, 163–5, 188, 190, 192, 209, 218, 221
pornography 32, 97, 207–10, 214, 216, 219, 221
postmodernity 17, 20, 109–11, 114, 117, 191

presumption 9, 12, 79–81, 89–92, 114, 118

safety 9, 54–5, 58, 60, 62, 64–5, 125, 141–2, 149, 160
satire 10, 152–4, 159, 161, 164–5
selfhood 9, 26–7, 34–6, 40
selfie 26, 34–5, 37–8, 43
serious leisure 9, 80–93, 194–5, 201, 204, 206
serious leisure perspective 81
sexuality 11, 127, 149, 207–9, 213–21
sexually explicit material 11
small fates 11, 166–77
smartphone 3, 45, 58, 60, 179, 181, 183–5, 187–9
snowboarding 67–78
sociality 136, 138, 142, 145, 154
sociology xii, 8, 12–13, 23–4, 37–8, 52, 64–5, 78–9, 91–2, 114, 116–18, 149–50, 222, 224
sport 1, 8, 10, 14, 19–20, 28, 51, 68, 70, 74, 78–82, 84–7, 89–93, 117, 120–9, 131–4, 144

technology xii, 3–4, 9–12, 16, 19, 26–7, 34–5, 38, 53–65, 76, 78, 94–5, 97–8, 102–4, 106, 108, 116, 121, 133, 136–9, 143, 146–7, 149–51, 161, 165, 167, 179–85, 187–9, 192, 207–13, 215–19, 221
tourist photography 67, 69, 75, 78
tourist videography 78
tweet 2, 122, 125–7, 130, 134, 169–70, 173–6, 183–4
Twitter 5, 10, 19, 22, 24, 82–3, 85, 89–91, 116, 120–2, 126–7, 129–34, 138, 166–77, 183–7, 189–91

Virilio 4, 8, 12, 14, 16–17, 19–25, 180–1, 192

wearable cameras 66–7, 69–71, 74–6
Web 2.0 37, 92, 95, 106, 172, 193

Žižek 15

Printed in the United States
By Bookmasters